ROUTLEDGE LIBRARY EDITIONS:
ADULT EDUCATION

Volume 13

WORKING AND EDUCATING FOR LIFE

WORKING AND EDUCATING FOR LIFE

Feminist and International Perspectives on Adult Education

MECHTHILD HART

LONDON AND NEW YORK

First published in 1992 by Routledge

This edition first published in 2019
by Routledge
2 Park Square, Milton Park, Abingdon, Oxon OX14 4RN

and by Routledge
52 Vanderbilt Avenue, New York, NY 10017

Routledge is an imprint of the Taylor & Francis Group, an informa business

British Library Cataloguing in Publication Data
A catalogue record for this book is available from the British Library

ISBN: 978-1-138-32224-0 (Set)
ISBN: 978-0-429-43000-8 (Set) (ebk)
ISBN: 978-1-138-31328-6 (Volume 13) (hbk)
ISBN: 978-1-138-31354-5 (Volume 13) (pbk)
ISBN: 978-0-429-45765-4 (Volume 13) (ebk)

WORKING AND EDUCATING FOR LIFE

Feminist and international perspectives on adult education

Mechthild U. Hart

London and New York

First published 1992
by Routledge
11 New Fetter Lane, London EC4P 4EE

Simultaneously published in the USA and Canada
by Routledge
a division of Routledge, Chapman and Hall, Inc.
29 West 35th Street, New York, NY 10001

Typeset in Garamond by LaserScript Limited, Mitcham, Surrey
Printed and bound in Great Britain by
Mackays of Chatham PLC, Chatham, Kent

British Library Cataloguing in Publication Data
Hart, Mechthild U. (Mechthild Ursula) *1948–*
Working and educating for life.
(Feminist and international perspectives on adult education)
1. Adult education. Related to employment
I. Title II. Series
374

ISBN 0–415–00558–2

Library of Congress Cataloging in Publication Data

0–415–00558–2

For my daughter Jenni

CONTENTS

Part IV Skills and knowledge

Part V Working and educating for life

ACKNOWLEDGEMENTS

I have to thank many people for helping me in large and small ways to write and finish the book, but special thanks go to the following friends: Peter Jarvis, for suggesting the idea of writing a book and for never losing patience as deadlines kept eluding me; Mel Paul, for her untiring support, helpful criticism, and her belief in the importance of my work; Lori Rosenblum and Kathy Earnest for reading parts of the manuscript and helping me with comments and suggestions; Jim Hart for readily making available his scholarly expertise; Beverly Firestone for her creative ideas and her empathetic understanding of the difficulties of writing a book while being immersed in other major responsibilities; and Marlene Stern for being a friend whenever that was what I needed most.

Thanks also go to the members of my family in Germany for their unwavering love and support in ways too numerous to count; and to my daughter Jenni whose existence has been an ongoing source of inspiration.

Finally, I want to thank the members of the DePaul University Research Council for acknowledging my work with a grant, and my students at the School for New Learning whose courage and dedication to learning never cease to amaze and inspire me.

INTRODUCTION

Adult education and the future of work

ADULT EDUCATION AND THE VIEW FROM ABOVE

It is impossible today to talk or write about work, or the relationship between education and work, without taking notice of the current dramatic shifts and changes affecting the organization and distribution of work, and the nature and actual content of work and work-related skills, knowledge and experiences. Not surprisingly, the literature (educational or sociological) which explicitly deals with these changes is therefore always full of predictions or prognoses concerning the future of work. Such speculations deserve to be looked at more closely because they shed light on well-entrenched assumptions about the nature of work and of society, and they therefore reveal pervasive concepts and ideas, and well-established ways of seeing work and society. In other words, these prognoses have a tendency to clarify society's fund of interpretations and assumptions about experiences and conventions concerning productivity, work and leisure, because their outline becomes more distinct when projected on to the map of a yet unknown future.

The reality of work has a multitude of dimensions, all of which ultimately come together in the fundamental question of the nature of human existence, and of the collective context all human beings find themselves in, i.e. the nature of society. Work never simply signifies strictly economic realities, but always contains a net of relations into which the entire range of human experience is woven. Even more importantly, the way work is organized, the actual form it takes, and the relations it establishes ultimately express the way a society structures its relationship to nature – a relationship which is the very foundation of all other relations: of human beings to each other, and to themselves. To address the issue of work, and the future of work, therefore means to deal with some fundamental questions. What are our cultural assumptions about work and production? What are the technical as well as ethical problems associated with current developments?

On the whole, adult educators appear far from meeting the challenge of these questions. It is only on rare occasions that one finds an honest assessment of the difficulty and complexity of the situation, and a probing into deeper-lying issues. Adult educators have traditionally identified themselves as practitioners, bringing a healthy down-to-earth attitude to their task and leaving theory to the few specialists (who, by implication, are the less practically inclined members of the profession). It seems that this attitude is exacting its price because it makes the field as a whole, as well as individual representatives, ill-equipped for the task of coming to grips with complexities and ambiguities. Pragmatism does not excuse one from asking questions since practical action is soaked with theoretical assumptions, pre-definitions and tacit interpretations which can only be recognized and evaluated by assuming a theoretical stance. The most self-assured pragmatism might very easily rest on bad theory, and thus lead to bad practice.

In this book I will assume such a theoretical stance, ask some questions rarely asked, raise some issues which for the most part remain unrecognized, and discuss problems which are left unformulated in most adult education writings. My point of departure will be a critique of the view from above, that is, the one-dimensional identification of education with the needs of business and industry. I will show how such a view results in distorted interpretations of current developments, misrepresentations of facts, in a disregard of some fundamental aspects of work and production, and in the failure of asking questions which arise from the actual experience of work, i.e. from the concerns and problems of the workers themselves.

The view from above leaves out or misrepresents the experiences of the majority of people. It is a distorted and distorting view, although not altogether untrue because it is, after all, anchored in the same material conditions that affect everybody. The view from above is equivalent to mainstream thinking and signifies a certain theoretical approach whose mode of social inquiry is – like any other mode – governed not only by questions asked, but also by 'the questions *not* asked, and the relationship between them' (Giroux 1983: 48). The particular relationship of margin and centre, or of above and below, which is structured by mainstream thought, reflects larger social hierarchies. Mainstream thinking repeats in thought what is happening in reality, and its own structure prevents a critical illumination of this reality.

The perspective taken in this book is not a mainstream one. 'Mainstream' implies a middle position, a typical and therefore generally valid representation of society and its problems. It presumably excludes extreme positions which, by nature, cannot be representative of the typical case. In the process of truth-seeking the experiences of those at the margin, or at the bottom of the social hierarchy, are consequently considered irrelevant. However, the hierarchy of relevancy and irrelevancy does not reflect the natural order of things but rather social and historical circumstances, that is, social conventions. This hierarchy is therefore rooted in the material conditions of society. Mainstream thinking simply uncritically reflects this hierarchy and always assumes the view from above which is the view of those who have an interest in keeping the material conditions of society the way they are because they profit most from them. It is, of course, by definition the predominant view and as such does not need further justification but can rely on the entire matrix of socially sanctioned norms and values. A mainstream position hardly ever needs to be explicitly justified.

THE VIEW FROM BELOW

In this book I will focus on those questions that cannot be asked within the parameters of mainstream thought in order to reveal inequalities and power hierarchies, and to arrive at a fuller and more truthful picture of reality. Moving those questions to the centre of analysis means presupposing a different perspective and a different view, as well as consciously adopting a standpoint which does not simply rely on unquestioned assumptions, but which is explicitly justified. Such a different view does not merely add another version to the pluralism of descriptions of the reality of work but instead disrupts the usual boundaries of these accounts, rearranging and expanding their structure, and contributing to a more comprehensive and inclusive picture. Disrupting and rearranging boundaries means, above all, looking at the experience of those who are usually left out or misrepresented in general analyses. Again, those experiences need to be made accessible not simply because we need to round out the picture, but because they contain answers to questions which are fundamental and therefore of general concern. As Adorno (1974: 125) described it, 'the division of the world into important and unimportant matters, which has always served to neutralize the key phenomena of social injustice as mere exceptions, should be followed up to the point where it is convicted of its own untruth'.

In our society partial views can so easily be presented as generally valid because they rely on a culturally predominant dualistic perception of the world. It is 'the other' which remains silent, that with which one cannot identify because it is declared to be fundamentally different. Although a society's sanctioned outsiders may vary throughout history, their exclusion from general analyses never has to be justified. Consequently, the interests or experiences of all outside or marginal groups and categories of people are implicitly or explicitly branded as irrelevant, partial, and therefore non-representative.

By examining the nature of the relationship of margin and centre, created by these divisions and ordering perspectives, a different picture emerges. Feminist theory offers descriptions of this problematic relationship between margin and centre, inside and outside, particular and universal of established social interpretations. Bell Hooks (1984, preface), for instance, writes about the experience of Black Americans for whom 'to be in the margin is to be part of the whole but outside the main body'. She continues (ibid.):

> Living as we did – on the edge – we developed a particular way of seeing reality. We looked both from the outside in and from the inside out. We focussed our attention on the center as well as on the margin. We understood both. This mode of seeing reminded us of the existence of a whole universe, a main body made up of both margin and center. Our survival depended on an ongoing public awareness of the separation between margin and center and an ongoing private acknowledgment that we were a necessary, vital part of that whole.

In a similar vein, but in more philosophical terms, Hartsock (1983: 285) equates assuming a standpoint with assuming the standpoint of 'the oppressed':

> The vision available to the oppressed group must be struggled for and represents an achievement which requires both science to see beneath the surface of social relations in which

> all are forced to participate, and the education which can only grow from struggle to change those relations. ... As an engaged vision, the understanding of the oppressed, the adoption of a standpoint exposes the real relations among human beings as inhuman, points beyond the present, and carries a historically liberatory role.

It is common in feminist theory to speak about a 'double' or 'dual' perspective assumed by the writer or researcher. In Hartsock's words (1983: 285):

> ... rather than a simple dualism, [such a view] posits a duality of levels of reality, of which the deeper level or essence both includes and explains the 'surface' or appearance, and indicates the logic by means of which the appearance inverts and distorts the deeper reality.

However, as indicated in the previous quote, this is not simply an intellectual device. Clearly, if the writer or researcher is not a member of the oppressed group, she has to achieve actively such a dual perspective in order to be able to identify with the oppressed. Such an effort requires leaving behind the dualism of 'thinking and being, of knowledge and action, of theory and practice, of subject and object, of sameness and difference', 'a dualism which hardly ever allows a process of cognition which is both comprehensive as well as differentiating' (von Werlhof 1985c: 27). Such a double or comprehensive/differentiating view starts from the assumption of human commonality rather than unbridgable difference or 'otherness' – which is precisely what makes it all-encompassing. In the research process the researcher tries to see sameness and similarity in the other rather than difference and otherness. She tries to see herself from the outside, see the difference and otherness in herself:

> That what is 'other' is, from this perspective, only a different aspect of one's self, and I see myself in the other, and from her/his perspective.
>
> (von Werlhof 1985c: 27)

Neither the comfortable middle position (which in reality is upwardly mobile) nor the allegedly unifying view from above can achieve such a dialectical consciousness and corresponding analyses which are capable of seeing totality as well as the relationship among the parts that make up totality.

In this book I will assume a dual perspective by identifying with those whose lives are most affected by the current changes and developments, but who appear as inanimate objects in writings on the future of work, and of work and education. In Part I, I will focus on those categories of people who have most consistently been left out of general theories and accounts: women and Third World people (men and women). Within the current context of a global restructuring of the economy, Third World peoples' lives are affected the most, and in the most detrimental ways. The reality of their ongoing and intensifying impoverishment is glibly denied by their summary categorization as cheap labour. As I will discuss in Parts I and III, such talk relies on the continued power of well-entrenched imperialist patterns of thought and action, and on a hierarchical and dualistic view of the world. Furthermore, the new international division of labour is inseparable from sexual divisons of labour, in old as well as entirely new guises. An understanding of the close link between the new international division of labour and the old as well as new forms of sexist divisions of labour both here and in the Third World are therefore fundamental to an understanding of the issue of work, and of the future of work and education.

The reality of most people in the Third World, and of women and their work everywhere, gives 'us' a glimpse into 'our' future (Mies 1983: 119). The people in the Third World are already living and working under conditions which seem to converge more and more with conditions of large groups of people in the industrialized countries of the West. And, as my discussion of the 'housewifization' of labour will show (Chapter 3) men's work is to a great extent already 'femalized', i.e. male workers can see their own future as devalued labourers in the already devalued female workers.

Thus, by looking at the experience of those who are the most marginalized and who are considered the exception to the norm in mainstream writings, a picture emerges which is fundamentally different from that painted by mainstream accounts. It is a picture that reveals the key phenomena of social and economic injustice: the disappearance of the classical wage worker, accompanied by the mushrooming of precarious work relations, and of a workforce which is alternately characterized as marginal, contingent, or disposable; a growing instability of people's employment situation and prospects; a worsening of working conditions; a deterioration of the social relations in which work is embedded; a continuing trend towards devaluing or cheapening human labour in the form of the 'feminization of poverty' and 'housewifization' of labour in general. Finally, a picture emerges which reveals a society deeply divided, stratified, and increasingly polarized, not only in terms of a 'declining middle' (Kuttner 1983), but also in terms of racial, sexual, ethnic and national polarization.

PRODUCTION FOR PROFIT AND PRODUCTION FOR LIFE

In our society work is directly related to buying power, and to the place held in relation to the employment structure as a whole. Work and power therefore determine the degree of membership in society. As I will discuss in Part III, in the wake of changing and developing economic structures, definitions of what constitutes the actual social community, who was to belong and who was to be considered 'outside,' also changed. The nineteenth century norm of full social membership, the 'white male worker over 21' (James 1975) is still tenaciously being held on to, although beleaguered by the new majority of women, immigrants, and so-called minorities. The following quote not only indicates the omnipresence of this norm, but also the attempt to uphold it even in the face of changing empirical realities, if only at the level of language:

> The workplace of the future will change, too. First-time workers, workers whose first language is not English, increasing percentages of *nonwhite, nonmale* (sic) workers and illiterate workers will characterize tomorrow's workforce.
>
> (Spikes 1989: 11, my emphasis)

Some themes consistently recur in the literature on work, the future of work, and education and work, particularly in more explicitly philsophical treatments of the subject. These themes seem to express a fund of culturally shared assumptions about the nature of work, and, by implication, about the nature of human existence and of the human community. In other words, economic developments of work are overlaid with ideological, religious, and spiritual developments that all combine into currently prevailing notions and realities of work. As I will discuss in Part III, these core assumptions pivot around the problem of 'necessity', or 'necessary labour', and, closely related, to the belief in the liberatory potential of technology. These two major themes are, in turn, symptomatic for a certain social attitude towards the natural world, an attitude which has its own history and tradition in Western culture, and which is one of the primary pillars of Western civilization's self-identity.

The themes of necessity and freedom, of production for profit rather than for life, of dichotomous world-views and a related epistemology which mirrors the relations of ruling, centre on the exclusive and uncritical acceptance of an industrial-patriarchal concept of work. This concept is characterized by an excessive emphasis on control, and by a division of labour and control over labour. Such a division, only imperfectly grasped by the terms manual and mental labour, results in the creation and organization of meaningless, and in many cases destructive, work. Underneath the emphasis on control lies the idea of liberation from necessity through technology, resulting in a dichotomous division between the social and the natural world, with all its destructive consequences for the natural environment and those human beings who must be 'naturalized' if this dichotomy is to be upheld. I will discuss the erroneous belief that industrial production, or production for profit and the accumulation of capital, is independent from the production for life (Chapters 6 and 7). This belief culminates in the idea that technology will eventually 'free' us from the ties that bind us to nature. Such beliefs are illusory, and constitute an inversion of the actual relationship between commodity and subsistence production, or production for profit and production for life. Furthermore, beliefs like these contribute to the degradation of labour (and the labourers) directly associated with 'necessity', and to the ongoing devaluation of human labour in general.

Work is therefore not simply an economic category. It is a major nodal point for a number of fundamental relations: to the self, to others, and to nature. The structure of these relations is historically determined, and the reality of work, of its internal and external features and dynamics, and of the nature of the relations that are governed by it, therefore provides us with the most important information not only about the economic, but also about the social and cultural life of a society. Educational institutions or programmes fully participate in this life, as it is their primary task to train, educate and socialize competent members of society.

THE POVERTY OF EDUCATION

Educational institutions, programmes, and approaches are consequently soaked with the same general cultural assumptions and beliefs about work and production that underly other social and economic institutions. This is manifested in many different ways. For instance, the adult education enterprise defines 'competent' primarily in terms which reflect a narrowly instrumental as well as starkly individualistic approach. Since the overall social, political, and cultural context is entirely taken for granted, to be competent therefore either means merely to function within this pregiven context, that is, if one is placed at the lower ranks of the social hierarchy, or to 'make it' by climbing the ladder towards individual success. This notion of competence is undergirded by the ideology of economic growth and competitiveness, an ideology which never appears to be worthy of questioning. Training and education are therefore presented as politically neutral processes which are self-evidently oriented towards individual success and overall economic growth. Consequently, educational proposals and programmes related to the issue of work and of workplace education entirely lack the dimension of critique. Likewise, the meaning of 'competent' does not include the ability to reflect critically on the overall economic and political context of work and production, or on the experience of work itself.

The appearance of political neutrality can be upheld only by the construction of powerful taboos concerning certain issues and problems. It is the most important questions which remain unasked: the hierarchical occupational structure, the unequal distribution of jobs and joblessness, the continued existence of sexual and racial discrimination, the exploitativeness of the international division of labour and of the division of labour betwen men and women, and the ongoing destruction of the environment. The most stringent taboos concern any mention of the structural and, in many cases, direct violence that characterizes the working conditions of millions of people.

Furthermore, in the literature dealing with work and education the overall hierarchical and polarized occupational structure is replicated by dualistically dividing the world of work into jobs and careers, with quite different programmes and proposals for corresponding educational preparation (Chapters 4 and 5). 'Career' is equated with 'good work' *per se*, leaving no space to develop a vision of work which is not individualistic, class-based, or patriarchal.

I want to question the limitations of such an approach. I also want to question an economic orthodoxy that places its main concern on 'economic growth,' measured in abstract indices of a Gross National Product (GNP) which has no real meaning in terms of social and individual well-being. In the words of an ecologist:

> *Gross* National Product – for once a word is being used correctly. Even conventional economists admit that the heyday of GNP is over, for the simple reason that as a measure of progress, it's more or less useless. GNP measures the lot, all the goods and services produced in the money economy. Many of these goods and services are not beneficial to people, but rather a measure of just how much is going wrong: increased spending on crime, on pollution, on the many human casualties of our society, increased spending because of waste or planned obsolescence, increased spending because of growing bureaucracies: it's all counted.
>
> (Jonathan Porrit, quoted in Shiva 1989: 6–7)[1]

Other aspects of this orthodoxy, such as full employment, or free trade have likewise become increasingly unsound in the light of current realities but are still tenaciously held on to (Barbier 1986), and still underpin the majority of adult education proposals. Furthermore, the full employment scenario is tied to a myopic focus on the formal economy and on employment conditions within large bureaucratic organizations. Ignored are therefore the growing numbers of precarious work relations, and the myriad old and new forms of informal work, 'shadow work' (Illich 1981), unpaid or unremunerated work, that is, work relations which do not fit either of the two major categories of jobs or careers. Consequently, the content of work and of corresponding work relations associated with 'women's work', i.e. work relations which are subsistence-oriented, non-industrial and non-instrumental, are disregarded as well – leaving a vast potential of truly productive or good work unexplored.

I would like to stress that throughout the book my focus will be on the normative context of educational programmes and proposals rather than on their actual content. I realize that in many ways I will do injustice to the practical, short-term usefulness of the work of many adult educators by insufficiently addressing the dimension of content. Undoubtedly, many aspects or details of various adult education programmes may indeed be quite effective and reasonable, not only from a managerial perspective, but also from a perspective of individual survival. This aspect of usefulness needs to be honoured. On the other hand, a critical and comprehensive point of view which is responsive to the moral implications of education must question the relevance of programmes based solely on immediate practical utility as too confining. Just as education means more than adjusting people to the status quo, the genuinely human dimension of the notion of survival also means more than the ability to function within a pre-given, taken-for-granted context. Education refers to a form of peaceful change, where latent possibilities are drawn out, rather than to an adjustment to brute facts. As regards the issue of work, the latent possibilities include a dignified human existence, at peace with nature and with other human beings, where good work is part of a communicative–collaborative effort. Such work would be judged in terms of its productive contribution towards the sustenance and improvement of the human community rather than in terms of individual–psychological or economic pay-offs. Consequently, the economy would be embedded within the community rather than set apart from it.

THE SEPARATION OF WORK AND LIFE

Adult education seems to see its task as essentially pre-defined: to train and educate human capital. Since neither questions concerning the various divisions of labour, nor the complexities of the world market arise, the only difficulty facing education is to teach the right kind of skills. While vocational education has always been burdened with the problem of accurately predicting work-related skills, this problem is today exacerbated by the accelerating pace of change taking place with respect to content and organization of work and corresponding tasks and skills. (In Chapter 4 I will discuss some of the proposed solutions to this difficulty.)

An over-emphasis on skills, and, above all, on (perceived or real) skill deficits, keeps the actual experience of work walled off. Where education's task is interpreted mainly as training for the right kind of skills, basic or advanced, and 'right' is interpreted as helping towards finding or keeping a job (or making a career), the questions and problems bundled up in the everyday experience of work are either trivialized or silenced. Within the reductionist confines of a purely economistic understanding, work is seen as separate from life, and is looked at in terms which divorce it entirely from its final purpose. Such an understanding shapes educational practices which uncritically accept the current organization of the experience of work. As I will discuss in Part IV, these forms of organization greatly diminish the possibility for the worker to learn and grow.

Looking at work from the perspective of its learning potential is fundamentally different from looking at it simply in terms of skills needed in order to perform well on the job. The latter view reduces work from a rich, multi-layered experience to a one-dimensional means–ends relationship between worker and skills, where workers need to acquire certain skills in order to become employable and to contribute to an increase in productivity. Workers are therefore viewed primarily as carriers of skills or, more frequently, skills deficits. Consequently, the workers' own purposes and interests become either irrelevant, or they become direct objects of manipulation and control. The control of workers' feelings or needs is a new development in the history of labour discipline, representing new and highly effective forms of worker control (Chapter 9).

Overall, the adult education enterprise does not acknowledge the challenge of these issues as a challenge to rethink work and education, and to assist people in their attempts to live and produce in a free and dignified way. Instead, adult educators seem to offer their services in the production of a docile labour force by unquestioningly accepting the ideology of abstract, quantifiable growth and productivity. Such thinking feeds into the traditional adult education emphasis on efficiency and control, an emphasis which greatly contributes to the reproduction of forms of consciousness, dipositions, and values necessary to maintain the *status quo*. Adult education therefore supports the formation of an industrialized mind which is becoming incapable of experiencing its own experience, i.e. of organizing the structure of experience in accordance with a reflected upon and understood reality.

THE GLORIFICATION OF TECHNOLOGY

Instrumental reason is the prime mode of rationality underlying adult education practice, structuring all experiences in terms of means–end relationships. It permeates adult education vocabularies, approaches, explanatory systems, models and theories. The predominance of instrumental reason is reflected in the emphasis on skills, efficiency and control, and also in the entrenched individualism of adult education philosophies which emphasize self-directedness or the individual growth of isolated learners who strategically organize or 'manage' their own learning within the confines of their own privately determined goals.

Today it is no longer work at the assembly-line which represents the most efficient and scientifically designed form of production, but work mediated by the computer. Although neither assembly-line work nor computer-mediated work is representative of all work under capitalism, both express the logic of capitalist production most unequivocally. They exemplify the rationality that underlies the overall production process, and embody its epistemology and reflect its tie with class divisions, and with other divisions of labour that are woven into class inequities.

All strands of current thinking on the issue of work come together in the idea of an entirely technologized workplace with its main protagonist, the 'knowledge worker'. The knowledge worker presumably represents not only all the most important future work-related skills, but also the clean and intellectually challenging workplace of the future. The notion that most work will be knowledge work is highly questionable. So is the idea that work which deals with the symbolic representations of reality is work of a higher order and requires 'higher' skills than work which comes in direct contact with material reality.

My critique of knowledge work (Chapter 8) is not meant to dispute the many powerful uses of new technology, but is meant to bring into focus how a one-sided glorification of technology is accompanied by a loss of vital educational and Utopian potential. It is also meant to make visible again the underlying *social relations* within whose context new technology was produced, and which this technology itself contains. The glorification of technology is linked to a kind of thinking where people regard the products of their labour, and the specific social relations that govern their productive activities, as things which follow their own laws of development, outside of human interference. As I shall describe in Part IV, such thinking, and the forms of consciousness that constitute it, pose fundamental questions for education because they close off the most important avenues for learning.

THE DEVALUATION OF EXPERIENCE-BASED KNOWLEDGE

A related problem which directly affects education is the devaluation or dismissal of experience-based knowledge, accompanied by a loss of certain experiences, and of vital human competences, knowledge and skills which are gained through these experiences. For example, the move from a direct, physical involvement in the material underside of production to a manipulation of its symbolic representation is not a simple or neutral process of change, or an exchange of one set of skills with another (invariably presented as higher or more advanced). This change involves a loss of knowledge and competence which cannot simply be considered obsolete or dysfunctional. Such knowledge, and related skills and competences, are tied to a relationship (or the possibility of a relationship) between the worker and their knowledge, themselves, and the processes and objects of their work which is in many ways more human, and more 'progressive' than the relationship of objectification and detachment which replaces it.

In the last part of the book I will therefore ask the following central questions: what experiences lie buried in those forms of work, production, and corresponding knowledge and skills which are either ignored by the current predominant models, or which are degraded and devalued by existing ideological beliefs and assumptions? What is the educative potential of these experiences, and what kind of educational approaches, programmes, and processes would do justice to these experiences?

Part I

SEXUAL AND INTERNATIONAL DIVISION OF LABOUR

1

THE NEW INTERNATIONAL DIVISION OF LABOUR

INTERNATIONAL ECONOMIC REORGANIZATION

The so-called 'third technological revolution' came about within the context of a reorganization of the international division of labour.[1] Beginning in the late 1960s, and becoming more apparent in the 1970s, the post World War II period of expansion was coming to an end (Frank 1983: 188). Safa (1986: 63) lists six major economic conditions that led to a reorganization of the old international division of labour:

> (1) full employment, particularly during the economic boom of the 1960s; (2) a dwindling supply of immigrant labour, particularly after the passage of the Immigration Act of 1965, which greatly limited the admission of unskilled immigrants; (3) high wages, brought on by a scarcity of labor and the increasing strength of unions and of the working class in general – workers' demands for fringe benefits such as paid vacations, sick leave, and medical insurance drove labor costs even higher; (4) growth of the welfare state, which provided members of the reserve labor force, particularly women, with an alternative to poorly paid, manual labor [Santa Cruz Collective on Labor Migration 1978]; (5) technological changes, which facilitated the development of a cheaper and faster international cargo transportation system; and (6) the de-skilling of work (or the 'massification of labor') through relatively simple stages, each performed by a different operator.

In the industrialized countries a decline in investment and the rate of profit was met with a variety of deflationary measures aimed at lowering the costs of production. These monetary austerity policies led to a reduction of real wages (especially in the US and in Great Britain), and a deterioration of the welfare state (Frank 1983: 190). Another major strategy – which is at the core of the New International division of Labor (NIDL) – was the promotion of 'export-led growth', a new model worked out by the OECD (Mies 1986: 113, Frank 1983: 190). Particularly labour-intensive industries (textiles and garments, shoes, toys, electronics) moved their production to Third World countries offering 'cheap labour', but also a number of other benefits like 'tax-holidays' (especially in the Export Processing Zones), as well as ready-made infrastructures including:

> ports, airports, railways, cheap electricity, cheap water, and free land, among other things, and often they [national governments] even build the factory buildings and lend international capital the money or guarantee private loans to them in order to set up production in their countries to export to the world market – in competition with other countries that bid to do the same.
>
> (Frank 1983: 191)[2]

'Run-away shops' exported jobs especially to small countries (which had fewer possibilities for import substitution, or small, limited domestic markets) but also to larger countries like Mexico (Safa 1986: 62–3).

Although these new world market factories constitute a partial industrialization of the countries of the Third World they offer them little control. As Fernández-Kelly (1983: 100) pointed out, these plants are not 'factories in the traditional sense of the term. Rather they are departments belonging to large corporations which (because of the fluidity of contemporary investments), can be relocated'. These global factories constitute a transfer of stages of production where raw material and unfinished parts are shipped to Third World countries where the products are assembled and then exported. Aside from the multinationally owned global factories of the export-processing zones, similar arrangements of production for export in Third World countries come in the form of joint ventures with nationally owned subcontracting firms, and foreign owned subsidiaries and branches. Furthermore, the term 'run-away shop' directly refers to the current high mobility of capital which would be impossible without the new information and communication technologies (Bluestone and Harrison 1982). As Bluestone described it in an interview with *Working Papers*, labour-saving technology may be less threatening to working people than the new 'technology of management', i.e. 'the revolution in the technology of transportation and communications, and its consequences for the mobility of capital' ('An interview with Bennett Harrison and Barry Bluestone' 1983: 43). Harrison and Bluestone are here referring to a different but closely related phenomenon: parallel production or the production 'of identical products in plants in different locations' (Haas 1985: 19). Ford's 'world cars' strategy, for instance, combines parallel production with 'outsourcing' or 'subcontracting to multiple suppliers': 'The Ford Escort uses parts, plants and assembly operations in 15 countries outside of the US including Austria, Belgium, Canada, England, France, Italy, Japan, Northern Ireland, Spain and West Germany.' (Haas 1985: 19)

In cases like these, advanced technology provides a mechanism for keeping wages low, 'undermining union leverage by maximizing its ability to pit workers in different factories against each other and minimizing its vulnerability to strikes' (Haas 1985: 19).

'Capital mobility' refers not only to a world-wide fragmentation of the production process (including the dispersion of location and stages of production), but also to the increasing orientation of large corporations, particularly conglomerates, towards short-term fiscal rather than long-term production decisions. For instance, businesses whose rate of profit falls below an acceptable 'hurdle rate' are 'traded in' instead of being reinvested with capital as an effort to improve productivity (Haas 1985: 22). US Steel is the most prominent example of an entire branch of manufacture being disinvested because 'US Steel is not in the business of making steel. It is in the business of making money' (Chairman Roderick to *Business Week*, quoted in Haas 1985: 24; see also Bluestone and Harrison 1988).

However, even purely fiscal manouvres and decisions ultimately depend on something being produced somewhere – and hopefully under the most cost-saving conditions. Thus, whether parallel production, outsourcing, or the establishment of free trade zones, the ultimate motive is to find labour which is as cheap as possible. Only this constant search for cheap labour can explain the frequent shifts and relocations that continue to occur, where US companies may even 'come home' again once products are developed enough to 'lend themselves to cost-saving automation' as reported in the *Chicago Tribune*, (22 November 1987). As the same article states, 'routine, labor-intensive assembly continues to be pulled abroad'.

The effects of the new international division of labour on the majority of the working population seems to be twofold: the spatial division of labour has seriously undermined the bargaining power of the traditional industrial working class in the industrialized countries, i.e. has generally 'cheapened' wage labour. A concomitant phenomenon is the growing importance of the so-called informal sector of the economy (see Ferman *et al.* 1987). Secondly, the new international division of labour 'has included a sharp reconstitution of gender for certain ages and social classes in specific countries [Froebel, Heinrichs and Kreye, 1980]' (Momsen and Townsend, 1987: 79). This reconstitution of gender takes on seemingly contradictory forms: on the one hand women are heavily drawn into paid employment, especially in the global factories of transnational capital (thus creating an entirely new industrial female work force), on the other hand women are pushed out of traditional productive functions and increasingly deprived of any access to cash. In the following, all these trends will be discussed from the perspective of underlying unifying dynamics provided by the mechanisms of the world market into which all kinds and forms of work and work relations are increasingly integrated.

HOUSEWIFIZATION OF LABOUR

A group of West German sociologists at the Bielefeld Center for Sociology of Development uses the term 'housewifization' of labour to draw attention to the changes in the nature of all work relations (male as well as female), and to the fact that behind all these changes lies a systematic utilization of the sexual division of labour to cheapen both male and female labour.[3] As I shall discuss below, this also means that despite the continuing impoverishment of growing numbers of people all over the world, the forms of labour as well as exploitation that comprise survival production are nevertheless distinctly different for men and women.

The particular achievement of the theories and analyses represented by the 'housewifization thesis' lies in the deliberate attempt to see trends and phenomena in their relation to each other, i.e. to see the structural and historical links between First and Third World, paid and unpaid work, market and non-market production, men and women, Black and White. Consequently, when seen in relation to each other the common ground of these varied phenomena becomes visible: their integration into a 'world capitalist system'

(Wallerstein 1974) which subjects them to the same underlying dynamics. True to this dialectical method of analysis, the characterization of femalized labour is therefore seen less in terms of specific tasks or kinds of labour, but in terms of *work relations*. Thus, the housewife is considered above all a structural category, making it possible to see the underlying organizing principle of the (capitalist) sexual division of labour behind male labour as much as behind female labour although both retain fundamental differences.

Furthermore, when seen within the overall context of political, economic, and social theory, the housewifization thesis overcomes the limitations and theoretical shortcomings of mainstream as well as Marxist analyses. In so-called 'general' social science, discussions of female labour, or the sexual division of labour, are almost entirely absent. The exceptions are only proving the rule. Apart from feminist scholars who are by definition outside the main stream, there have been a handful of writers who specialize in women's work as a separate issue deserving special attention but not representing the general case. In most cases, however, the category 'women' suffers from theoretical–analytical neglect.[4]

Marxist analyses of capitalism, especially of capitalist exploitation exclusively focus on the waged worker and thus consider wage labour the only kind that is exploited under capitalism (and therefore worthy of analysis). However, the Bielefeld theorists give detailed analyses and descriptions of major trends in industrialized and underdeveloped countries which reveal that it is the housewife and not the wage labourer who is the paradigm of exploitation under capitalism (see the contributions in Mies, Bennholdt-Thomsen and von Werlhof 1988).

Earlier I noted the rapid growth of so-called 'precarious work relations' in the industrialized nations. This phenomenon is frequently although inadequately called the growth of the 'informal sector'. In underdeveloped countries a similar phenomenon is usually referred to as 'marginalization'. In the most general terms marginalization refers to the overall worsening of life conditions of large and growing numbers of people, i.e. to conditions of poverty, ill health, unemployment, etc. The term generally does not refer to work although in reality poverty or unemployment signify a wide range of work activities. These may include illegal labour, contract-based labour, homework, credit-based production, migrant, seasonal, temporary, and part-time labour as well as small trade and other forms of self-employment. To this we have to add subsistence labour and housework. All these activities are precarious in the sense of being unprotected by contracts or legal regulations, highly unstable, characterized by hazardous work conditions, and, above all, by their minimal or non-existent cash value.

Although 'descriptively telling', the concepts of the informal sector and of marginalization have 'little explanatory value' (Momsen and Townsend 1987: 56). The observation that many of these forms mentioned above are non-waged carries more promise, although it also misses important dimensions of informal labour activities (see Smith 1984). The summary term 'non-waged labour' is unable to explain, for instance, the mechanisms underlying the general trend towards marginalization of all labour, including wage labour. The characteristics of certain kinds of wage labour are often similar to certain kinds of non-waged labour precisely because of the same underlying dynamics (see below).

Let us first consider 'normal' wage labour which traditionally has been associated with good pay (or a family wage), a labour contract, union organization, stability, promotional opportunities, and a number of legally regulated protections. Historically, the prototype of the wage earner (the proletarian in Marxist, the middle class family man in mainstream sociologist literature) has been classified as 'free' in a double sense: he is free from the means of production and therefore free to sell his labour power on the market. Secondly, as a legal person or free subject he can freely enter a labour contract with the owner of the means of production.

The typical wage earner is of course the result of a prolonged and multi-layered historical process, including the struggles of the workers themselves for the freedom to vote (i.e. to become full legal citizens), to form trade unions, to be paid a family wage, to have working conditions which comply with government regulations, and, finally, to receive a number of benefits such as social security, unemployment benefits or health insurance. These are all ingredients of conventional assumptions about a decent working life and modern standards of living. Although they are typical for a numerically rather small group of mostly white and mostly male workers in industrialized countries, they have traditionally been taken as the norm, as representing the essence of capitalism or the free enterprise system. The creation and spread of such waged work conditions has therefore also been the traditional concern behind Third World development efforts.

In contrast with normal wage labour, abnormal or marginal wage labour has no job stability or security, no union support, no promotional opportunities, no benefits, no access to training and education. Instead of being stable, long-term and legally or contractually protected, abnormal or informal labour activities are frequently illegal, never stable, with wages paid below subsistence minimum, and often 'unfree' in a double sense: the workers are often not free from the means of production (e.g. the homeworker knitting on her own knitting machine, the peasant with her/his own little plot), nor free in the sense of entering a labour contract as the latter is replaced by forms of direct or indirect coercion. In the US, the most prominent examples of this type of work can be found in the sweatshops of the garment industry (see *New York Times*, 16 November 1987) where many undocumented workers are employed, the conditions of agricultural migrant labour, but also in programmes like 'workfare' (see Kuttner and Freeman 1982).

Informal labour is the counterpart of formal or normal wage labour just as the housewife is the counterpart of the male breadwinner. The formal economy has always had an informal underside. It is one of the major theoretical breakthroughs of the 'Bielefeld approach' to see housewife and proletarian, unpaid subsistence worker and industrial wage labourer as the two extreme poles on a continuum of forms of work under capitalism. *Both*, free wage labour as well as the many different forms of unfree and unremunerated labour are recognized as 'pillars' of capitalism (von Werlhof 1988a). In other words, the (in the classic sense) free wage labourer is no longer considered the normal base line from which all other forms of labour and production must inevitably be classified as abnormal or deviant, not 'really' capitalist, perhaps 'pre-capitalist,' or 'not-yet' capitalist.

As the term 'housewifization' indicates, the labour and work relations of the housewife are considered exemplary, or prototypes for all those work relations that cannot be subsumed under the normal case. According to the Bielefeld theorists, the housewife becomes an analytically important category when both, the formal characteristics of housework as well as the housewife relation (or the work relation within whose parameters housework takes place) are considered *prototypes* of unfree labour under capitalism. This means, among other things, that housewifization can affect men's as well as women's labour.

CAPITALIST UNFREE LABOUR

In what sense is housework unfree labour, and in what sense is it the prototype of capitalist unfree labour? First of all childbirth and the raising of children can be considered the most important task of the housewife. Motherhood is the core of true womanhood as the ideal developed especially in the nineteenth century. Furthermore, motherhood is interpreted as a 'natural' expression of femininity which, in turn, is anchored in female biology, foremost in woman's childbearing capacity.[5] Thus, woman is bonded to her uterus, and the inherently social–cultural work of bearing and raising children is 'naturalized' into an expression of female biology. Furthermore, she is bonded to her uterus as her major 'means of production' as she is expected to produce children. She can therefore not be considered to be free from the 'means of production', i.e. her own childbearing capacity. However, to speak of female childbearing capacity as a 'means of production' makes sense only within a social-historical context in which

> women were socially separated from their uterus, the control of which was handed over to individual men and the state, whereas women were left with its possession as a 'means of production' for new life appropriated by others after its 'production'.
>
> (von Werlhof 1985b: 28)

Since the use of women's means of production has been allowed only within marriage, they have been tied to husbands and home, adding a further dimension of unfreedom that is similar to bonded labourers.[6]

The idea that housework and mothering are somehow an expression of female biology legitimizes the subordination of women, and the exploitation of their labour by 'naturalizing' housework, and to a large extent all women's work. This is the same as to say that women's work becomes socially devalued. In a market society where social value is directly measured in monetary equivalents, anything that is 'naturally' available and can therefore be appropriated free of cost is essentially worthless (see also von Werlhof 1988).

The cult of true womanhood and, consequently, the notion of the housewife whose 'natural' calling it is to care for husband and children, is inherently tied to the rise of the bourgeoisie and the development of capitalism. The proclamation, and realization for some, of the ideals of 'liberty, equality, and fraternity', the battle-cry of the new class, was therefore linked to the legal, material, and ideological dispossession of women, and to their transformation into unfree or bonded labourers.[7] Far from being the epitome of backwardness, as the housewife is frequently stigmatized, she is as modern as her male counterpart, the free wage labourer.

The development of the housewife and the proletarian has taken place over a prolonged period of time marked by considerable struggle and resistance. This process had its beginning in the sixteenth century when a basic change in the social division of labour took place. New forms of *sexist* division of labour developed, aimed at a continued 'taming' of European women (a taming which had begun with the witch hunts), and destroying major areas of female autonomy and independence. This process culminated in the complete 'domestication' of the women of the bourgeoisie in the nineteenth century when the Victorian ideal of true womanhood had taken its final hold on the minds of the members of the upper classes (see Kessler-Harris 1982). From there it could unfold its hegemonic power, lending itself in complex ways that interacted with a multitude of other social myths and realities to the control and appropriation of female labour. To mention only the most extreme examples: it could be used to justify the violation and extreme exploitation of Black women under slavery as totally other and outside of the very possibility of living up to the ideal. And it could lend justification to the confinement, and the stifling of desire and intellect of White upper class women assigned the task to perpetuate and keep pure the patriarchal property line. Finally, the ideal lent itself to a pacification of male workers whose demand for a family wage represented their aspiration to have 'their' women at home just like the bourgeoisie, and to reserve their claims to the better paid jobs (for a discussion of the family wage debate in the US see May 1985; see also Mies 1986: 108–10).

It is important to keep in mind that the relatively expensive and unprofitable family wage had to be subsidized by the super-exploitation of the European colonies, very much like the original accumulation of wealth and capital which was based on the ruthless plunder of non-European countries (Mies 1986, Galeano 1973, von Werlhof 1985b). The production of the 'ladies' of the bourgeoisie and the 'naturalization' of their work and existence is therefore historically linked to the 'naturalization' of non-European peoples into 'savages' (Mies 1986: 95).

THE ALLURE OF CHEAP LABOUR

When today labour is 'housewifized' rather than 'proletarianized,' this means, among other things, that the *cheapness* of labour has attained primary economic importance. The housewife, whose work is (ideally) entirely free of charge, must inevitably become the ideal form of labour, representing the highest degree of cheapness.

Housewifized labour therefore has two major dimensions: it is socially devalued, and it is associated with the idea that the cheap labourers have somehow access to resources outside the wage relation to cover their reproduction. In the face of often massive counter-evidence, this idea functions as a device for 'exterritorialization of costs which otherwise would have to be covered by capitalists' (Mies 1986: 110). This trend constitutes a major feature of the new international division of labour (NIDL). As Smith (1984: 69) notes in reference to the period of the late 1960s and early 1970s.

> while most attention among US scholars continued to be directed towards the so-called realization crises, U.S. firms were increasingly engaged in searching out and securing areas of investment in which subsistence costs to be met exclusively through wages were considerably lower. Through this well-rehearsed strategy, domestic production in high-wage areas could be cut back even while profit levels were maintained or enhanced. While academics were continuing to concentrate on the problems of increasing accumulation at given levels of subsistence, U.S. firms (and those of other industrialized areas of the world) were taking steps not to enhance productivity at a given level of subsistence but to actually decrease the level of subsistence that the overall wage packet was expected to cover.

Labour, whose subsistence cost is presumed to be covered by resources other than wages, is cheap. However, because cheapness always signifies that wages cover only a fraction of the worker's subsistence, he or she is inevitably forced to engage in non-wage activities in order to stay alive, or otherwise to exist barely at extreme poverty levels. The poor and the unemployed may be engaged in a multitude of activities since any one activity will yield too little for survival. 'Marginalized' labour therefore always consists of a combination of work or work relations. Consequently, in some form or other, paid work is always combined with unpaid work. The two are principally inseparable. These combinations manifest themselves in historically and culturally changing forms, as the particular nature of a certain combination depends on a variety of circumstances, in particular on the cultural and political characteristics of a country, and on the degree of industrialization or capitalization of its economy.

In the history of capitalism a combination of work or production relations is not a new phenomenon, nor is it typical only for marginalized labour. As the discussion of the historical twin of housewife and male breadwinner has already indicated, and as will be discussed in a later chapter, capitalism itself is characterized by the separation of subistence and commodity production. Although commodity production has been singled out as the major distinguishing feature of capitalism, subsistence production never ceased to exist. Instead, it always combined with commodity production within a hierarchical relationship. Within this relationship, subsistence production assumed a subordinate position. Because it also simultaneously became privatized, capitalism gave rise to the illusion that commodity production, the 'actual' capitalist form of production, is independent from production for subsistence (see Chapter 6 for further discussion). In Bennholdt-Thomsen's words (1984: 262), 'only capitalism gives the impression that production can be independent from its basic purpose, namely the production of life'.

In one way or other, all combinations of work contain this original relationship of dependency and hierarchy. Both these aspects need to be kept in mind. A statement like the following, for instance, takes cognizance of the fact that labour always appears in the form of a combination, but it is somewhat misleading with respect to the actual nature of the dependency relationship involved: 'Reproductive activities – even those that apparently fall outside of the wage – are possible only insofar as they come in contact with the capitalist wage relationship' (Smith 1984: 67). This means that all forms of labour, even unpaid or unremunerated, are ultimately tied to the (cash-based) market economy. While it is true that non- waged work can only exist because of waged work, the latter is similarly dependent on the former. Although the market predominates as the principle of organizing labour and the various divisions of labour, non-market activities continue to be the material 'ground' of market activities. It is in these non-market activities where labour is oriented towards immediate survival, i.e. where people and social relations are produced and reproduced rather than goods or pieces of technology.

While the cheapness of women's work is legitimized by the many ideological and material mechanisms provided by the idea of the housewife, the cheapness of other categories of people relies on a multitude of racist and nationalist-imperialist assumptions which bear some major similarities to those underlying the view of women as housewives.[8] This is not surprising, as they share the same historical–cultural framework.

Thus, the notion of 'cheap labour' is intimately tied to the history of colonialism and neocolonialism, particularly in its latest version of the NIDL which is characterized by the economic and political supremacy of Western industrialized countries. It is first of all strongly related to that part of the ideological heritage of colonialization which viewed the peoples of the colonies as savage, backward, or, in the somewhat milder terminology of today, as less developed. In all cases, these peoples were and still are, very similar to women, perceived as closer to nature, and therefore more removed from culture and civilization. As I will discuss in a later chapter, such characterizations deprive these peoples of their claim to full membership in civilized society, thus rendering them either altogether worthless or at least cheap in terms of their *social* value. Second, utilization of 'cheap' Third World labour continues the exploitation of the peasant status of the majority of people in this area. The integration of underdeveloped countries and their people has always signified a double strategy of making it impossible for the peasants to continue living off their land while at the same time insisting on their peasant status, mostly through expropriation or expulsion of peasants from their land (see, for instance, von Werlhof 1985b, Payer 1979). This strongly parallels the reasons given for declaring women's wages to be supplementary income. The workers who were fully integrated into commodity production would be declared peasants who presumably still had their plot of land for growing their subsistence food. Thus it was justified paying them minimal wages.

2

THE EXPORT OF SEXUAL INEQUALITY

THE CREATION OF THE PEASANT HOUSEWIFE

Apart from the overall cheapening of human labour, there is a new tendency to deliberately utilize existing ideologies, particularly the ideology of the Western housewife, to restructure divisions of labour for greater capital accumulation. One of the most striking examples for the importation of the image of the housewife into a social context where she appears entirely out of place is provided by von Werlhof (1985c) in her study of forms of labour (and corresponding divisions) in the Venezuelan countryside. She reports how, in a newly created model cooperative in the region of Yaracuy, women were from the outset defined as housewives, making it possible for men to use their labour power arbitrarily as well as free of cost. Women were first of all legally excluded from becoming official members (or 'socios') of the cooperative, thus making them directly dependent on their men. Furthermore, it was expected from women that they be principally capable of doing all the work the men were doing (as they were required for helping out during the harvest season, or to take over when their men got sick) plus all the immediate subsistence labour or housework. In such a way, 'women were defined as housewives in this cooperative because they were thus made an ever-ready and available labour reserve, which did not even need to be paid at all' (Mies 1986: 133). They were therefore also fully integrated into the Venezuelan and international agro-industry.[1] Apart from this unpaid work women were, of course, responsible for actual domestic labour as well. This last reservoir of subsistence production became an additional object for further 'development' ideas. Through adult education programmes (brought to them by social workers) women were systematically prepared for assuming contract-based homework (e.g. the production of dolls).[2] This is not an isolated example. On the contrary, the growing phenomenon of 'housewife credits' can be considered an attempt to tap into the last reservoir of subsistence production, creating the 'paradox of the wageless commodity producer'. As von Werlhof describes (1983: 70):

> To be a housewife therefore does not mean not to produce commodities but to be considered a subsistence producer despite producing commodities. A housewife has to accept that she is not treated like a dependent commodity producer but as an independent subsistence producer. It is this process of transformation that we call 'housewifization' and that, in a certain sense, also affects men who are transformed into wageless but monetarily recompensed commodity producers ('peasantization' instead of 'proletarianization').

The example of the Venezuelan model cooperative is not an isolated one. Many studies exist on the effect of 'development' or 'modernization' on Third World women which reveal alarmingly similar patterns of changing the sexual division of labour in the direction of making women extremely dependent on men by depriving them of their independent productive roles, thus creating a sex-specific access to money and technology.[3]

Although at first glance the creation of the 'peasant housewife' seems to be entirely different from the creation of a new industrial female labour force in world market factories, a second glance reveals that the same underlying assumptions of women as housewives are played out in different ways. The fact that 80 per cent of the workers employed in factories owned or controlled by transnational capital are women is therefore entirely consistent with the housewifization thesis.

THE NEW FEMALE INDUSTRIAL WORKER

The massive employment of women in the factories of transnational capital cannot be explained by a shortage of male labour (see Cunningham 1987: 303), but by the international division of labour which is characterized by its ongoing search for ever cheaper sources of labour. Here we find the most 'important clues as to why women are employed rather than men' in certain industries

(Cunningham 1987: 305). He observes (ibid.) with respect to the foreign-controlled industrialization of Brazil:

> Over the 1960–80 period there was a substantial increase in direct manufacturing employment associated with the expansion of dynamic industries and with the restructuring of traditional industries. This suggests that it was the creation of 'new' areas of work with significant proportions of women employees observed in some sectors. Further research is required on this point, but there does appear to be some evidence that employing more female workers gave employers an extra opportunity to contain wage costs.

Mexico provides a particularly striking example. After the United States terminated the *Bracero* Programme which regulated the legal entry of Mexican agricultural workers into the US, the Border Industrialization Program, and later the 'In-Bond Plant Program' or *maquiladora* was implemented as a means of alleviating the growing economic problems, particularly massive male unemployment. These programmes constitute a collaboration between multinational corporations, the Mexican state, and private enterprise (Fernández-Kelly 1983). Due to advantageous tariff regulations, fiscal incentives, and a variety of other bonuses offered by the Mexican government,

> ... the border industrialization project was likely to provide major benefits for the business sectors of the world by reducing the costs of production through a combination of advanced technology and the employment of Mexican labour which would offer proven efficiency and lower relative cost. Moreover, the plan was a logical solution for those foreign firms which were unable to penetrate international or domestic markets because of high manufacturing costs and their impossibility to sell at competitive prices [Flamm and Grunwald 1979, p.3]. By permitting the duty-free importation of machinery, equipment, and raw materials along the Mexican border on the condition that everything produced was exported, the Border Industrialization Program would enable these firms to compete in the international market.
>
> (Fernández-Kelly 1983: 27)

However, by recruiting a labour force which until that time had not even appeared on the books as 'economically active,' i.e. women, and particularly young women between the ages of 16–25, male unemployment not only remained high, but actually increased (Fernández-Kelly 1983: 38). This is a pattern that occurred in other parts of the world as well, especially in Asian Export Processing Zones (Morello 1983). Although the substantial wage differential between male Mexican and American workers had been advertised as one of the major incentives for foreign industry to relocate along the Mexican–American border, transnational capital obviously considered women an even cheaper labour force. Eighty-five per cent of the *maquiladora* workers are therefore women, directly contributing with the cheapness of their labour to a 'booming export industry' (of mainly textiles and electric or electronic goods), accounting 'for about half of US imports from underdeveloped countries under assembly industry tariff provisions, as compared with only ten per cent in 1970' (Fernández-Kelly 1984: 230). Currently, plans exist to create 'new *maquiladoras*' in the interior of Mexico paying wages 'closer to the average Mexican manufacturing wage' with some of the plants even offering training. Significantly, employment in these factories is geared towards men (*Business Week*, 14 November 1988).

Whether within the free trade zones, in multinational-controlled plants or in domestically-owned subcontracting factories,

> ... 80 to 90 percent of the light-assembly workers are women. This is a remarkable switch from earlier patterns of foreign-controlled industrialization. Until recently, economic development involved heavy industries such as mining and construction and usually meant more jobs for men and – compared to traditional agricultural society – a diminished economic status for women. But multi-nationals consider light-assembly work, whether the product is Barbie dolls or computer components, to be women's work.
>
> (Fuentes and Ehrenreich 1983: 12)

It is important to have a closer look at this interpretation, and at the explanations generally given for the creation of this 'whole new category of industrial workers' (Safa 1986: 65).

IN SEARCH OF A DOCILE LABOUR FORCE

The perspective assumed by corporate managers, and comments made by feminist analysts sometimes appear to converge when the latter try to explain why businesses prefer to hire young, inexperienced, and 'unskilled' women. Fernández-Kelly (1983: 193–4), for instance, states (indirectly contradicting her own detailed analysis) that 'women are a docile, manipulable, easily replaceable work force. Flexibility of this kind is good for business'. Arizpe and Aranda (1986: 177) refer to women's socialization for 'absolute obedience, docility, service to others' and maintain that 'it is precisely these qualities that make young women so attractive a work force'. In a similar vein, Wong (1986: 213) reports that

> ... in Singapore, or elsewhere in the developing world, foreign corporate managers consider women workers to have special qualities – docility, diligence, and 'the swift fingers' and tolerance necessary for repetitive tasks that make them especially suitable for unskilled work in the export-processing industries.

Finally, Fuentes and Ehrenreich (1983: 13) explain the preference for women in the following way:

> Multinationals want a workforce that is docile, easily manipulated and willing to do boring, repetitive assembly work. Women, they claim, are the perfect employees, with their 'natural patience' and 'manual dexterity.' As the personnel manager of an assembly plant in Taiwan says, 'Young male workers are too restless and impatient to be doing monotonous work with no career value. If displeased they sabotage the machines and even threaten the foremen. But girls, at most they cry a little.'

Let us first look at equating women's 'special qualities', their 'patience' and 'manual dexterity' with 'unskilled', boring' and 'monotonous' work, and secondly at equating these qualities with 'docility' and 'manipulability'. The ease with which these equations are made by personnel managers and feminist analysts alike points to a shared view of skills and abilities such as patience, attention to detail, care, or manual dexterity, as well as of the context within which they are produced, as being of less or low value. Considering that these workers were raised within peasant families, these abilities also bear the positive mark of a work experience that is use-value or subsistence oriented and can therefore not simply be viewed as carrying the stigma of oppressive patriarchal relations. Only in the context of a highly alienating, fragmented, and exploitative production context are these special qualities transformed into 'unskilled', boring, and monotonous work. The restlessness of the male may testify not only to his greater sense of power, nourished by a wider range of options, but also to the absence of such a subsistence orientation, making him therefore less useful for transnational capital, but also, as we shall see, less useful in terms of contributing to the survival of his family. It is important not to make the mistake of devaluing such special qualities because they are useful and therefore exploitable by business.

Second, the above-mentioned statements (admittedly out of context) do not sufficiently distinguish what is business' perception of women as docile and manipulable, how this perception functions and manifests itself in hiring practices as well as in the organization of work, and to what extent women put up with these jobs because they are trained or socialized for obedience. All statements, even in their context, at least to a certain extent imply the latter. It seems that such a subtle blaming-the-victim attitude is more revealing of the authors' hidden class bias than of the actual reality of the women involved.

Several factors need to be considered if we want to attain a critical understanding of the mechanisms behind the creation of a female work force in export-processing and other multinational-controlled industries. Business hiring practices (i.e. active and direct exclusion of certain categories of people), their perception and consequent treatment of the categories of people they do hire, and the options available to them – all have to be considered together with larger social and economic pressures that may be at play in a certain locale or region before the 'docility thesis' can be affirmed or rejected.

Thus, business management may adequately assess the cultural context of socialization as a highly authoritarian or patriarchal one (to what extent such an assessment is itself informed by Western concepts of patriarchal authority is another matter). It is also possible to explain the preferential hiring of women by examining the business context itself for which 'cheap female labour' is being sought. Such an approach would seek to pick apart the complex process that translates young peasant women's qualities and abilities into preconditions for a highly controlled and militaristically organized work environment (see Fuentes and Ehrenreich 1983).

What is the connection between these highly undesirable work places, excruciating working conditions and the idea that they are particularly fit for women? To ask this question means to avoid the pitfalls of a subjective interpretation which seeks the answer in the socialization patterns of the workers themselves, and it throws a different light on the frequently raised claim that factory work helps to integrate backward women into the process of modernization, moving them on to the path of emancipation and upward mobility. At the same time, it would be foolish to disregard the potentially emancipatory effect of living away from the personalized, intensive supervision of the family, to earn an income of one's own, however minimal, and to be able to contribute to the financial well-being of the family.

The existence of this emancipatory potential seems to be a major reason for the strict and harsh forms of labour discipline found in these factories. Obviously, business does not completely trust the docility of its workers. The possibility of workers attaining an identity as industrial workers and making demands for better wages or working conditions may also be a reason behind the practice of pushing them out after a few years of employment. In addition, seniority itself might translate into higher wages. Thus, with only certain exceptions (see Fernández-Kelly 1983), young and unmarried women are preferred over older women, or women who are themselves heads of households. In the strawberry agribusiness of Mexico, for instance,

> ... work is not given to women heads of households, nor to the poorer male and female labourers – those who most require an income. Rather, since the survey shows that the majority of the workers do not support themselves, it suggests that jobs are given mostly to young women from the mid-level peasant families, whose wages serve to improve their families' standards of living.
>
> (Arizpe and Aranda 1986: 191–2)[4]

This provides business with two major advantages: first, it supports the claim that the women do not need an income which would cover their subsistence needs since they 'have' their own families to support them. Second, because of this confirmed dependence of the workers on their families, workplace control and discipline are bolstered by patriarchal family control. In other words, patriarchal discipline and labour discipline neatly complement each other. These workers are therefore not 'free' in the previously discussed classical meaning of the word. No doubt, the assumption that these women are all going to marry at some point and will be taken care of by a husband, and that they therefore do not have any 'career aspirations,' is another handy piece of ideological justification for keeping wages low and working conditions dismal. This idea has been particularly pernicious in the case of young women working in the electronics industries in South East Asia where the work frequently leads to early invalidity. Once the workers are used up, they are presumably to be taken care of – at no cost to business – by their husbands (Grossman 1979).[5]

However, in the face of shrinking male wages and/or high male unemployment, it becomes more and more difficult to uphold the claim that women are 'supplementary' income earners. In fact, as the example of the *maquiladoras* illustrates, the creation of a new female labour force intensified male unemployment and made women's income the only or most important one. In Fernández-Kelly's words (1983: 57–8), for instance, women's employment in the *maquiladoras* represents 'a convergence between labor market conditions and familial needs', resulting in 'a swift transformation of women into the main providers of stable and regular income (however small this may be)'. Despite diminishing empirical validity, the concept of 'supplementary income' remains an effective piece of propaganda that weakens men's and women's bargaining power in the market-place.

The Western idea of the housewife dependent on her husband has another side, however, which also comes into play in the various labour practices of multinational or foreign-controlled factories. As Grossman (1979) reports, Western concepts of femininity are systematically employed (in the form of beauty contests, sewing classes, and the like) as mechanisms of control, i.e. as a way to *create* the desired docile and manipulable labour force. Again, these practices do not testify to the docility or pliability of Third World women, but rather to the oppressive content of the image of the housewife. This oppressive content, particularly the notion of true womanhood, is systematically played out to once again 'tame' women, this time in order to make them more useful to capital.

It may also ultimately be irrelevant whether business correctly assesses young females as docile or not. By preferentially recruiting young women within a context of poverty, male unemployment, and the absence of any other source of income, these young women are more likely than not going to take these job offers regardless of their own individual socialization. If this takes place in a cultural environment where women's status is low, and their labour therefore already devalued, business will simply have an easier time in justifying the super-exploitation of 'cheap' female labour and perhaps can rely on greater collaboration of individual men, for instance fathers or priests (Arizpe and Aranda 1986: 185). For the most part, the new industrial female labour force is recruited in a context as described, i.e. where other avenues for income, be it through a wage-earning husband, be it through a better-paid job, are effectively cut off. The following quote contains the whole 'saga of downward mobility' for women:

> It is evident from the testimony of workers that women seek *maquiladora* jobs compelled by their need to support families whether they be formed by parents and siblings or by their own children. Male unemployment and underemployment play an important part in this. Multinationals tend to relocate assembly operations to areas of the world where jobless people automatically provide an abundant supply of cheap labor. Sandra's longing for male economic support and regrets over the irresponsibility of men represent a personal counterpoint to a structural reality where men are unable to find remunerative jobs while women are forced, out of need, to join the ranks of the industrial labour force.[6]
>
> (Fernández-Kelly 1984: 244)

This writer entirely disproves the idea that factory work is a first step in the process of 'upward mobility' (1983, 1984). Judging from her own report, however, as much as the segregation of the labour market on the basis of sex is instituted from above, it nevertheless draws on, and is in need of a silent or open support of individual men. Clearly, as long as men, be it as fathers, brothers, or husbands, themselves cling to a notion of 'typical woman's work', and 'women's proper sphere', any possible solidarity with women is seriously undermined. For instance, the pressure coming from husbands and fathers on women 'to leave their jobs to adjust to a conventional understanding of what gender roles should be' (Fernández-Kelly 1984: 244) directly cements the very ideology of women as housewives, i.e. as supplementary income earners, that is used to superexploit them as wage earners. To what extent this pressure, and this active withdrawal of solidarity, psychologically undermines women's self-esteem as industrial workers, thus contributing to their 'docility,' is a question worth asking.

In the studies consulted, men's perspective on the actual content of women's new wage work is not discussed. In other words, it is not clear whether the deliberate recruitment practices of business to hire only women was complemented by men's perception of these jobs as being only good enough for women. If we consider, however, that the idea of women's proper role is intimately tied to the idea of women's work, it would be surprising for such an evaluation to have been absent, thus making it easier for corporate managers to superexploit women. We can therefore speak of male collaboration even in cases where the immediate interests seem to clash (e.g. between corporate managers and fathers or husbands) because they are united by the common interest to control women, their labour, and the products of their labour. Although the individual household, or the family, is the primary organizing and controlling agent of the use of female labour, existing power relations between the sexes, tied to concepts of women's proper role, provide a handy leverage for outside business or market interests.

THE POLARIZATION OF WOMEN AND MEN

The make-up of household structures varies considerably in composition and structure, even within the same region. This makes it problematic to generalize about relations between the sexes and corresponding divisions of labour. If we go beyond the boundaries of a region, and especially of a nation, these variations become even more problematic because they are bound up with cultural and historical differences. Generalizations become even more difficult in reference to much broader categories like 'Third World'. However, the continued integration of all parts of the world into a global economy, i.e. into the 'world capitalist system' (Wallerstein 1974), has an alarming levelling effect by creating or introducing a new kind of sexual (or sexist) division of labour which increasingly polarizes men and women everywhere.

Ideologically speaking, this can only be seen as the *combined* result of imposing both, a Western concept of femininity (and corresponding images of the modern woman, above all, the modern housewife), as well as a concept of masculinity. However, while the cultural imperialism behind Western concepts of femininity has enjoyed much critical attention by Western and Third World writers, the corresponding reality of importing Western notions of masculinity suffers from considerable critical neglect. It is interesting to note how the concepts of 'tradition' and 'modernity' have attached themselves in different ways to the concepts of femininity and masculinity. Women are either negatively singled out as 'traditional' (in the sense of being backward), or positively burdened with the task of upholding (now sacrosanct) tradition. Haraway (1988: 84), for instance, discusses the many conflicting notions associated with nature/culture and feminine/masculine which 'lace into networks with each other'. This makes it possible to look simultaneously at women as 'civilizing agents' who preserved and are expected to uphold purity on the one hand, and as irrational, backward creatures in the clutches of their own nature, on the other. It is, of course, always the men who set the terms of what is traditional and what is modern.

Explicitly or implicitly, the divisions between men and women along the lines of modernity and tradition always confirm the inherently *Western* view that 'the growth of culture through domination of nature ... was the increasing assertion of masculine ways over irrational, backward-looking women' (Jordanova 1980: 61). Barbara Christian (1983: 146) reports how male Black intellectuals during the 1920s and 1930s held a similar view, expressed by the the concept of 'negritude':

> One major image of negritude was the African woman idealized as mother earth, the source of all life, who in her traditional gendered sphere remained intact, untouched by the West. Revered as mother, powerful in her sphere of magic, she provided a source of cleansing for the men who had ventured out and were tainted by European education, religion, ideas, money.

Although the proponents of 'negritude' reversed the values placed on tradition and on modernity, apparently speaking against the typical Western dualism of nature/woman/backwardness and culture/man/progress, they still fed on the same underlying dynamic dualism.

As regards our discussion of housewifization of labour, it appears that 'there must have occurred a parallel process of "masculinization" of men, laying the basis for the now developing polarization and fundamental interior separation between men and women as hierarchically opposed "caste"-like classes defined by birth' (von Werlhof 1985b: 33). This process has an economic and an ideological dimension. As previously mentioned, development planners and strategists, as well as government and business representatives generally provide men with 'access to money, new skills, technology, wage-labour, and productive property' whereas women are 'increasingly defined as "dependents," that is, housewives, irrespective of the fact that in many cases – as, for instance, in Africa – they still play the most crucial role in subsistence production' (Mies 1986: 115). Thus, world-wide women are increasingly divided in terms of access to cash, which has a number of material as well as cultural consequences. First of all, it leads to an increase of the overall workload for women (Momsen and Townsend 1987: 58–61). By drawing men increasingly into production for exchange, the work previously done for immediate consumption becomes an additional responsibility of the women. Momsen and Townsend (1987) discuss the problematic nature of assessing or measuring women's productive contribution. Not only are different definitions adopted by different countries to measure economic activities, but many areas of women's work, especially in 'agriculture, domestic service and income-generating activities' are 'quite commonly missed' (Momsen and Townsend 1987: 42).[7] Once all those activities are taken into account, a picture emerges which reveals the sharp delineation of women's and men's access to income:

> ... women represent 50 per cent of the adult world population and one-third of the official labor force, they perform for nearly two-thirds of all working hours for which they receive only one-tenth of the world income: but they own less than one percent of the world-property.[8]

These statistics not only reflect the fact that women perform an inordinate amount of unpaid or unremunerated work, but also that they receive considerably lower wages than men in cases where they are employed. This has a material as well as an ideological dimension, contributing not only to the 'feminization of poverty' but also to a deeper-lying cultural division between the sexes.

Money, the 'queen of the commodities' (Marx) does not only represent purchasing power but accords its owner social value. Consequently, activities that are rewarded with cash likewise carry higher social appeal than those that are performed for free. In a market society the worth of everything is determined by its price-tag, and the smaller the cash equivalent, the more the object or activity measured in those terms becomes *socially* worthless. This is why in such a society the 'good life' is equivalent with the 'affluent life', i.e. with the possession of (dead) things (Bookchin 1982: 221). Here, the corrosive cultural effect of money as a new source of status and individual power for men, but not for women, becomes relevant. This manifests itself in a number of ways. For instance, men may develop a disdain for subsistence labour because they are 'spoiled' by wage labour. To what extent this produces disdain or contempt not only for women's work but also for women in general whose diminishing access to cash devalues their labour as well as their status, i.e. to what extent this further separates the sexes, is a point worth speculating about (see von Werlhof 1985b).

However, the underlying issue is not so much this new kind of sexism (which must be considered more as a consequence than as a cause), but a loss of orientation towards use-values, subsistence, and production for immediate survival. This loss occurs on the individual level, i.e. on the side of individual men, but also on the socio-cultural level where a whole culture begins to devalue such a subsistence orientation. It seems that the possession of money not only leads to an increase in individual power, but money itself signifies the cultural power to obtain things. These things are not only 'dead' (and the act of acquisition is always an inherently unproductive one), but within the context of poverty they are also frequently entirely useless. In a way, the possession of money doubly corrupts. Behind the complaints of women that 'men spend their money on "bachelor consumption goods" such as cigarettes, palm wine, clothes, and, less often, bicycles and radios' (Trenchard 1987: 164) lies a recognition of this corruption of a use-value orientation to work and life. Where male status may previously have been associated with 'hospitability, responsibility for family and village',

> ... the owners of the new status symbols have become individuals, but not in the sense of being able to freely develop their personality; mass media and political power determine the choices available for this new identity. They have become individuals in order to be able to consume. They do not participate any longer in the work of securing the existence of the family. They have now become independent from the family as a production unit, bonded by the need to survive. Women now take over the work of taking care of themselves, their children, and the old.
>
> (Mansfeld 1983: 51–2)

In such a way, men also become 'men' in the proper sense of being not only different from, but also superior to women. The influx of Western culture of Rambo-style machoism that contributes to this process of masculinization through the media cannot be overestimated. Because of the close association of male sexuality with violence, such cultural colonialization may partially explain the overall increase of male violence against women world-wide. However, we cannot dismiss another possible explanation of this violence. Not only do men continue to get poorer all the time, meaning that their economic power base, and thus leverage over women, is also shrinking, the process of their 'masculinization', i.e. their withdrawal from the work for immediate subsistence or survival simultaneously makes them more dependent on women, and on the survival work of women. Without a real power base men may therefore resort to direct violence as the only way to secure access to women's services and labour (Mies 1986).

3

A NEW SEXIST DIVISION OF LABOUR

THE MYTH OF THE SUPPLEMENTARY INCOME EARNER

In this chapter I want to summarize the major points made in the preceding one by looking at the situation of the United States (and other industrialized countries) from the standpoint of a new sexist division of labour that is no longer characterized by sex-specific work content or tasks, but by sex-specific work relations (Bennholdt-Thomsen 1988). As we shall see, this approach will overcome the usual (and false) division between women's wage and non-wage work, and, consequently, between 'housewives' and 'working women'.

Earlier I mentioned the growth of precarious work relations as part of the growth of the informal sector. In connection with the rapid expansion of the service sector, these developments account for a large part of women's employment. Overall, the service sector represents by far the largest growth in female employment. Smith (1986: 130) describes how the conditions of the service sector, i.e. a low capital-to-labour ratio and a highly competitive business environment 'strongly encourage employment practices that allow overall wage reduction and increases in the size of the labour force simultaneously'.

Thus, a not only 'cheap' but also 'flexible' labour force is needed to meet the requirements of low wages as well as 'rapid expansion and contraction of the labour force to match fluctuations in demand' (Smith 1986: 130). We do not need three guesses to determine that it is women who are once again considered the ideal labour force, and it is therefore not surprising that the majority employed in this sector are indeed women. However, as Smith (1986: 122) describes, '... women's labor has been the major contributor to employment growth in the most rapidly expanding sector of the economy, yet the experience of women wage workers continues to be that of the most marginally employed.'

Smith (1986: 122) comments on the fact that more and more women enter the labour force in the following way:

> ... Despite women's vastly increased participation in the labor force, the nature of jobs offered them in the growing service sector is shaped by the presumption that women still have access to sufficient support beyond their own earnings and are at best only partially committed to wage labor.

This 'presumption' is only a short step away from the argument that women prefer part-time work because it enables them to combine wage work with 'family responsibilities' (an argument Smith herself convincingly disproves). In other words, part-time work offers women a way to solve their 'role strain'. Both attempts to explain the combination of increased women's employment and continued or renewed devaluation of female labour as cheap and flexible are too one-sided to grasp the interplay of forces and mechanisms that together produce a marginalized female labour force. To speak of presumptions on the side of corporate management that women have access to other sources of income (i.e. are housewives) and are therefore paid less than men is not only rapidly losing any empirical basis (in the form of a disappearing 'family wage'), but has hardly ever been true for a considerable portion of the female population. Massive corporate resistance to the 'equal pay for comparable worth' campaign illustrates particularly well that the issue of pay equity is not primarily an ideological one. Rather, ideology is used as a cover for blatant financial considerations.

As reported in *The New York Times* (4 September 1984), critics of equal pay for 'comparable worth' are quite blunt about their financial (rather than ideological) reasoning: 'If comparable-worth policy was applied to private business, ...it would raise the cost of production, bringing higher prices home and hindering American competition abroad'. The same report warns against the danger of inducing employers to 'reduce the number of women's jobs in order to hold down costs', 'to lower men's salaries,' and to 'help white middle-class women at the expense of minorities'. Women are obviously 'not seen as fully entitled to fair wages' (Feldberg 1986: 174), and the socially and economically rooted inequities of existing racial, sexual, and class divisions are ideologically displaced by labelling women's demands for pay equity racist, anti-male, or class-biased.[1]

Furthermore, the emphasis on explaining women's low economic status in reference to their (actual or potential) existence as housewives neglects the fact that women have always been employed. They have also been the first industrial workers (Kessler-Harris 1982). As previously mentioned, the fully-fledged figure of the housewife did not come into being before the nineteenth century, and became a reality for only a minority of middle-class women during the peak of industrialization (Kessler-Harris 1982, Jones 1986). Black women have a highly contradictory relationship to the concept of the housewife. As Jones (1986) reports, Black women have simultaneously been prevented from becoming housewives and have been blamed for taking away the 'provider role' from their men. Their long history as domestic workers working for White middle-class women adds an additional conflict-ridden dimension to the reality of the Black housewife (see Rollins 1985). Black women's earnings today, and the over-representation of Black women in female-headed households which are disproportinately poor is particularly illustrative of the purely ideological nature of the above-mentioned presumption that women have access to other income, or that poverty and bad working conditions are an outcome of individual preference. In fact, Black women have a history of practically continuous employment, as well as a history of being the major, if not the only provider for their families (Jones 1986). However, rather than being offered a family wage, they are alternately portrayed as emasculating their men, or as passive and helpless poor mothers whose only salvation lies in a full-time male bread-winner.[2]

The example of Black women in the US teaches us several things. First of all, women's marginal employment status cannot simply be explained via their housewife status. In other words, the conditions of the housewife, i.e. her social status as well as the nature of her work do not in and of themselves explain the condition of women as wage-earners. In fact, as Cockburn (1983: 199) observes, 'woman's economic disadvantage in employment adversely affects her standing in life outside of work'. Second, the history of Black women's work has not only been continuous but also covered a wide range of activities which can certainly not be summed up under domestic labour (Jones 1986). This history reminds us most urgently of the necessity to see women's work from a historically as well as geographically comprehensive perspective, i.e. to keep in mind the history of colonialism and neo-colonialism. When seen from a world-wide perspective, women do the same kind of work as men, except they do more of it.[3] This 'more' does not only mean a heavier work-load, but also an additional domain of work that is rarely, and in some cases never, performed by men. Furthermore, and most significantly, women work almost consistently under worse conditions than men.

THE SEXUAL DIVISION OF WORK RELATIONS

By paying special attention to this last point, Bennholdt-Thomsen (1988) proposes to investigate the sexual divison of labour according to *work relations* rather than *content*. She considers the external and internal circumstances that structure the social and task-specific dimensions of work to be more indicative of the sexual division of labour than the actual tasks performed (as well as the attitudes women bring to their jobs). The overall major parameters of work relations that should be considered are 'differing contracts and conditions of employment, different forms of organization of the work process and different mechanisms of coercion. ...More specific factors include (sex-specific) assignments to certain phases of the production process, the level of income, access to benefits and social security, and the overall temporal structure of the employment situation' (Bennholdt-Thomsen 1988: 120–1).

Although no comprehensive study exists which investigates the sexual division of labour in those specific terms, there is ample documentation of the fact that women predominate in jobs which are on the negative side of all of these factors. Overall, women work under the most stressful conditions, are assigned to the most repetitive or monotonous phases of the production process, are over-represented in part-time, temporary or intermittent labour which is especially low paid, offers little or no access to benefits, is unprotected by contracts or labour regulations, and is therefore particularly hazardous to women's health (see, for instance, *Toward Economic Justice for Women* 1985, *Working at the Margins* 1986). Black and White women's situation seems to be converging more and more, although, as Jones (1986: 305) describes in great detail, Black and White women have quite different patterns and life histories of employment.[4] In other words, the existence of similarities in work conditions should not be taken as equivalent to similarities with respect to the entire context of women's lives. Furthermore, detailed studies are needed today on the issues of desegregation and resegregation among the sexes as as well as races within occupations. As Glenn and Tolbert (1987: 319–20) write:

> ... the growing similarity in the distribution of majority and minority women among broad occupational categories ... disguises the continuing differences among groups at the finer level of specific occupations. Broad occupational categories, such as clerical work, are made up of jobs differing in skill, discretion, authority, and relation to technology. If we look at the distribution of racial ethnic women in specific clerical specialties, we see that they are concentrated in more routine, largely manual jobs. Moreover, the jobs that racial ethnic women have entered tend to be those which are being negatively affected by office technology – jobs that are being deskilled by automation (e.g., filing) or reduced in number by more advanced systems (e.g., key-punching).

Many studies on women's work and on the sexual division of labour provide useful documentation of sex-specific work relations, although they usually do not single out these aspects as the most important characteristics of the sexual division of labour. Thus, characterizations of women's jobs as 'dead-end,' 'unstable and among the lowest paid' (Fox and Hesse-Biber 1984: 99), offering 'less variety, diversity, interdependence, and control both within and across employing organizations' (Hall 1986: 217, citing Baron and Bielby 1982) are presented as only some among many other characteristics of women's employment situation. Most importantly, rather than being considered prime indicators of the underlying sexual division of labour they are investigated as examples of discrimination on the job.[5]

Obviously, these general characteristics of women's work conditions also function as mechanisms for producing and keeping a subordinate and relatively powerless labour force, i.e. they are coercive mechanisms of labour discipline (Bennholdt-Thomsen 1988). The previously mentioned assumption that women are not entitled to decent living wages is both an expression of the equation money = social status and power, as well as a way to maintain women's reduced access to full membership in society. The other major important ingredient of a sex-specific labour discipline is likewise a symptom of and a means for social (and individual male) control of women and their labour. This is the sex-specific organization of women's time that combines 'flexibility' with monotony, disrupted and fragmented employment with 24-hour availability. Although the *external* structuring of women's overall time – a double day, temporary or intermittent employment, short-term and part-time work – is empirically connected with the reality of many women as mothers and housewives, for others it functions ideologically as a stigma that affects all women regardless of whether they cook and clean or not, raise children or not. As Bennholdt-Thomsen (1984: 254) observes, to be a housewife is not a decision women make, but an 'image that persecutes women like an infectious disease'. Internal structuring of time like speed-ups, especially in the form of 'voluntary' speed-ups associated with piece-work, monotony or repetitiveness that are typical of work affected by automation and computerized technology feeds on another aspect of female labour.[6] The fact that women are expected to put up with stress and monotony is akin to the 'docility thesis' discussed earlier. Hall (1986: 195), for instance, states that sex-specific 'socialization patterns ... interact with the opportunity structure to yield traditional "feminine-type" jobs offering low pay and little opportunity for advancement'.

Apart from the questionable, although revealing, equating of 'feminine' with 'low-pay' and 'little opportunity', a more important aspect is entirely ignored by the socialization approach. Employers single out women not only because they take advantage of (presumed) 'feminine traits', but because they are able to take advantage of women's overall weak and vulnerable economic and social position. It is this position, the 'common third factor' (Bennholdt-Thomsen 1988) rather than individual socialization or internalized role expectations that determine the condition of women's paid and unpaid work. Seen from this angle, an explanation has to be sought for the fact that certain groups are *excluded* from these kinds of jobs, an approach which would yield more interesting results than explanations focusing on why women are *included*.

WAGED HOUSEWORK

The dialectic of inclusion and exclusion is a historically changing and shifting social process. It feeds on sexual, but also on racial and national differences in a variety of complex and changing combinations. Thus, instead of seeking an explanation exclusively in the 'internal conditions' of those occupying the most disadvantageous positions, it is more revealing to look at the interest behind such placement. History provides useful examples for such an approach. In the following I want to compare a citation from a Nazi propaganda brochure justifying a policy of ruthless exploitation of female labour with an 'explanation' of an American electrical firm for differential placement of women workers. In the first case, fragmented assembly-line work is justified in the following way:

> Because so little thinking is involved, the unskilled task ties a woman only loosely to her job and above all *only loosely to its purpose*. In her fantasy she enjoys visions of her children's happy faces while she is toiling for them ....
>
> (quoted in Tröger 1984: 256)

In the second case, the American firm 'claimed that the concentration of women in the electrical department was not discriminatory because'

> ... there are some things about the job that appeal to the females such as: clean working conditions, routine work, which once learned, gives the female the opportunity to plan the family budget, menu and other responsibilities directly related to family ties.
>
> (quoted in Bergmann 1986: 101)

The decisive factor in the analysis of women's paid work is therefore the overall subordinate position of women rather than the content of their work or their individual attitudes towards employment (Bennholdt-Thomsen 1988: 114). Thus, it is false to separate housework and employment, or housewives and workers. Analyses which attempt to explain the low and super-exploited status of women as wage earners exclusively from the perspective of their activities as non-wage earners, i.e. housewives, therefore yield only distorted interpretations, because

> ... the characteristic hallmark of women – a natural resource equally good for any kind of activity, free of charge or for the lowest possible pay – is dictated to women because of their sex; *it is not acquired as specific type of skill or qualification.*
>
> (Bennholdt-Thomsen 1988: 119, my emphasis)[7]

Likewise, the meaning of 'housewife' is therefore not determined by specific activities (as already implied in the above-mentioned quote) performed by the housewife but rather by the *conditions* under which these activities are performed, and by the *social relations* that characterize it (Bennholdt-Thomsen 1984: 179). Housework and paid work are both linked together in a 'mutual relationship that contains the moment of structural violence' simultaneously forcing women into a housewife existence and into marginal employment conditions (Bennholdt-Thomsen 1988: 113). Women are driven into these situations neither because of a personal preference, nor because of a 'role change', but because of the inseparable combination of lack of access to decent, well-paid employment, and their subordination as housewives.

Within this overall matrix of coercive relations the exclusive responsibility of women for the work with children, and the isolation of mothers in the patriarchal nuclear family are of central importance, but 'all other mechanisms combine to prevent women from freeing themselves from this situation' (Bennholdt-Thomsen 1988: 121). Again, it is not mothering work *per se* (and concomitant attitudes towards waged work), but the fact that women have exclusive responsibility for this work, and for the organization of work with and for children (ibid.).[8]

Whatever it is that gets characterized as sex-stereotyped or even 'feminine' (work, attitudes, occupational status, etc.), it must be seen as a crystallization of social expectations placed on women correctly perceived as subordinate, and therefore exploitable, in particularly intensive and advantageous ways. Thus, only because women as a sex are devalued can all their work be devalued as well. Consequently, the jobs offered to women prevent them in advance from establishing an independent economic existence (Bennholdt-Thomsen 1988: 125).

THE SUPERQUALIFICATION OF WOMEN

Women are confronted with expectations that are rather abstract, particularly as regards the demands for flexibility and availability which structures all women's work relations. This expectation, and the concomitant utilization of women's labour has a total, if not totalitarian dimension which makes it entirely justifiable to say that women are considered (and treated) as natural resources. Not only in the family, but also in the workplace are women never simply 'workers', but always female human beings, i.e. their sexuality is utilized as well, as is their feminine sensitivity, their 'affiliative skills', and the like. In Verena Fiegl's words (1990), women never simply sell their labour power as a commodity, but always their whole person as 'the commodity female labor power'.[9] The widespread and persistent problem of sexual harassment is the most illustrative, but not the only testimony for this total utilization of women in the workplace (McKinnon 1979; Bergmann 1986).

The situation in the family is very similar. There women are expected to do the work of sustaining 'the physical, financial, and emotional health of the household' (Lloyd and Niemi 1979: 315). In other words, women are not only responsible for physical tasks like cooking, cleaning, shopping, doing the laundry, etc., but also for the psychological and sexual tasks of keeping the family together, and its individual members happy and satisfied, in short, to do the 'relations work'. Women are therefore expected to provide healthy meals, and to produce healthy and happy children who will turn into well-adjusted adults.[10]

Apart from the totality of expectations placed on women within the family, the formal characteristics of housework are worth looking at from another angle as well. The modern housewife not only combines a great variety of tasks, from cleaning, cooking, financial planning to tutoring and nursing, but also the ability to pay attention to and to take care of several tasks at one and the same time (soothing a crying baby, answering the phone, watching food cooking on the stove, etc.). As well as the many specific skills that go into the perfomance of these tasks, the successful housewife must also have a kind of attitudinal super-skill: she must be willing and ready to be principally available for any (new) demands placed on her during a 24-hour day. In other words, she must be flexible in a small and a large way. She has to adjust her overall life-plan to the phases when children are born and have to be raised; if she is seriously interested in a (male-specified) career, she is faced with the often agonizing decision of not having children at all – a decision men hardly ever have to make. Furthermore, women often have to adjust their employment decisions to 'husband's career patterns, the amount and type of time demands on the husband (shift work or overtime work), and geographical mobility requirements' (Hall 1986: 196); women's work days also have to move with the rhythm of children's and husband's daily routines and needs.

The growing phenomenon of homeworking adds another dimension to this situation. Here women are employed either under the sweatshop conditions of the 'underground economy', or they become part of the new 'electronic cottage industry' which draws mainly on a (White) middle class female labour pool. It is easy to imagine that the stress level of women increases when their paid work is very likely constantly interrupted by children and other family members and may perhaps have to be moved into the late evening hours, thus lengthening the work day even more.

All these characteristics – the broad spectrum of knowledge and skills, as well as universal and permanent availability – are captured in the following description:

> Everything that women do must bear fruit and it must be gratis, like the air we breathe. This applies not only to producing and rearing of children, but also to the sundry housework and wage labour, the emotional care bestowed on colleagues, the friendliness, submissiveness, being-always-at-other's disposal, healing-all-wounds, being-sexually-usable; the putting-everything-again-in-order, the sense of responsibility and self-sacrifice, frugality and unpretentiousness, the renunciation in favour of others, the putting-up-with and helping-out-in-all-matters, withdrawing oneself and being-invisible and always-there, the passive being available and the active 'pulling-the-cart-out-of-the-mud' – the endurance and the discipline of a soldier. All this makes up the feminine work capacity. It is the most general and the most comprehensive work capacity imaginable, because it draws in and mobilizes the whole person.
>
> (von Werlhof 1988a: 179)

It is consequently wrong to explain the cheapness of female labour in terms of women's lower productivity because they are hampered by childcare and domestic duties.11 Likewise, the idea that women's labour is less valuable because it is mainly unskilled denies the fact that 'employers reap the benefits of skills learned by women as daughters, wives, and mothers in the family without granting these formal recognition' (Beechy 1987: 165). In fact, as the above-cited quote illustrates, women are a highly trained and disciplined labour force.

A MODEL FOR THE FUTURE?

The usefulness of women's superqualification has been noted by some writers who see it as a model for better future work relations. It appears in calls for training people for future 'flexilives' (Handy

1984), to train them in an attitude of flexibility and adjustability to permanent change, to attain 'generic' rather than specific skills. All these demands are strongly reminiscent of the skills of the housewife. In an article significantly called 'Working Like Women' Sheila Rothwell (1986: 220) summarizes this 'discovery' of women's labour capacity remarkably well:

> Before we seek too far for dramatically new patterns [of work], however, the patterns of women's working lives should be examined more closely. In many respects the greater flexibility of these, the balance of responsibilities between employer, family, local and personal needs, between extra income and other priorities, demonstrate different 'opportunity-cost' trade-offs, which may vary at different stages of the personal, job and family life-cycles, but are more fitted to the needs of society and individuals at the present time.

Rothwell here entirely confirms, albeit uncritically, the 'housewifization thesis' proposed in the preceding section. In the absence of an understanding or analysis of the relationship between women's promising flexibility and their greater exploitation based on the sexist division of labour, her proposal to consider women as new 'role models' for men not only reinforces women's dismal social situation but also creates an illusion of a future greater equality between men and women. The examples of active male resistance to become or work like women are too numerous to nourish any belief that this will happen easily, or that it will happen at all.[12] The same examples show that such resistance has always been based on well-entrenched and socially strongly reinforced notions of male superiority and power over women rather than on a rational assessment of the situation in terms of employers' attempts to squeeze an extra amount of life out of men. In other words, male resistance to capital has frequently assumed the form of bonding with other men *against* women.

Faced with a shrinking pie, this struggle may become even more fierce and violent, fuelled by a growing social acceptance of violence against women, and by the increased social use and exploitation of all aspects of female existence for profit or male self-aggrandizement. Rothwell indirectly, and correctly, points to an overall cheapening of all labour, men's and women's. She does not address the fact that the social appeasement that will be necessary because the former model of social norm and respectability, the male (White) breadwinner and head of the household is losing ground, will structurally and ideologically be dependent on the inferiority of women. We can only expect the division and alienation between the sexes to become wider rather than narrower, supported by an 'alliance of interest' (Bennholdt-Thomsen) between corporate management, labour representatives, the state, the church, the medical establishment, and individual men, and enhanced by the continued militarization of Western culture.

Thus far my analysis of women's work has stressed the dialectical unity of women's waged and non-waged work in the form of 'wage-house-work' (Bennholdt-Thomsen 1988), where women's waged work must be considered 'paid housework rather than free wage labour' (von Werlhof 1988b: 176). Neither housework nor waged work alone can be seen as the primary *locus* of female oppression, because the conditions, surrounding circumstances, and social relations that characterize women's labour are ultimately based on the social evaluation of women as an inferior sex.

To the extent to which it is the stigma of the housewife and mother that follows women everywhere and brands them as inferior or cheap wage labourers, housework nevertheless remains a critical factor for understanding women's overall situation. However, it is not the social position of the housewife as 'a married woman who holds no paid job and who works within the home performing services for her own family' (Bergmann 1986: 200) that holds the key to women's oppression; I hope I have sufficiently pointed out that this definition of the housewife is descriptive at best, and only with respect to a numerical minority of women. What needs to be explained, and what therefore holds the key to a full understanding of the sexist division of labour, is the fact that housework is stigmatized as not socially necessary, therefore unpaid and, consequently, invisible labour. The question that has to be asked is therefore why 'the housewife' is such an infectious disease that afflicts all women regardless of their actual situation or work reality. The ultimate ground for this disease is therefore not to be sought in the characteristics of women themselves, but in the overall social ascription of women to housework, and in the overall social devaluation of the tasks and responsibilities that are summarized by the term.

This necessitates looking more closely at the content of housework – again not for the purpose of seeking parallels between these activities and those performed on 'typical women's jobs', but for the purpose of investigating more closely the particular kind of work which so obviously deserves no formal social recognition, and which turns those who perform it into less than full members of society. In a later chapter this theme will be taken up again, and the reasons for the underlying social devaluation of 'women's work' will be explored in some detail.

Part II

THE DIVIDED CURRICULUM: CAREERS AND JOBS

4

GOOD WORK AND LIBERAL EDUCATION FOR CAREERS

LIBERAL EDUCATION: ÉLITIST OR TRANSFORMATIVE?

The current debate on the crisis in higher education has many facets, generating apparently divergent positions and proposed solutions. The common theme, however, is the changing relationship between higher education, or the world of academia, and society. Significantly, 'society' has become largely equivalent with business or the corporate world. In his discussion of the changing relationship between the university and society from medieval to contemporary times Dole (1980: 334) states that where 'the university and society were once one and the same, business and society are now one and the same, with universities unable to meet the expectation of business, hence those of society as well' Dole (ibid.) considers this new 'organic fit' between industry and the modern world as the major reason behind the establishment of higher education programmes offered by industry itself.[1] He sees these programmes (and representative institutions) as having the considerable advantage of being unburdened by the weight of divergent academic traditions, or by inflated public expectations concerning the university's 'social-corrective role'. These programmes can afford to be directly responsive to the needs of the day, and to pick and choose from those academic traditions whatever contributes to the efffectiveness of their educational efforts. Increasing calls for greater partnership, joint ventures, or collaboration between business and colleges or universities can therefore be interpreted as an answer to a growing competition between traditional institutions of higher education and industry.

Proposed and actually-forming alliances between colleges and industries raise a number of fundamental questions, above all the question concerning the meaning of education under the auspices of a new 'organic fit' between institutions of higher learning and corporate America. Thus far, the heritage of a non-technical, non-industrial and above all non-instrumental liberal arts education is still alive enough to have to be reckoned with.

The concept of liberal education is strongly tied not only to the social-corrective role of the university, but also to the social-Utopian tradition of Western intellectual thought with its emphasis on a critique of the status quo, and on speculating about what could be and what ought to be. One of the most significant strands in the current movement to adjust colleges and universities to changed social and economic circumstances is the re-structuring of the concept of liberal education itself. In particular, selling the concept as direct preparation for careers, especially by higher education institutions which are trying to appeal to a growing number of non-traditional adult students, represents an interesting new twist in the old vocational/liberal studies debate. It is worth looking at this debate because it has already wrestled with all the major issues which are currently reopened albeit under changed overall circumstances.

The history of the vocational/liberal studies debate is tightly woven into the history of a struggle between conflicting and contradictory traditions and values in American society and culture. Wirth (1983) describes this history in terms of a value conflict between an economistic or technocratic orientation towards society and its problems, and a critical, or democratic orientation based on the values of a populist, grassroots participation of people in social, political, and economic institutions. Although closely related, the concepts of 'liberal' and 'vocational' cannot be assigned unequivocally to either one of these value orientations, but the shifting and changing interpretations of these concepts bear out the same tension. It is the tension between the critical potential of the concept of liberal education and its inherent elitism which reserved this tradition for the few; between an élitist anti-vocationalism which refused to tether the cultivation of the mind to any utilitarian requirements, and a class-biased vocationalism which explicitly excluded aspects of a liberal education because it 'would ruin a good field hand' (Myrdal, quoted in Shor 1986: 50).

Neither 'vocationalism' nor 'liberalism' therefore signify monolithic educational programmes, nor irreconcilable dichotomies. In fact, as Green (1968: 99–100) points out, the difference between liberal and vocational is 'vague and imprecise', because liberal studies have always been 'vocationally oriented' by – however implicitly – preparing the student for a vocation or profession. Entwistle (1970: 63–5) describes how the concept of liberal education has drawn its rationale from the concept of a 'non-producing class', e.g. the Platonic guardian, Aristotle's citizen, the Renaissance courtier, and the English squirearchy, but that such a 'cultivated existence' had 'a function which had a political, and hence economic value'. He further describes how Newman, the founder of the modern idea of liberal education, entirely denied this economic or 'vocational aspect'. However, the meaning of 'vocational' here has the connotation of *jobs*, and of education as short-term preparation for *making a living* for which liberal education was considered irrelevant if not an obstacle because, as so vividly expressed in Myrdal's phrase, the cultivation of higher-order intellectual abilities could not be reconciled with menial labour.

Historically, the concept of liberal education has therefore always oscillated between its adaptive–elitist and its critical–transformative potential, never completely giving in to one or the other of its two poles. This is becoming less true today where the adaptive as well as élitist tradition of liberal education seems to be gaining the upper hand. By structuring it directly along market lines, the dynamic tension between liberal and vocational education has essentially been neutralized.

The concern for a class-biased vocationalism that prevented a comprehensive understanding and critical assessement of the whole of industrial reality is most clearly expressed in Dewey's writings. Since Dewey is claimed as a proponent of liberal education, his thoughts deserve some commentary in the present context of the discussion. One of Dewey's primary concerns was the education of a citizenry who could grasp the powerful influence which social and political institutions have on individuals, and therefore ground the notion of individual freedom in the ability to control collectively those institutions (Bernstein 1967: 139). Dewey's 'liberal' view of education as contributing to the full development of individual potential was therefore always complemented by his concern for an education that stressed the ability to share with others in the *common* task of shaping truly democratic institutions. This would allow for such individual development and freedom not only for a select few but for the entire population. Because he recognized the negative as well as positive potential of economic institutions to hinder or to contribute to individual freedom, Dewey's own programme took the aspect of vocational preparation very seriously. Such preparation included, however, the ability to evaluate critically the world of work for which the students were prepared. This meant to attain a comprehensive view of the entire economic structure including a critical perspective on its hierarchical organization. Neither strictly technical preparation for jobs as proposed by many of his progressive contemporaries (see Wirth 1983), nor preparation for professional or managerial work could therefore claim candidacy for the title 'good' or 'liberal' education, since the positions at the top necessitate positions at the bottom and therefore presuppose an undemocratically structured world of work. As Wirth (1983: 78) pointed out, instead of simply asking 'are our children good enough for industry?' Dewey posed the equally important, and truly liberal–critical question: 'Is industry good enough for our children?' Only an education that would seriously address this question could be called an education that *sets people free.*

LIBERAL EDUCATION FOR BUSINESS CAREERS

During the 1960s, the critical potential of liberal education was recognized by a student population dissatisfied with the hollowness of the American dream that had shrunk to a simple call for more, and which had become increasingly callous towards phenomena of social and economic injustice. However, in contrast with today's calls for 'liberal learning skills', the content areas of the liberal arts, especially the humanities and social sciences experienced an upsurge in appreciation. Despite the élitism, racism, and sexism built into the academic practices of research and teaching, and into the content of the liberal arts disciplines themselves, 'elements of critical thinking' are 'inscribed in the traditional curricula' (Aronowitz 1980: 46). This critical potential of Western intellectual tradition, with its grand themes of justice, freedom, and democracy, was seized upon in an attempt to re-appropriate it, make it accessible and of practical relevance to hitherto excluded groups and segments of the population. During the 1970s, the era of careerism and vocationalism, and 'the triumph of training over education' (Shor 1986: 52), the importance of the liberal arts disciplines receded into the background, discarding the critical themes of justice and freedom.

Recent attempts to give liberal education a new legitimacy by framing it in terms of a more effective career preparation are therefore a far cry from its renaissance during the 1960s.[2] In current proposals for 'liberal learning for business careers' (Jones 1982), the tension between a practical preparation for productive work in society and a critical understanding of the way society organizes and distributes work has vanished. So has the tension between individual freedom and the recognition and assumption of shared tasks within a democratic community.

Whether it concerns the education of managers or of professionals, liberal learning is proposed as the best or most effective response to a 'crisis', be it 'a crisis of confidence in professional knowledge' (Schon 1983), in management, or in organizational theory and practice (Marsick 1987b).[3] The crisis is brought about by 'rapid, complex change in organizations, people and their work', (Marsick 1987a: 10) calling for new ways of dealing with knowledge and information, new kinds of knowledge and information, and different ways of organizing the workplace and managing employees. Previous forms or 'paradigms' of training and educating professionals and managers are considered inadequate for dealing with change because they emphasize technical knowledge, narrow specialization, and a mechanical, Taylorized workplace organization characterized by a hierarchical, non-participatory structure of management. In all of these proposals, a comprehensive analysis of change in terms of its many ties to larger social, economic, and political developments, is missing. In particular, the question of larger social divisions and hierarchies with which the manifold causes and manifestations of change are inevitably bound up is not addressed at all, severely limiting the value of programmes and proposals presumably representing new paradigms.

Despite a vocabulary of reflection, participation, and empowerment, underlying structures of a hierarchical and unequitable organization and distribution of work remain intact. This is particularly apparent in proposals that directly link education or learning with upper-level positions in management or the professions. In these proposals the idea of learning for social and individual empowerment has to a large extent shrunk to learning for positions of power. This is reflected in a corresponding notion of work, and of 'good work', which essentially becomes equivalent to professional and managerial work, set in sharp contrast to 'jobs'. Liberal education or liberal learning is proposed to serve as a preparation for 'good work' rather than jobs (Chickering 1981). He simply asserts (ibid. 6) that current changes in the work force, particularly the shift to the 'service worker' and the 'knowledge worker' 'require a shift in the way we think about work and jobs' and swiftly moves his focus to the 'professional'. He avoids the problematic question of the benefits of a liberal education for people who have, or who are prepared for, jobs which, we can safely assume, will be the reality of the majority for some time to come.

In such writings the world of work is essentially collapsed into upper-level leadership positions within the occupational structure. By combining not only 'good work' but also 'individual success' with these positions, proposals like Chickering's fully operate on the basis of a highly conventional notion of individual success. The underlying view of the model adult is a competitive, upwardly mobile individual. The characteristics of such a successful individual actually magnify prevailing stereotyped definitions of masculine qualities into exemplary social behaviour, significantly reducing the possible realm of meaning of 'good work' and of 'success'.[4] I believe (and the writing of this book is an expression of this belief) that we can arrive at a notion of 'good work' which is not constructed from the privileged, exclusive reality of a male-identified élite, thus freeing the notion of success from its bond with an inherently unjust, stratified social reality, characterized by an unequal system of rewards and privileges.

It could be argued that these writers' explicit concern is with the élite, and that they want to ensure that our leadership is an enlightened and responsible one who could greatly benefit from a liberal education oriented towards 'cultural sophistication and cross-cultural understanding, empathy, understanding and respect for others, loyalty and intimacy, sense of self in a social–historical context, clarity of values and integrity' (Chickering 1981: 3). Such goals, however, are confronted with the question why these important educational goods are apparently of value only for a small élite. In training/education schemes oriented towards job preparation and 'work readiness' the idea and ideal of liberal education are strikingly absent – an absence which testifies to the critical, and hence potentially 'subversive' elements of the liberal tradition. As one writer observed: 'It is hard to find examples in education history of people being kept in their place with liberal arts' (Shor 1986: 50). Are those who are stuck with jobs expected to lack the qualities that a liberal education is to produce? It seems that cultural sophistication, clarity of values and similar goods are reserved for activities to take place after working hours. However, the above-mentioned qualities associated with a liberal education are tied to an existence that is both *social* and *productive*. To presume that they can become objects of private pursuits disconnected from inherently social–productive activities, inexorably pushes them into the sphere of *private consumption*.

FROM LIBERAL EDUCATION TO LIBERAL LEARNING

Chickering and others who link liberal education directly with careers, work with an already reduced notion of liberal education as liberal *learning* where certain general and broad skills called 'liberal learning skills' are distilled from the traditional content areas of the liberal arts. As one writer emphasizes, 'liberal learning is *not* specific coursework' (Jones 1982: 2). Rather, the content areas comprising the liberal arts are arenas of practice for students to 'ask questions, to exercise judgments based both on facts and values, and to analyze problems' (ibid.: 6). Consequently, while liberal learning skills cannot be entirely dissociated from content, this content has value only in as much as it contributes to general skills which can be applied in many different or divergent contexts.

From an educational perspective, the dissipation of content, and the distillation of de-contextualized liberal learning skills signifies a thorough restructuring of the concept of liberal education which has a number of far-reaching consequences. These revolve around the relationship between a substantive content as represented by the knowledge areas of the liberal arts, and the procedures of analysis, synthesis, and evaluation that are inscribed in their structure. Undoubtedly, the broad cognitive skills that are placed under the rubric of 'liberal learning skills', which together comprise a questioning, reflective, and evaluative habit of mind, can be developed and sharpened only around and through a substantive content. However, such substantive content comprises symbolic expressions of a cultural heritage and a common past which provides the grounds for socially shared norms, assumptions, and procedures. These are, above all, the content areas of interpretative sciences such as history, philosophy, literary criticism, etc. A great portion of the knowledge content of the liberal arts therefore deals with questions and themes that relate to a quest for cultural-social self-interpretation and self-understanding. Such questions directly arise out of the communicative or consensual foundation of a shared stock of knowledge and experience.

The critical potential of a liberal education is directly related to this consensual basis. In fact, the very meaning of 'critique' or 'critical' refers to the process of questioning the reality and validity of a social consensus concerning beliefs, values, and assumptions. In particular, critique aims at the illumination of a false consensus which, within a hierarchically organized, divided and stratified society, is but the consensus of an élite. The actual content around which such a pseudo-consensus is built, i.e. the pre-given context of established norms and associated values, opinions, and beliefs is as much an issue here as are the procedures of analysis and critique. The process of establishing the truth of opinions or the rightness of norms is a collaborative–communicative one, aiming at a new and authentic consensus about what constitutes the truth or what can and should be considered generally acceptable norms. In other words, these procedures themselves have a dialogic structure that directly arises out of the communicative structure of the themes, contents, and issues themselves.[5] The ability to engage in those consensual procedures encompasses more than either context-free cognitive–analytic skills or context-bound concrete and specific knowledge, but draws in a person's entire motivational structure. Above all, it creates a sensitivity suffused with respect and co-operation and one which recognizes the damaging effect of power on all aspects of social and individual reality.

When the selection of content becomes an essentially arbitrary matter because conceivably many different kinds of content could serve the same purpose, the communicative or consensual structure of content becomes frozen into a means–end relationship. The liberal learning skills, already severed from their context, are further instrumentally related to greater work efficiency or career preparation. As previously mentioned, a liberal education has always been vocationally oriented, but it has always had an overflow of content which had no immediate relevance for the students' vocation or work, but which was meaningful as preparation for membership in society or the general human community. Although in reality true and full membership has traditionally been reserved for White property-owning men, the underlying idea of 'the rights of man' to participate in public life as a free citizen as developed by liberal philosophy in the eighteenth and nineteenth centuries has always been confronted by demands which seized upon its inherent claim of being a *universally* valid ideal. To be prepared for such general membership, however, implies knowing about the history, the traditions, and the meaning of cultural artefacts of the society one is to become a member of, and not simply the ability to function effectively in the position in which one is placed or which one wants to attain. In particular, 'membership' implies taking notice of a shared heritage, and of moral–practical implications that affect all members.

We can therefore speak of a twofold transformation and thinning out of the concept of liberal education. First, by severing skills and procedures from their content-context, and secondly, by assessing the value of these skills primarily in terms of their contribution to more efficient work performance. A third aspect has to be added as contributing to a further gutting of liberal education. To the extent to which the recent emphasis on the value of liberal learning constitutes an attempt to adapt to a crisis, its legitimation is tied to the extrinsically given 'need to be more effective in an economy that for the first time is truly international'.[6] Or, in Aronowitz and Giroux' words (1985: 180), 'the formation of a critical cadre able to span a wide area of political, cultural and social knowledge is an absolutely essential condition for crisis management'. However, to span such a wide area of knowledge does not mean to transcend the narrowly utilitarian context of corporate education. As the dean of the Arthur D. Little Management Institute correctly points out, traditional MBA programmes train people for being 'a brand manager at General Foods'. The new approach, strongly oriented towards 'an international environment, instead prepares the students to be 'the managing director of the Tanzanian Tobacco Company, or some such thing'.[7]

Symptomatically, the broader, more general abilities that are considered relevant for the new manager become increasingly narrower as one descends the occupational ladder. The instrumental core of the 'liberal learning for business careers' approach emerges more clearly, however, once the outer layers of the meaning of 'liberal' have been peeled off, and the liberal learning skills are codified into discrete, observable behavioural objectives.[8]

In proposals for new 'workplace basics', normative issues associated with moral-practical conduct like 'motivation' and 'interpersonal communication' are further reduced to strictly adaptive attitudes. Here a *general*, broad liberal arts education is only faintly echoed in the *generic abilities* to be developed by the majority of workers.[9] Qualities like cross-cultural understanding or clarity of values and integrity that were still included in the preparation for successful professional and managerial performance (Chickering 1981) are obviously no longer necessary for effective performance in subordinate positions.

5

EDUCATING CHEAP LABOUR

THREATS, CRISES, AND OTHER LOOMING DISASTERS

In Part I the economic reasons for the need for cheap labour were discussed in some detail.[1] I want to refer the reader to this discussion and here only add a few points. In his essay 'Education and the Sony War', Joel Spring (1985) summarizes the economic developments which have taken place since 1960. The fact that American companies were losing ground in international competition due to delayed capital investments and declining productivity led to a twofold appeal to education: better basic skills training or 'career preparation' in order to expand the pool of workers qualifiying for low-level jobs thereby keeping wages from climbing, and 'increased graduation requirements in mathematics, science, and other academic fields', producing new graduates who 'will lead US industry to victory in the worldwide technological competition' (Spring 1985: 124).[2] He continues (ibid. 124–5):

> Both of these trends in educational policy are designed to provide US business with an expanded pool of potential employees – and consequently a decline in wages. This will be particularly true if high unemployment continues to characterize the 1980s. If these two trends are successful, the market will be flooded with high school graduates with good work attitudes and minimum basic skills for entry-level positions and with highly qualified scientists and engineers.

Shor (1986: 128) makes a similar point in his discussion of the 'real needs' of business:

> One is a limited supply of highly-trained personnel. A second is an oversupply of middle- and lower-range labor. A third is high-level research and development in a handful of major universities. A fourth is a curriculum which adjusts students to the labor market, as well as to the domestic and foreign priorities of the corporations. A fifth outcome is education as a business activity itself, an open market for business goods and services.[3]

It is against this background that I want to examine the proposals and arguments presented for training and educating the future labour force. By keeping in mind business' overall concern for a large pool of workers with good work habits and basic skills, a critical look at the arguments put forth reveals a number of glaring inadequacies, and above all a lack of analyses which would do justice to the complex interplay of the multiple factors and relationships contributing to the current situation, a complexity which is not explained by simply painting the picture of a 'looming human capital crisis' (Perelman 1984). One of the consequences of describing and explaining work-related developments within these narrow parameters is an overall structure of argument that is ridden with contradictions, and marked by unwarranted assertions, stated but unproven relationships between isolated facts, an absence of concrete and specific evidence, and a reliance on emotionally charged language.

The overall tone is generally set by a vocabulary which 'preys on the anxiety of a generation that has finally got the news that America in the new era is *Hard Times*' (Aronowitz 1980: 45). Thus, we hear of *A Nation at Risk* (1983) of a literacy *crisis* or even a literacy *breakdown*.[4] Perelman's *Learning Enterprise* (1984), for instance, is replete with a vocabulary that can only promote anxiety. The first chapter is titled 'Threat', depicting the dangers of a 'looming human capital crisis', speaking of 'the threat of turbulent, even violent social upheaval', and of 'a threatened professional class' (ibid. 1-5). Lee (1988: 28) speaks of a 'quiet crisis in basic skills tightening its grip', 'setting off alarms', and putting America's workforce in 'grave jeopardy'. *Business Week* (19 September 1988) devotes an entire issue to 'the decline of America's workforce', the 'monumental mismatch between jobs and the ability of Americans to do them', which is 'threatening' the nation's 'ability to compete' (Bernstein 1988).

It is worth looking at the argument in some detail. In *A Nation at Risk*, for instance, the decline of the American educational system is deplored, thereby holding it fully responsible for current economic problems. Consequently, so the authors of the report argue, the only road to economic recovery is improved schooling, education, and training. In short, the educational system is both 'the problem and the solution to the economic crisis' (Shor 1986: 108). No proof is offered for this causal connection. Rather, it relies on its considerable emotional appeal which is drawn from many sources of actual and potential fears and worries of a population confronted with the dismal state of public education, the diminishing power of unions to protect pay cheques or jobs, with worker displacement, unemployment, and a fast rate of obsolescence of work-related experience and skills. This report, like others, seems to draw its persuasive power primarily from the presumed direct connection between the 'economic crisis' and a deficient human capital. Once that connection is made, the primary task is to present information on demographic trends (who *are* these deficient workers?) as well as changing and increasing skills requirements for the jobs of the future (what *are* the skills needed by the future workforce?). However, precisely because the relationship between education/training and jobs (in the form of performance, work-related tasks and skills, employment opportunities, etc.) is far from unidirectional and clear-cut, concrete, detailed, and convincing evidence cannot be brought forth in favour of this connection.

This is one of the reasons that facts and myths are so enormously entangled in these accounts. The overall message is all too clear, however: the problem of threatened economic competitiveness or economic decline resides with the individual. In other words, the entire weight of the current 'productivity decline' is placed on the shoulders of 'an unproductive population' (Shor 1986: 110). Questions of international economic competition that have led to a new international division of labour, plant closures and relocations due to high capital mobility forever in search of 'cheap labour', urban decline leading to geographical and social isolation of large inner city populations, sexual and racial discrimination – to name only a few factors which directly contribute to the current reality of work – all these questions are ultimately reduced to the simple explanation that people lack certain skills. While the concerns with illiteracy, lack of so-called basic skills, and with uncertainty about skill requirements of future jobs are all highly legitimate, the mystification of the true causes of these and other problems makes training proposals which idealize the complex and ambiguous link between work and education highly dubious (Gleeson 1986: 56). Without a clear understanding of these causes, however, proposals for various training schemes and programmes will contribute mainly to 'reducing expectations, limiting aspirations, and increasing commitments to the existing social structure' (Shor 1986: 38–9) by feeding on justified fear and anxiety about future survival possibilities.

THE WHITE MALE WORKER – A VANISHING SPECIES?

In a special report titled 'Human capital: the decline of the American workforce,' *Business Week* (19 September 1988) depicts the problem as one that arises because 'employers must now dig deeper into the barrel of the poorly educated' because labour markets have tightened (Bernstein, p104).[5] The 'decline' is brought on by the fact that the future workforce will consist of a higher percentage of women, minorities, and immigrants and a correspondingly lower percentage of White men. As described by Dole (1989), these are the 'populations where the human resource investment has been historically inadequate – women, minorities and immigrants'. In a similar manner, Chynoweth (1989: 1–2) cites five 'facts' in connection with the claim that 'a gap is emerging between the relatively low education and skills of workers entering the labor force, ... and the advancing skill requirements of the new economy': a slower growth of the population and the workforce, a rise in the average age of the population and the workforce, women constituting almost two-thirds of the new entrants into the workforce, minorities assuming a larger share of new labour force entrants, and immigrants representing the largest share of the increase in the population and the workforce. The relationship between these facts and the claim of a widening skills gap is tenuous at best, nonexistent at worst.

A relationship is established mainly by the quasi-automatic association of women, minorities, and immigrants with low-grade human capital. Additionally enveloped by a language of threat, gloom and doom, existing prejudices against women, minorities, and 'aliens' are easily mobilized. I believe that these are, above all, the fears of White men who, in the future, will no longer be the majority of workers (although still favoured by employers, see below). Such fear is expressed, for instance, in the language used in the following quote, where the authors warn of the 'increasing percentage of *non-White, non-male* workers and illiterate workers' (Spikes 1989: 10, my emphasis), creating an immediate and unquestioned association of non-White and non-male with less valuable than male and White, particularly by placing these terms in juxtaposition with 'illiterate workers'.

On the whole, the arguments in favour of a declining human capital are based on vast generalizations which are only partly supported by factual evidence. For instance, to label categorically women as 'low-skilled' or 'uneducated' can only be called absurd. As reported by Cyert and Mowery (1987: 119): 'The secondary educational attainment of female workers exceeds that of male workers, which suggests that women in fact may be better prepared to deal with the workplace of the future'.[6]

Although without a solid empirical base, the structure of the argument is revealing. It appears to serve primarily an ideological function as it directly feeds into a notion of skill which is 'saturated with sexual bias' (Phillips and Taylor 1980: 55). Not only are skills in general sex-stereotyped as typical women's and typical men's skills, but – as the current debate on 'comparable worth' reveals – the unilateral equation of women's work with low-skilled labour weaves in and out of skills' definitions and corresponding wage differentials.[7] Ironically, the same skills that were previously expected from women as practically natural givens, above all manual dexterity, patience, and attention to detail (see Chapter 2) now reappear as 'higher skills' for which the (male) workers have to be retrained. The switch from handling '100-pound wire that was 6 inches in diameter' to the use of fibre optics 'which means splicing very delicate fibres – like a brain surgeon, almost' is interpreted as a 'skills gap' and illustrated with the picture of a White, male, intellectual-looking worker (Bernstein 1988: 105). The hundreds of thousands of South East Asian women doing the intricate wire bonding work in the microchip industries of multinational corporations were certainly never compared with brain surgeons, and their skills were likewise not considered 'high'.[8]

The picture painted of minorities is equally one-sided, overgeneralized, and therefore highly misleading. The existence and growth of the Black 'underclass' (Wilson 1987) cannot be denied, and should cause alarm and outrage. However, the over-emphasis on Black teenage pregnancy, high-shool drop-out rates, the references to crime, drug-use, and single-parent families paints an overall picture of total 'disorganization' and 'disintegration', directly feeding off White racist fears. In addition, the situation is not deplored because of the human suffering involved, but because it places an immense burden on American businesses. 'Explanations' of this problem consist of vague references to 'racism', mainly, however, the reasons are found to lie in 'cultural factors, and in the frustration and apathy' on the side of the members of the underclass itself (Garland 1988: 123). Why the cities are in decline, why large numbers of minorites are geographically isolated, without access to decent schooling, job opportunities, or to information about the latter – these questions are not addressed. Neither is the part 'the economy' itself may have played in this demise.

There is another hidden dimension which needs to be addressed. In discussions emphasizing the high illiteracy rate and general cultural disorganization of 'the disadvantaged' it remains entirely unclear to what extent these people are not part of a general labour surplus that will most likely never be absorbed or even tapped into. We need to look at this situation not only within the context of the world market and the global economy which is characterized by an overall trend towards a growing labour surplus, but also in the light of the above-mentioned upward moving 'flashpoint' indicating 'full employment'.[9] Johnston and Packer's comment (1987: 91), that the 'unprecedented opportunity' for minorites to enter the labour force 'over the next 13 years' is a 'sanguine outlook' which is 'far from assured', is one of the more realistic statements found in the literature.[10] While these authors indirectly support my point, their explicit emphasis lies on an accurate assessment of the workings of a segregated labour market and the mechanisms of discrimination (ibid. 91):

> ... given the historic patterns of behavior by employers, it is more reasonable to expect that they will bid up the wages of the relatively smaller numbers of white labor force entrants, seek to substitute capital for labor in many service occupations, and/or move job sites to the faster growing, more youthful parts of the country, or perhaps of the world.[11]

Furthermore, the history of discrimination against minorities regardless of educational background or preparation is similar to that of women. As reported in *Business Week* (5 February 1990), for instance, 'a surprising number of college-educated blacks have remained mired at the bottom of the economic ladder' (p. 18).

According to Census Bureau data,

> one out of three black male college graduates earned wages in 1987 that fell below the poverty line of about $12,000 for a family of four (compared with one of six white male college graduates). Worse, nearly half of the black female college graduates earned similar poverty-level wages.
>
> (ibid.)

Perelman (1984) also indirectly supports the view that not much is to be gained by concentrating on 'the disadvantaged', although he approaches the issue from another angle. His main concern is to provide an argument for building a large, comprehensive adult education 'learning enterprise', modelled after the (idealized) 'free enterprise system', and built on the principles of privatization, decentralization, and open competition. His concern with an undue emphasis on youth and the disadvantaged, and a corresponding neglect of the 'masses of workers in the middle' (ibid. 22) by adult educators can be interpreted as a practical business decision since the 'mainstream of work-force adults' (ibid. xvi) is certainly a more likely and reliable clientele than the 'disadvantaged' who are generally 'hard to reach'.

The information regarding immigrants likewise becomes a bit less clear-cut than the equation 'immigrants = unskilled = bad for business' suggests. Contrary to the evocation of hordes of aliens ill-equipped for future high-skill jobs, Johnston and Packer (1987: 93) state that 'on balance, levels of immigration of 450,000–750,000 will benefit the country'. This is not surprising, since immigrants are an instant cheap, and above all, disciplined labour force, often desperate enough to work for lowest wages, and under worst conditions. As *Business Week* (13 June 1988) reports, 'tough immigration laws may be the last thing we need', and 'Washington may already be recognizing the need to import more workers' (p. 22). Significantly, in both reports the (generally low) educational level of the immigrants did not enter into the argument. Furthermore, Johnston and Packer (1987: 93–4) describe a situation of little or no competition between Mexican immigrants and native minorities, thus testifying to a highly segregated and segmented labour market where different kinds of work are reserved for different kinds of people.

A WIDENING SKILLS GAP?

If we look at the statistics and numbers presented, there is no doubt that the skills of the future will look different, and in many cases require higher levels of literacy. It is not clear, however, precisely how large the increased demand will be, and, more importantly, how many workers will be needed to fill these jobs requiring higher literacy levels. As stated in Chynoweth (1989: 13), 'depending on the definition, estimates of national illiteracy range from as low as 0.5 percent to as high as 50 percent of adult Americans.' Apart from different kinds of definitions that may exist concurrently, any one definition is prone to change as well. As stated by Harmann (1987: 3):

> The attempt to define literacy is like a walk to the horizon: as one walks toward it, it continuously recedes. Similarly, as groups of people achieve the skills formerly defined as literacy, altered circumstances often render definitions obsolete. New definitions replace the old ones as new goals are set. People considered literate by a previous yardstick are now regarded as illiterate.[12]

Lee (1988: 28), for instance, who talks about a 'quiet crisis in basic skills', does not state what percentage of the actual workforce is and will be affected by illiteracy or what the ratio of available jobs and illiterate workers will be. Very similar to *Business Week*'s (19 September 1988) alarmist report, an impression is created of an overall workforce plagued by illiteracy, and of a school system that churns out more illiterate than literate students. Lee cites an example, however, which throws some light not only on the magnitude of the problem, but also on the *real* crisis: A New York telephone company tested 21,000 applicants to fill 780 vacancies. He reports, (1988: 29) 'only' 16 per cent, i.e. 3,360 of those applicants, or more than four times as many as were needed to fill the jobs, passed the test. Can this really be interpreted as a 'widening skills gap', or do we have to focus our attention on the 'widening jobs gap' instead, where 21,000 applicants are competing for 780 positions? This does not take away any importance from the fact that a high number of people are lacking basic literacy skills – but this is a problem that needs to be discussed and addressed in its own right rather than misinterpreted as a danger to productivity and economic growth.

In general, numbers of workers involved, as well as the actual skills requirements are entirely blown out of proportion. It also remains unclear (and undiscussed) from which groups of people the new job entrants will be recruited. 'The workforce' is a mythical construction, as we need to talk about a labour market which is highly segregated, divided, and stratified. Thus, to say that 'of all the new jobs that will be created over the 1984–2000 period, more than half will require some education beyond high school' (Johnston and Packer 1987: 97) does not state whether this trend is new or one that affects the groups of people deplored as unskilled. It plays, however, into the 'higher skills' argument. As the statistics presented by Johnston and Packer (1987: 97) show, if ranked by percentage of growth, the top 50 per cent of all jobs that are growing include lawyers and judges, scientists, technical and health professionals, managers, writers and artists, etc., but do not even include the fastest growing occupation, i.e. services. Obviously, these occupations have traditionally not been drawing from 'women, minorities, and immigrants'.

The overall picture regarding past, current and future levels of educational attainment of the workforce as a whole, or of certain special groups like women or minorites is far from equivocal. First of all, since the 1950s there has been a steady and continuous rise of educational attainment. As reported in Cyert and Mowery (1987: 66), the share of the labour force without a high school diploma declined from 50.3 per cent in 1959 to 18.5 per cent in 1986. In addition, the share of those with at least a college degree doubled over the same time span. Likewise, Perelman (1984: 15), after deploring the 'looming human capital crisis', complains of an overabundance of 'college-educated members of the workforce' and warns of 'a rising tide of overeducated and underemployed graduates'. In her discussion on the reasons for growing workers' alienation, Munelly (1987: 80) summarily states that 'workers are now more highly educated than at any other time in our history'. The evidence presented by Cyert and Mowery (1987) fully supports this view. This evidence also contradicts the portrayal of the workforce of the future as deteriorating because of the higher percentage of women and minorities. In fact, as they write (1987: 67), 'changes in the racial and gender composition of the future US work force will have a minimal impact on aggregate levels of secondary or postsecondary attainment'. Not only will the increase of minorities be relatively small (a rise from 13 per cent in 1984 to 15 per cent in 1995), but the educational gaps between Whites and minorities have been narrowing (ibid. 66, 70).

Above all, no solid evidence exists for the claims about an overall decline or deterioration of the workforce, and discussions on the growing illiteracy of large numbers of Americans, or on the 'widening skills gap' need considerable qualification. The same is true for the claim that the jobs of the future will require higher skills. Johnston and Packer (1987: 100), for instance, make the following statement:

> Although the overall pattern of job growth is weighted towards higher-skill occupations, *very large numbers of jobs will be created in some medium to low-skilled fields*. In absolute numbers, the biggest job creation categories will be service occupations, administrative support, and marketing and sales, which together account for half of the net new jobs that will be created. In the service category, the largest groups are cooks, nursing aides, waiters, and janitors. Among administrative support jobs, secretaries, clerks, and computer operators predominate. In marketing and sales, most of the new slots will be for cashiers. With the exception of computer operators, *most of these large categories require only modest levels of skill*.[13]

The authors continue (1987: 100) by stating that even for those moderately skilled jobs 'workers will be expected to read and understand directions, add and subtract, and be able to speak and think clearly'. In other words, the overall expectations may be higher with respect to previous skill levels, although the skills themselves are fairly 'basic'.

The discussions on lack of basic skills among workers already employed and among new applicants fairly consistently point to large numbers of both these groups to show some deficiencies in written communication and computational skills. As reported by Cyert and Mowery (1987: 25), the Office of Technology Assessment estimated that roughly 20 per cent of those displaced from employment from 1979–84 'could be characterized as deficient in basic communication and computational skills'. This is consistent with the example given above about the New York Telephone company. Undoubtedly, lack of basic literacy skills constitutes a problem for the workers involved, as they may not find new employment, or lose their jobs because of the difficulty in retraining them.[14]

Again, these figures do not in and of themselves testify to the 'decline of human capital'. They testify, above all, to large numbers of jobs which did not draw on the human capacity to think. We do not find even a hint of criticism of design and organization of work as contributing to the 'decline' of basic skills in mainstream literature.[15] On the contrary, past efforts to adapt a workforce to the highly fragmented, Taylorized and regimented conditions of factory life is now considered simply 'inopportune'. In the words of one adult educator (displaying total obliviousness to the ethical implications of his statement):

> We (sic) can no longer rely on brute strength and brawn, or completion of rote, assembly line tasks to survive and prosper in the twenty-first century. We can no longer afford to let abstract thought processes atrophy in a large percentage of the population.[16]

Apart from testifying to the general moral bankruptcy of bottom-line thinking, this quote illustrates particularly well the above-mentioned 'view from above', expressed in a strong class bias evoking an imagery of mindless manual labourers.[17] In the light of all this, I find it extremely hard to empathize with the 'plight of business' which has to deal with so many illiterate workers, nor am I impressed by the figures that are so frequently cited on how many dollars US corporations spend on training. Obviously, the assumption is that 'society' as well as individual workers 'owe' it to business to provide a fully prepared, ready-made labour force, and with enough surplus labour to keep wages down.

Within the context of the present discussion it is important to emphasize, first of all, that the millions of workers who lost their jobs over the last 15 years were not displaced because of their lack of basic skills (apart from the fact that only 20 per cent were shown to be deficient) but because of various structural changes like plant closures, relocations, and workplace automation. Second, it is not clear how many of these displaced workers can or could be reabsorbed into the active labour force anyhow, regardless of their levels of skill, especially considering their age. Third, the obstacles many of these workers face are frequently caused by new jobs being geared towards quite different populations than those who have been displaced. This is true particularly with respect to the fastest growing sector, i.e the service sector which, as discussed in Chapter 3, favours the employment of women.

Nevertheless, a concern with lack of basic skills is highly legitimate. In a society that is becoming increasingly more complex, everybody should be equipped with more than 'basic' literacy skills, and the fact that so many Americans lack even these is an indictment of the society as a whole rather than of the illiterate people themselves. Furthermore, to have minimal basic skills at least gives people a chance to find employment, although this is no guarantee since the relationship between skills and jobs is far from being unidirectional.

RE-SKILLING, DE-SKILLING, AND THE KNOWLEDGE WORKER

Arguments concerning a 'widening skills gap' not only rely on the above-cited figures concerning deficiencies in basic skills, but also explicitly or implicitly evoke the need for 'higher skills'. Through a variety of rhetorical means the overall picture that is painted for the jobs of the future is one of generally higher-level skills, i.e. abilities that go beyond reading, writing, and computing, primarily in connection with high technology and 'knowledge work'.[18] The definitions of what constitutes 'higher skills' are as volatile as those describing basic literacy. While these definitions are highly context-specific, they are often presented as objectively given, generally valid requirements for jobs of the future. Perelman (1984: 10) is particularly optimistic about large numbers of people in the future being employed in 'knowledge-related work'. This fits well with his interest in building a huge adult 'learning enterprise' but contradicts the usual predictions of where most jobs of the future will lie.

Perelman's optimism is unfounded for another reason as well. To be employed in knowledge-related work by no means automatically translates into 'performing functions that require uniquely human intelligence, imagination, and creativity' (ibid. 10). This may be true most likely for a small élite of workers, especially when one considers the continuing trend of new information processing technology to become 'people-literate', i.e. to take over more and more of the functions of human intelligence – a point which Perelman (1984: 19) himself stresses. This may leave only rather passive and assisting or 'processing' functions to the 'knowledge worker'. Contradicting most of his argument, Perelman (ibid. 47) even states that

'Pac-Man may be more relevant to tomorrow's functional literacy than some high school math courses'. I would like to claim that instead of requiring intelligence, creativity, or imagination, Pac-Man strengthens precisely the opposite: to react without interference of thought.

Perelman's idealism concerning knowledge work feeds into the overall tendency to equate work dealing with various aspects of a symbolically mediated material, i.e. language, numbers, etc. with higher skills. The underlying assumption seems to be that the very contact with the symbolic expressions of human intelligence, no matter on what level, requires equivalent knowledge or intellectual processes. However, the nature of the contact with the products of human intelligence needs to be considered before the assertion is warranted that higher skills are required (see also Chapter 8). I want to claim that underlying this equation lies the usual glorification of technology rather than a sound understanding of levels of skill. One wonders why the skills of the secretary typing the manuscript of a philosophy professor or of a scientist were never considered to be of a higher order although she certainly works with the results of human intelligence and imagination. In general, a direct, unequivocal association between high technology and higher skills is entirely unwarranted. Such an equation functions mainly as an ideological device to portray the workers of the future as ill-equipped, thereby blaming them not only for the problems of the economy, but also for their own potential 'personal failure' in obtaining adequate employment.

The calls for higher skills are part of the larger argument concerning the 'de-skilling' or 're-skilling' of work, particularly in connection with the introduction of new technology into more and more workplaces. The arguments and counter-arguments for and against re- or de-skilling are manifold, contradictory, and highly confusing. The de-skilling argument was first presented by Harry Braverman (1974), and has been taken up and criticized by researchers investigating the effect of new technology on women's office and clerical work (see, for example, Machung 1984). The re-skilling argument has so far mainly been presented in literature identifying with the business perspective and emphasizing the positive aspects of new technology on work (for references see Carter 1987: 202–3 and Zuboff 1988).

The effect of the introduction of high technology into various workplaces is therefore highly varied, depending on a large number of factors, including the particular category of workers affected by these changes. In general, available evidence seems to suggest that the various re-skilling and de-skilling processes set in motion by the introduction of new technology not only occur along the lines of pre-established divisions but also contribute in their own particular way to the overall trend towards a polarization of the workforce. A study conducted by Appelbaum (1987) on the introduction of new technology into the insurance industry, for instance, shows that this change displaced a significant number of minority women who had only recently entered clerical positions and performed the more routine jobs which could be automated most easily. Simultaneously, new highly skilled clerical work, the result of automating the more routine aspects of professional work and making them part of clerical work was available primarily to White women with the necessary class background and credentials.

However, while the skills requirements rose, making work available for certain groups of women (while diminishing employment opportunities for others, or pushing them into newly available low-skilled and poorly paid jobs), clerical work as a whole remained sex-segregated and essentially dead-end. We can here speak of a trend towards polarization characterized by an elimination of middle-level (professional) positions and thus of the career path from clerical to professional work (Appelbaum 1987: 196). Polarization therefore occurs not only in terms of wages, work relations, and skills or expertise, but also in terms of dead-end and upwardly mobile positions, all of which occurring along old class, racial, and sexual lines.

There is ample evidence to show that the processes described above are characterized by considerable internal struggles where skills are often redefined by the more powerful groups to exclude the weaker ones from moving out of dead-end jobs, or from entering more prestigious positions (Cockburn 1983, Bergmann 1986, Game and Pringle 1983, Phillips and Taylor 1980). In other words, the distribution of kinds of work, and of access to work or employment is strongly related to the fact that the labour market is divided by class, race, and sex. This means that access to jobs, requiring higher skills is unequally distributed along the lines of class, race, and sex, that 'higher skills' are not necessarily equivalent to higher-level or more prestigious jobs (including higher levels of autonomy or authority), or that they constitute more opportunity for advancement.

In fact, evidence exists for both de- as well as re-skilling of work, depending greatly on the particular area or occupation under scrutiny (e.g. banking vs. industry), as well as on the size and structure of an office or firm where new office technology is introduced (see, for instance, Zuboff 1988). The picture is further complicated by the fact that not all researchers base their discussion on the same definition, emphasizing different factors or aspects, depending on their particular interpretation, interests, as well as tacit cultural assumptions. Thus, while some researchers discuss the increase or decrease in the *technical* aspect of skills, others emphasize the aspect of *autonomy* and *control* as important indicators for de- or re-skilling (see, for instance, Carter 1987).

THE NEW NATIVES

In the light of the considerable qualifications that have to be made about the wholesale portrayal of 'the American workforce' of the future as seriously deficient, one has to find the reasons behind painting these gloomy pictures elsewhere. In fact, by coupling the unabashedly admitted corporate need for 'cheap labour' with the alarmist language of decline, threat, and crisis (used by corporate leaders and adult educators alike), a picture emerges that is not unlike 'the native problem' of the colonial era, and not unlike the debates on Third World development, characterized by a vocabulary of 'integration' and 'modernization'.

In more familiar adult education terminology, the new natives are the 'disadvantaged' stratum of society, the 'special populations', and all those classes or groups who have not yet managed to 'enter' the mainstream of American society, who are still 'outside', do not yet fit. They constitute the internal Third World of 'not yet developed' or 'underdeveloped' segments of the population.

This analogy is not far-fetched. In fact, the tenor of proposals aiming at the 'integration' or 'development' of certain segments of the population bears striking resemblance to the structure of argument that supports the concept of 'cheap labour' which in an earlier chapter has been criticized as inherently imperialist. The unproblematic presentation of the (male-identified) successful individual as a societal model for good work, and, by implication, for the good life, is structurally analogous to the notion of the superior White man whose mission it is to civilize the natives in the name of progress.[19] In both cases, the missionary efforts of civilizing the natives or of making the underprivileged 'work ready' ultimately aim at a better utilization of these groups, without, however, eradicating the dichotomous divisions. This has been observed with respect to vocational training schemes, in which

> ... trainees are made more aware of what mainstream society expects of them, in terms of attitude, behaviour, motivation and so forth, but which as *outsiders* is nevertheless beyond their reach.
>
> (Gleeson 1986: 57)

The vocabulary of 'integration' is particularly noteworthy. For instance, the context in which a proposal to 'integrate Blacks and Hispanics fully into the workforce' (Johnston and Packer 1987) is made is reminiscent of 'integrating' the native population into the world market, or of women into the male-defined and hierarchical employment structure without the natives becoming White, or women's position in the labour market becoming structurally equivalent to that of male workers. In cases like these 'integration' is entirely defined in terms of those in positions of power, i.e. of those who constitute the norm from which the 'non-integrated' obviously deviate. However, the structure into which those groups are to be integrated produced their very 'outsider status' which is now being deplored. 'Integration' therefore stands mainly for a greater use and exploitation of 'human capital'. Furthermore, notions of cultural superiority are an integral part of the 'colonial structure' of adult education proposals dealing with the disadvantaged. The following quote, for instance, reveals such parallels with the colonizers' belief in their own cultural superiority, leading to attempts to reform and 'raise' the cultural level of the natives at least to an extent where they could be 'integrated' enough to become profitable:

> Before minority unemployment can be significantly reduced, there must be change in the cultural values that make it seem more attractive to sell drugs or get pregnant than to do well in school and work at McDonalds.
>
> (Johnston and Packer 1987: 115)

At least, the authors of the Hudson report are open about the extent to which the disadvantaged are to be integrated, and the kind of success towards which they can aspire.

The 'get tough' and 'shape up or ship out' language of what seems to be a new wave of mandatory training for the underdeveloped segments of the population further testifies to the basically authoritarian attitude represented in those programmes, ranging from suggestions to 'close the worst schools, fire incompetent teachers, and expel disruptive students' (Johnston and Packer 1987: 115) to 'Learnfare' programs 'in which AFDC [Assistance to Families with Dependent Children] parents who have not completed high school would be required to register for adult education/GED programs, followed by mandatory registration in job search/skills programs' (*Online*, vol. 5, no. 6, January 1988). Passages like the following, for instance, give further testimony to such an inherently authoritarian structure, giving credence to the statement that '"illiteracy" became the rubric under which all forms of repression were subsumed' (Aronowitz 1980: 45). Hugh Gordon, personnel director of Lockheed, Atlanta:

> we (sic) need ... to cut the problem into digestible hunks; perhaps divide the illiterate into several 'strata' and then provide prescriptive evaluation and instruction plus mastery testing to solve it.
>
> (Summary report on the National Alliance of Business conference 1985)

Gone is the rhetoric of 'cultural sophistication', of 'empathy' or a 'sense of self' (Chickering 1981) which took the sharp edges off career education. Gone also the concept of liberal learning. We are here not talking about labour that is held in high social esteem, or about 'good work' or careers, but essentially about the production of 'flexible and adjustable human capital', i.e. *cheap labour* whose task it is to restore profit margins. In sum, if today US companies are reclaiming lost markets and staying 'profitable during periods of weak demands' ('Going for the Lion's Share', *Business Week*, 18 July 1988) because they drastically 'slash' payrolls, they are depending on a well-adjusted, unaspiring if not downwardly mobile labour force. In fact, the ground has already been well prepared,

> ... as competitive pressures from overseas have inspired (sic) employers to resist wage demands, as painful memories of staff cuts, layoffs, and plant closings have led workers to temper those demands.
>
> (*Business Week*, 27 May 1988, p.24)

THE FLEXILIFE OF THE GENERIC WORKER

The universal portrayal of the workers of the future as dismally unprepared for the new demanding jobs can be seen as a way to enlarge the pool of minimally skilled entry-level workers without the intention of absorbing them into the labour market. In fact, even the most conservative reports do not envisage a full employment scenario (see, for instance, Johnston and Packer 1987) and hope for an unemployment rate around 5 per cent. Thus, all indicators point in the direction of generally stagnant high unemployment with only slight fluctuations, and increasing forms and numbers of under-employment. Confronted with the considerable uncertainty and instability as regards employment projects, the current strong emphasis on training for jobs tends to translate into the reality of training instead of jobs, of 'learning now, jobs later' (Shor 1986: 131). This policy is officially legitimized by referring to 'constant change' where no one can predict with certainty what kind of jobs, requiring what kind of skills will be available in the future. Shor (ibid. 114) astutely observed that these training schemes are attempts to 'blur the troubling link between education and employment'. He continues (ibid.):

> A weak job market amounted to a moving target which the pistol of education kept missing. Less direct aiming and less shooting meant more credibility to school and society both.

This is the place for 'generic skills' to enter the picture. Generic skills are, above all, meant to contribute to intellectual ('learning how to learn'), psychological ('ready for change') as well as geographical *mobility* and *flexibility*. In other words, generic skills training is proposed as a means to adjust labour 'to long-term uncertainty in the job-market' (Shor 1986: 119).

This is precisely the ideological core of the general or generic skills argument. Those who try to hold on to the continuity of their life history and experience are now met with the indictment of being 'habit-bound', or of 'fearing change' (Johnston and Packer 1987: 68). Again, this rhetoric is reminiscent of the imperialist or patriarchal language that speaks of tradition- or custom-bound peasants, natives, or housewives unwilling to be 'integrated' into the process of modernization. The rhetoric of constant change, flexibility and mobility today has replaced the older one of responsibility and commitment, and a corresponding indictment of irresponsibility and lack of commitment levelled against those who changed jobs frequently on their own account. Furthermore, the calls for flexibility is reserved exclusively for the workers themselves, a perfect illustration of the 'view from above'. In light of such an entrenched idea, to require business or 'the economy' to adjust to the needs of its workers appears scandalous.

Dewey's concern for truly educational principles in the context of a vocational education which adapted workers to the existing industrial regime, today attains a new urgency, as well as an additional twist. It is no longer sufficient to educate a work force which can adapt and live with the regimentations of factory life. This would directly contradict the need for flexibility and versatility. What is called for is a psychological, mental and behavioural preparation for living with instability, and for being able to think of oneself in terms of a renewable, exchangeable and updatable resource rather than in terms of a human being with unique experiences, hopes, wishes, and dreams.

The psychologically (as well as socially), highly problematic aspect behind the euphemisms of 'constant career change' and 'multiple-option flexilives' (Handy 1984) is rarely addressed. For instance, the built-in obsolescence and proposed throw-away nature of one's work-related experiences and competencies may seriously conflict with a psychological and social need for constancy, or for continuity in one's personal history in order to be able to develop and sustain a sense of self, and a supportive community. Handy (1984: 163), who sees the 'flexilife' as not only inevitable, but also an ultimately desirable form of future existence, asserts this necessity for 'a sense of person', but nowhere addresses the question of how this sense is to be achieved. It seems that it is to remain a privilege of the 'professional' to develop a sense of self through her or his work, and to cultivate an identity that is tied to her or his work experience, to a sense of creativity and purpose, including the experience of accumulating, developing and deepening her or his competence – some of the prime characteristics of 'good work'. To be sure, under conditions of corporate industrialism and of generally alienated labour, these aspects of good work have long since been eroded for the majority of the working population. The new and universal emphasis on flexibility and mobility seems to add, however, the finishing touch, extinguishing the last traces of the 'traditional work ethic (which) stressed the integration of work and personal development' (Carlson 1982: 135).

Personal development is part and parcel of the communicative-collaborative aspect of human work (Wirth 1983), which in most workplaces is expressed in informal work relations rather than in the formal organization of work itself.[20] Under conditions of the generic 'flexilife', inherently social, interactive relations are restructured into individual attributes like 'accurate empathy' (Klemp 1982), which can be packed up and carried into a number of interchangeable workplaces or environments. Equipped with her/his generic skills, which are 'durable, versatile, transferable, open-ended, and elastic', the worker becomes the ideal human capital 'virtually immune to obsolescence' (Klemp 1982: 53). This represents a dramatic intensification of the trend found in many adult education programmes towards packaging the curriculum, and towards fragmenting the educational content into individual, disconnected competencies which confront the learner as externally given, objectified behaviour, dissociated from subjectivity or unique experiential background. In many ways, the generic worker of the future, this 'human capital virtually immune to obsolescence', is strangely disembodied, with the possibility of interference by subjective, history-bound experience to a large extent eliminated.

Furthermore, the ideal worker becomes a self-sufficient nomad, migrating with moving job possibilities, keeping specific ties to neighbourhoods, friends and family suspended enough not to interfere with the need for mobility. Stable, long-lasting social networks may, however, become more important for people as the uncertainty of employment opportunities increases. They may be absolutely necessary for spiritual as well as material survival. People who are unwilling to move because they rely on established social networks rather than risking both unemployment and absence of such support, do not display rigidity, inflexibility or 'fear of change' (a reproach which is levelled especially against middle-aged and old workers, see Johnston and Packer 1987: 82–3), as much as a realistic assessement of actual chances for survival.

In sum, the new *generic worker* must be able to adjust to indeterminate change, and is characterized by low expectations regarding pay, work conditions, and above all job security. Ideally, a workforce of generic workers must be either suspicious or directly afraid of any unionization attempts. Finally, such a work force must be able and willing to shoulder an unusual amount of work, since in all likelihood the new jobs will not be enough for the workers to get by, but will have to be combined with other employment, (occasional, seasonal, temporary, etc.) as well as work associated with providing unpaid social and personal services. In short, the new workers will be 'working like women' whose 'flexible working patterns' (Rothwell 1986) have already made them into the preferred labour force in many instances (see Chapter 2).

This parallel has not passed unnoticed. As Handy, the proponent of 'multiple-option flexilives' and 'portfolio-lives' writes (1984: 162):

> [a flexilife] is, in fact, the kind of existence that the last few generations of women have been well used to, moving between work and family, mixing part-time work with home responsibilities, balancing career priorities with a concern for relationships in the home and, in many cases, having to abandon one for the other.

And, he continues,

> It is ironic that just as women have begun to win their fight to lead the kinds of lives that men lead, those lives are beginning to shift towards the pattern from which women are escaping.

In Part I, I discussed how women's 'flexilives', i.e. the unspecificity of their skills, and, consequently, their universal availability for any kind of task is part and parcel of the sexist division of labour, and of women's subordinate position in society in general. In fact, women's flexibility and versatility constituted a major component of the overall devaluation or 'cheapening' of female labour. This pattern is repeated in the calls for the new generic worker. Here, too, flexibility and mobility, coupled with low expectations and a high degree of adaptability to existing social structures have to be seen as part of the general trend towards devaluing all human labour, turning 'human resources' more and more into quasi-natural resources (see also Part III).

It is therefore not surprising that the question 'how do we produce such versatility?' (Ritchie-Calder 1982: 20) becomes an urgent one, and that, therefore, the generic skills package is generally characterized by a strong emphasis on attitudes. In fact, in generic skills training proposals, calls for behavioural training are directly linked to, and at times stressed over, other aspects of training.[21]

CONCLUSIONS

The preceding discussion revealed that currently predominating responses to changes in the global market system move mostly within a production-oriented paradigm of economic development, with an overwhelming emphasis on skills and techniques, preparing students for work in hierarchical organizations. Such a paradigm generates an interpretation of the current crisis which screens out the most important and most troubling aspects of this crisis: the increase in precarious, unstable work relations, the growing North/ South division, the feminization of poverty in conjunction with a new sexist division of labour, and the continued destruction of the environment.

Furthermore, a strictly technological–industrial model of work is reflected in a model of education that derives its prime legitimation from its direct individual or economic pay-off appeal. Today, the bond between education, training and work, always troublesome, complex, and contradictory, is mystified into a simple, direct, cause–effect relationship, drawing education increasingly into the narrow sphere of bottom-line thinking. Because of the overarching importance of the issue of work for adult experience, a narrow, instrumental view of work translates into a view of education which places 'immediate relevance' and efficiency above concerns for overall human development and well-being.

Despite the rhetoric of sweeping change, major themes and questions that testify to the true nature of contemporary social and economic developments escape a thinking whose vision is blurred by its obsession with 'productivity' and 'economic growth'. These are questions concerning the human and social consequences of economic decisions, the equitable distribution of resources, and long-term ecological sustainability. Adult education proposals that would seriously address these issues would not only be very different from those which emphasize skills, techniques, and an overall adjustment to a technologically defined change, but would also fill the meaning of practicality and relevancy with new content. Preparation for work would have to include the development of critical knowledge of the larger social and political context of work, production, and work relations. Models of work would have to be discussed that are outside the orbit of technological–industrial work and production and that are not tied to the orthodoxy of abstract economic growth. If we interpret the crisis as one of increasing poverty, diminishing natural resources, and continued ecological disaster, we have to look at the issue of work and of production quite differently. Ultimately, we need to arrive at a new understanding of growth and productivity which entails different ways of dealing with nature and with human beings, that preserves rather than destroys, and that produces human well-being rather than consumes natural and human resources.

Part III

WORK AND THE RELATIONSHIP TO NATURE

6

THE CHANGING FORMS OF SUBSISTENCE LABOUR

THE SEPARATION OF SUBSISTENCE AND COMMODITY PRODUCTION

> The modern world-system is a capitalist world-economy, whose origins reach back to the sixteenth century in Europe. Its emergence is the result of a singular historical transformation, that from feudalism to capitalism.
>
> (Wallerstein 1979: 271)

Although the transition from feudal to capitalist social and economic relations was a multi-layered, ongoing process whose temporal and geographical boundaries were constantly changing and shifting, the 'singular' dimension of the capitalist mode of production is described in the following way (Wallerstein 1979: 272):

> The usefulness of capitalism as a term is to designate that system in which the structures give primacy to the accumulation of capital *per se*, rewarding those who do it well and penalizing all others, as distinct from these systems in which the accumulation of capital is subordinated to some other objective, however defined.

To give primacy to the accumulation of capital means to emphasize production for profit rather than for use. Production for profit calls for and itself produces certain forms of organization of work, expressed in various forms of divisions of labour. These divisions have been described in terms of different sectors of production (agriculture, industry, commerce), in terms of class divisions (between property-owning and working class), and in terms of divisions into branches (textile, food, steel, etc.) 'which need different techniques and different skills and knowledge' (Bennholdt-Thomsen 1984: 263–4).

Apart from these divisions, capitalism is characterized by another split which is much more fundamental and far-reaching than all of the ones mentioned so far: it is the division of production into subsistence and commodity production. From the beginnings of manufacture, the production of commodities, or of goods produced for the purpose of selling and making a profit, was separated from the production for subsistence, or the production of goods for immediate use and consumption. Further, and most significantly, a concomitant split developed between so-called social production (in the factories) and private production (in the household), demarcating the onset of a new kind of economic structure. In pre-capitalist societies where surplus goods were exchanged or sold on the market rather than consumed by the producers themselves, *both* production for immediate use and production of goods to be sold were fully part of the *overall social production process*. Likewise, divisions of labour had the form of divisions of specific tasks all of which belonged to the same overall process of social production. Women and men were therefore both valued as social producers although their tasks and duties were quite sex-specific.

If we look in more detail at the meaning and actual content of subsistence production, we can see the vast implications of this subordination for the entire course of development of Western civilization.

The term 'subsistence production' needs to be clarified first, however. Political economists and development theorists generally use the terms in reference to the production by small peasants and by the 'marginalized' in the urban centres of the Third World.[1] A term commonly used in a parallel fashion is subsistence reproduction which refers mainly to the 'domestic' work of women in the Third, First, and Second Worlds (Evers *et al.* 1984). My own usage of the term is based on the theories of the 'Bielefeld Approach' (see Chapter 2) where it illuminates the usual 'blind spots on the map of political economy' (von Werlhof 1988b) because it is based on the recognition of the realities of women and Third World people, the most important subsistence producers today. In the debates at the Bielefeld Center of Sociology of Development the 're' of reproduction was considered misleading because it was still afflicted with the typical Marxist fetishization of industrial production as the 'actual' form of production (Mies 1983). Therefore, (ibid. 117),

> ... the term subsistence production delineates a 'front line' between capital and human beings that is different from the usual one between wage labor and capital. What confronts capital, what is permanently exploited, sapped, and undermined by capital is not really wage labor, but subsistence production; likewise, it is not really work *per se* but the life of the workers because it is the subsistence producers (women, peasants) rather than capital who can create *life* (human beings, food, 'happiness').

The new meaning of the term 'subsistence production' therefore included the work typically performed by women in order to make visible the work which *enters into* the production of life (usually referred to as 'reproduction of labor power'), or into subsistence production (in the narrow meaning of the term; Mies 1983: 117).

In its enlarged meaning, subsistence production refers to 'all labor which is spent during the creation and sustenance of immediate life, and which has this immediate purpose' (Mies ibid.). It therefore includes such diverse activities as pregnancy, childbirth and nursing, and work associated with making food, clothes, or shelter for immediate, private use. Apart from work oriented towards physical well-being, subsistence work also includes work oriented towards psychological and sexual well-being.

Subsistence producers are the ones whose labour and production is directly oriented towards life – its creation, sustenance and improvement. They are working with the two most fundamental productive forces: land and womb. All production is ultimately dependent on the production of new life, and hence on *living labour power* which alone can transform nature for human use and benefit, as well as on the earth with all her natural goods and riches. These are the ultimate 'production conditions', and they remind us most directly that we are not only dependent on ourselves but part of nature. Without 'food and new life, there would be no production at all' (von Werlhof 1985b: 16). This creates a paradox for capitalism, consisting

> ... in the fact that exactly those producers who are of the most vital importance for the general maintenance of capitalist accumulation would not 'really,' materially be separated from their means of production. The production for the direct maintenance and creation of new life which capital as past, 'dead' labor needs as desperately as the vampire needs fresh blood, could in spite of so many experiments in this direction never

> be organized *in abstraction* from nature, and in *full separation* from the natural means for this social production: the soil and the uterus.
>
> (von Werlhof 1985b: 16–17)

Marxist critics and capitalist defenders of the system are united in their portrayal of women, particularly housewives, and of peasants as backwards or traditional, and in general afflicted with attitudes which prevent them from being integrated into the process of modernization. Modernization is equivalent to the creation of an industrial production process characterized by 'abstraction from nature' and her limitations, and oriented towards purposes that are freed 'from the responsibility to maintain life and free to transform this life into dead capital' (von Werlhof 1985b: 17). Since it is this very process which creates the modern peasants and housewives, we can speak of the parallel processes of industrialization as well as 'peasantization' and 'housewifization' (ibid. 18). Therefore, behind the label of 'backwardness' or 'underdevelopment' lies the complex material and ideological achievement of capitalism to create modern peasants and housewives

> ... as producers who possess a certain part of nature as if it were a 'normal' means of production which could be transformed into capital through their labor, but which, at the same time, was 'still reluctant' to its immediate capitalization. It was this perspective on the soil and the uterus as a 'pre-form of capital' which defined them as means of production, but 'not yet normal' ones, 'still' depending on natural forces.
>
> (von Werlhof 1985b: 17)

As producers who were 'tied' to their means of production, women and peasants came to be viewed as part of nature herself. Within the developing view of nature in hierarchical opposition to society or culture, this meant to deprive those producers of their full entitlement to 'culture', i.e. of their full membership in a now 'civilized' humanity. Thus, another paradox emerged which defines subsistence producers as being outside the 'actual' capitalist economy, and therefore outside the core of progress and development, while simultanously calling for an 'integration' of these producers into the ongoing process of modernization. In the history of Western civilization, such 'integration' has meant mass expropriations, forced resettlements, forced production (slavery), and outright genocide of indigenous peasant populations and other subsistence producers like nomadic tribes or aboriginal populations. As is becoming ever more apparent, it has also meant the continuous and ongoing destruction of the material or natural conditions of life itself (Shiva 1989). Mies (1983: 24) therefore succinctly states that 'the secret of modernization is violence'.

During the rise of capitalism the true citizen, the true member of society and representative of civilization was the bourgeois, the member of the new property-owning class. Such membership was displayed and confirmed in the bourgeois public sphere (Habermas 1971). In the process of a continued expansion of socialized production, the meaning of 'public' began to merge with the meaning of 'social'. New social and political institutions developed and replaced the old ones. Once industrial production was considered to be the only true form of *social* production, the only true members of society became those who were 'free, equal, and fraternal', i.e. those who worked and produced in that sphere. Even today the prototype of the true member of society is the White, male, adult worker, earning a family wage in a stable, long-term job. A host of legal, political, and social institutions exist to reinforce this idea, and a whole system of norms which shapes individual identity and governs individual behaviour. Corresponding internalized expectations and self-definitions are often expressed by unemployed people when they cite a feeling of 'normlessness', and of experiencing themselves as 'non-persons,' (Watts 1983: 64, 107–8).

PRIVATE AND PUBLIC

It is important to note that the split between subsistence and commodity production does not simply divide men and women by assigning them to different 'spheres', that is, the private and the public sphere, as it is commonly described by Marxist and mainstream feminist sociologists. No doubt, the development of the two distinct social spheres of 'private' and 'public' does weave into the problem at issue here. The process subordinating subsistence production to commodity production was indeed paralleled by a process of removing subsistence production from the sphere of actual social production, i.e. by a process of privatization. This privatization of subsistence production contributed to *and* was a symptom of its devaluation, i.e. of its subordinate relationship to commodity production. As the two spheres developed historically, the private sphere became the sphere of individual freedom, private autonomy and true intimacy – at least for the male bourgeois who could rest from the pressures of the market in the bosom of the family. The ideological association of the private and the personal with the feminine, and the actual (or ideological) imprisonment of women in the domestic sphere, contribute to the highly ambivalent, contradictory character of the meaning of 'private' or 'privacy'. The private can mean a sacrosanct realm, outside the reach of law and government. It can also mean a context of rigid normative expectations which govern and control the behaviour of men, women, and children in a way which reflects the general social hierarchy between the sexes and ages. In particular, the most intimate aspects of women's lives, especially their sexuality and childbearing capacity, are highly controlled: through the institution of marriage, general social control (medical, legal, political) supports and sanctions direct personal control (husbands, fathers, brothers, sons).

According to Habermas' detailed historical account of the development of the two spheres, and of respective institutions, the idea of the private as a haven could take hold because production was gradually moved out of the household in the form of trade and socialized labour (1971: 43). The bourgeois ideal of marriage as a community of voluntary love and individual autonomy could therefore emerge in the seventeenth century (ibid. 64–5). From the perspective of female experience, this is an ideological achievement of the first order. As pointed out above, not only did production in the form of subsistence production never cease to take place in the sphere of the private, it also never ceased to build the very foundation of 'actual' social production.

However, to focus on the meaning and the relationship of the two forms of production rather than on the relationship of public and private does not mean to render sexual difference irrelevant. Although the concept of subsistence production first of all indicates the subordination of this production under production oriented towards profit, men and women are nevertheless differently located within this overall reality of subordination. In fact, as shown in Chapter 1, subsistence production, especially in its more current, eroded form of production for bare survival under conditions of extreme poverty is sharply sex-specific.

WAGED AND UNWAGED WORK

Just as commodity production and subsistence production cannot simply be ascribed to men and women, they are also not simply equivalent with waged and non-waged labour, although the typical subsistence producers, women (as housewives) and peasants, have traditionally performed non-waged work (and whatever remains of true subsistence production or labour today also remains unpaid or unwaged). Peasants and women continue to perform subsistence labour, and although it changed its character in the course of historical development, it nevertheless never disappeared. As Bennholdt-Thomsen (1984: 263) describes it:

> What does disappear in this change is the substance of subsistence production, meaning raw materials for food, for textile, and for house construction, all of which must be acquired as commodities in ever-growing amounts. But the *preparation* of food, clothes, and housing for immediate consumption remains and becomes almost exclusively women's work. While this work is time consuming and must be performed daily, it nevertheless appears as unimportant, invisible, additional work.

Under present conditions it is mainly women in the industrialized core countries who still perform subsistence labour. In peripheral countries where peasants (men and women) as well as women (as housewives or maids) have been the traditional subsistence producers, the increasing integration of peasant production into the world market (and thus into commodity production) has brought about a number of changes and divisions of labour that make a clear-cut distinction between commodity and subsistence production along the lines of paid and unpaid work nearly impossible. However, despite all these new forms of labour (neither 'typical' subsistence nor 'typical' commodity labour) actual subsistence work (with the characteristics mentioned above) still takes place. Although it may be difficult to clearly delineate subsistence and commodity labour with respect to their link to wages, or to the formal economy, it is less difficult to distinguish between the two along the lines of their overall purpose and orientation. Undoubtedly, all labour is today integrated into the cash nexus, and is dependent on and ultimately structured by commodity production, but not all labour *is* commodity production. Thus, the old relationship of hierarchy and subordination lives on, although in new, changed forms. As the discussion of 'housewifized' (and 'peasantized') labour has already shown, the process of capital accumulation itself upholds the difference because it is in need of its very existence.

However, as Smith (1984) describes, there exist a number of non-waged activities today which are quite dissimilar to subsistence labour and to housework, and which are actually forms of non-waged commodity production. Smith (1984: 65) distinguishes between housework and other subsistence-sector activities, i.e. 'the exchange of services that are absolutely necessary for the reproduction and daily survival of the work force' and 'an economy proper, involving the actual sales of services and goods'. She argues that housework and other informal labour activities have very different structural links with the formal economy, based on quite different historical and material circumstances (ibid. 66). However, she analyses the two (i.e. housework and other kinds of unwaged work) from the perspective of their particular relationship to waged work and to commodity production, and thereby entirely neglects the aspect of subsistence production, or production oriented toward immediate survival (or to basic needs) which still characterizes the content of housework. She describes housework as an unpaid service to commodities (especially so-called 'labour saving' household equipment like washing machines) which could not be used without the housewife's additional unpaid labour. Despite this structural link with commodity production, and despite its historically 'shrunken' form, housework still remains subsistence work.

Part of the reason why Smith does not see this as the main difference between housework and other kinds of non-waged work may stem from the fact that she does not give the production and reproduction of the next generation a place of special importance. Instead, she lists it in a way that makes 'childcare' equivalent to watching the washing cycle to be there in time when the laundry is done. Nor does she mention other aspects of housework such as psychological and physical reproduction of children and husband which are all work *on and with people* rather than commodities. It has been argued that the housewife herself produces commodities by raising the next generation to sell its labour power on the market. Raising human beings requires, however, an orientation towards sustaining life, and towards producing things for immediate use. This subsistence rather than commodity orientation proves to be essential in the work of raising children, because it alone guarantees future healthy workers (which can then be controlled and exploited as commodities). A parallel example is the continued importance of the existence of the peasants in the capitalist world economy because the qualities that are part of their subsistence orientation makes them particularly attractive to capital (von Werlhof 1985b).

THE EROSION OF SUBSISTENCE LABOUR

Just as the scope and content of subsistence production has changed, and has been stripped of many of the immediate productive functions, housework itself has undergone fundamental changes. This especially affects the much acclaimed 'use-value' orientation of the housewife which today has narrowed into a rather abstract 'needs-orientation'. In an earlier chapter I emphasized the abstract character of housework, manifested in the super-qualification of the housewife as being flexible and permanently available for the satisfaction of others' needs. As noted, this ability is required or expected from women at work as well, although it is not officially recognized as valuable (nor considered a skill).

To be available and to satisfy others' needs has a physical and a psychological dimension. The physical dimension is the so-called 'chores' of cleaning (objects as well as people), cooking, and general maintenance. Apart from cooking, they are the most despised, and the most 'feminine' tasks, i.e. they are rarely performed by men. There are only a few 'chores', however, which can clearly be delineated from their psychological dimension. In fact, to the extent to which all of women's work within the house has been interpreted as a 'labour of love', even choosing the right laundry detergent can be portrayed as having a major effect on the mental well-being of men or children. One of the core elements of the ideology of domesticity is that women's primary task is to produce happiness in the family.

There are, however, considerable differences between servicing men's and fulfilling children's needs. Apart from the major difference as regards sexual service, much of the emotional and psychological nurturance women are expected to give to men can be considered 'repair work', especially in the form of soothing a male ego that has been bruised in the world 'out there'. Of course, sexual subservience is part of this work which directly depends on an affirmation of women's inferiority. Because 'maleness' is by cultural definition in hierarchical opposition to 'femaleness', the need for an affirmation of this superiority is therefore an integral part of the male psyche, and the soothing of male egos is therefore fully tied to women's subordination. The very fact that men are officially entitled to this service is already an indication of their socially declared supremacy.

The situation with children is more complex, however. Children need to be *raised*, not simply nurtured. Their nurturance is – ideally – an integral part of the much larger and much more encompassing work of bringing them up. Work with and for children starts with the production of new life. This is fundamentally different from either the physical household maintenance chores or from the production of male happiness. The latter is a more explicitly *reproductive* task, the former, i.e. giving birth and raising children, are directly *productive*, although they contain many reproductive aspects. These reproductive aspects, e.g. cleaning and feeding children, putting them to bed, etc., are, however, inseparable from the overall productive aspect of raising a future capable and autonomous member of society.

All of these quite diverse aspects of housework, and the fundamentally different experiences they signify, are generally lumped together, listing shopping and doing the laundry together with 'childcare' under the same rubric of chores (see especially Bergmann 1986). In some accounts of housework as a special category, children are not mentioned at all. This is especially striking considering that the ideology of domesticity revolves around the institution of motherhood as woman's primary calling. Thus, we have discusssions of housework where the work with and for children is either absent, or blends in with other chores on the one hand, and feminist writings on the oppressiveness of the institution of motherhood and the family on the other. In both cases two separate issues are not sufficiently distinguished, i.e. the general circumstances as well as social relations within which housework and mothering take place, and the actual work itself. What makes housework a dirty job, and the raising of children a 24-hour juggling act, is not the work itself, but the constraining and alienating conditions under which it has to be performed.[2]

A confusion of the content of work with its oppressive conditions underlies, for instance, the calls on girls to take more science and maths in schools, or to establish childcare facilities. Although the immediately practical value of these measures cannot be denied, they will lead to the individual empowerment of only a limited number of women. These proposals, however, leave intact the deeper-lying social devaluation of work associated with housework and mothering. This leads to a division among women into those who managed to 'escape' their destiny and are now 'free' to realize their own true potential, and those who for some reason or other remain bound to 'women's work'.[3] To portray this situation as women simply making 'different choices' of course also denies the hierarchy of values into which different kinds of works are embedded. The continued vitality of this hierarchy, and associated concepts of femininity and masculinity pressurize every group of women into legitimizing their choice. The now liberated 'career women' are in constant need to prove their femininity despite the fact that they are not mothers, and the full-time mothers need to prove that their work is valuable in the face of massive social contempt. The third group that 'does it all' has to pay the price of chronic overwork and exhaustion (see Hochschild 1989).[4]

Furthermore, if the deeper-lying social divisions and evaluations of different kinds of work are not criticized and re-evaluated, it is unlikely to expect childcare facilities that are not intrinsically structured by the very same value system. In other words, if the content of labour associated with the fulfilment of vital needs and the raising of the next generation remains socially devalued, childcare facilities designed to 'free' people from this task will more likely than not reflect this devaluation. What needs to be questioned is the idea that women, or anybody, has to be *freed* from the responsibilities associated with housework and mothering. The language of 'childcare' already indicates the limitations and restrictions of such a solution because it reduces the work with children to the level of maintenance and babysitting, and therefore to work that can be 'contracted out', most likely to ill-paid female childcare workers.[5]

To some extent the language of childcare reflects the actual (and continued) erosion of the substance of housework, an erosion that is similar to the one affecting peasant production in the Third World.[6] Unstructured, non-regimented organization of time which is a fundamental requirement for the work with children becomes less and less possible with women's hectic work schedules. Mothers are forced to augment short periods of time by considering them 'quality time', trying to squeeze into one hour what they missed in the ten preceding ones (Schultz 1985). Apart from the institutional constraints of the patriarchal nuclear family, and the struggle of balancing paid and unpaid work, an increasingly unsafe environment considerably adds to the stress of mothering.

The conditions under which children have to be raised today reflect the overall social contempt for the kind of work housework represents. The fact that child-raising is so often lumped together with other 'chores' can be seen as a primary symptom for this contempt. Because the work of mothers brings them in direct contact with the body, and therefore deals with the biological or 'natural' aspect of human existence, it is easy to establish a link between chores and working with children. Ultimately, the identification of sexuality, birth and life with nature, and the social stigmatization of the latter as something that has to be suppressed at all cost lies at the core of the devaluation of women's work. As the idea of progress pivots around the dream of a total emancipation from nature, work that reminds us most clearly of the fact that we ourselves are part of nature cannot assume a place of high social esteem. Likewise, progress cannot be located in the sphere of 'women's work' or, more generally speaking, in the sphere of subsistence production. Rather, progress is seen as located in the sphere of technological application of science, i.e. in the sphere of industrial production. In the following chapter I will discuss how the association of basic needs with nature and necessity is intimately tied to the concept of (technological) progress, leading to a major paradox. On the one hand, the work most closely linked to basic needs and to the satisfaction of basic needs takes place within the private household, i.e. most decidedly outside the formal economy. On the other hand, it is precisely the realm of industrial production that is presumed to hold the key for an emancipation from necessity, and from the labour associated with it.

7

NECESSITY AND FREEDOM

NECESSITY, TECHNOLOGY AND BASIC NEEDS

The belief that technology will take over most of the still necessary labour underpins many proposals and writings dealing with the future of work. Visions of a future better society, where the problems now associated with work have either been ameliorated or eliminated, seem to be entirely affixed to the belief in continuous technological progress. This technological bias is inherently linked to a deeply engrained patriarchal bias. It is the source of much fogginess on certain issues because it carries the imperative to place taboos on certain ideas and corresponding human experiences, which are therefore never examined.

On a relatively superficial level, a considerable amount of confusion arises from the virtual absence of any specification of what precisely technology is to take care of in any future post-industrial, post-work, or post-technological society. In other words, the question of what humanity is to be liberated from is rarely addressed. The argument generally has a dual–causal structure: technology is to free humankind from toil and drudgery, because/and it will take over the production of 'basic necessities'. The underlying assumption is, of course, that the provision of basic necessities inevitably means toil and drudgery. Such a quasi-automatic association between slavish toil and necessity seems to be powerfully entrenched in our collective consciousness.

A further confusion stems from the recognition, on the one hand, of the link between necessity and biology as related to physical survival, and, on the other hand, from a practically exclusive focus on industrial labour which is only indirectly tied to issues of immediate survival. This is highly unsatisfactory. A wholesale portrayal of industrial production as taking care of basic necessities has to be reconciled with the fact that the overall purpose of production is precisely not oriented towards the satisfaction of human needs, but towards the accumulation of capital. Although need satisfaction cannot be bypassed entirely, it is one among many factors which economic and corporate planners have to include in their calculation of profit maximization. In fact, the history of colonialism and neo-colonialism is full of examples where subsistence economies which were precisely oriented towards need satisfaction were systematically destroyed in the process of being integrated into capitalist development (see, for instance Shiva 1989). This makes it possible for an impoverished indigeneous population to produce agricultural luxury goods like flowers and strawberries for export while the producers themselves go hungry. Moreover, many of the goods sold on the market are either useless, superfluous, or directly detrimental to human well-being when measured against real human needs. In other words, they are far from satisfying any 'basic', or even secondary needs.

Patriarchal writers seem unable to reconcile the undisputed continued necessity of biological/physical survival with the supremacy of 'industrialization', where work has presumably been removed from the sphere of 'biological imperatives' (Entwistle 1970: 16).[1] The rigid fixation on industrial labour as the only or most typical form of labour under capitalist conditions inevitably leads to difficulties in correctly ascribing issues of survival and, correspondingly, production for life, to the sphere of industrial production. Since no other sphere or form of production is recognized, in the mind of these writers it can only be industrial labour, in its living or automated form, which is to provide for the satisfaction of basic needs. This may partly explain why both, 'basic needs' as well as the activities subsumed under 'labour' are hardly ever specified. Just as basic needs are for the most part treated rather biologically as ahistorical, unchanging entities, the activities associated with their satisfaction remain equally vague and abstract. Partly, too, the stigma of irrelevance, and the general devaluation of labour associated with 'basic needs' (whatever they are) lives on in the refusal (and inability) to explore the actual content, and thus the actual human potential, of these activities.

The question of what is necessity, and what is the content of industrial production, as well as the question concerning the actual power of technology to satisfy 'basic human needs' cannot be faced and addressed within a framework of thinking which has consistently relegated those issues to the realm of 'nature', or to the netherworld of a 'domestic sphere'. In short, it is a thinking which has traditionally considered the issues surrounding life as outside the realm of important questions and concerns. The low value placed on human experiences and efforts concerned with staying alive and keeping alive has shaped perceptions, vocabularies, and conceptual hierarchies which miss, indeed must miss, the essence of those very questions. To address those questions would mean undoing centuries of ideological, economic, and political efforts to define women and 'savages' back into nature, and treating them, and appropriating their labour as an expression of their biology or of their semi- or subhuman condition, rather than as a vital form of production, and the very basis of all other forms of labour and production.

Although the problem of necessity figures prominently in discussions on the subject of work (and leisure), the question 'what constitutes necessity' is hardly explored. There seems to be unanimous agreement, however, that it is not only undesirable but also directly and irreconcilably opposed to freedom. Although some writers see necessity as primarily linked to physical or biological survival (e.g. Arendt 1958), others see it in the need to make a living, i.e. as removed from biology, although ultimately related to it. Gorz (1985: 70), for example, locates necessity primarily in the sphere of the 'economy' (and thus work) which he sees as opposed to 'life' where 'autonomy' reigns supreme. Regardless under which category – biology or economy – because of its devaluation as *coercive* and *compulsory*, necessity is placed in direct opposition to freedom.

I want to emphasize that I do not intend to discuss the concept of freedom, a task for which I would be ill-equipped. Rather, I want to probe into a deep-seated cultural attitude towards necessity which, by its very definition, is considered to be freedom's mortal enemy. More specifically, the freedom/necessity antithesis is here discussed from the angle of work, and the question pursued is above all how work is linked to these concepts. I want to examine further how the need to survive, and, consequently, how work oriented towards sustenance is organized in a way which reflects both the dichotomy between freedom and necessity, and the negative attitude towards necessity that accompanies it. Like Mies (1986: 126) I want to explore and evaluate

> ... the distinction between socially necessary labour and leisure, and the ... view that self-realization, human happiness, freedom, autonomy – the realm of freedom – can be achieved only *outside* the sphere of necessity and of necessary labour, and by a reduction (or abolition) of the latter.

Above all, I want to pursue the practical consequences that result from the dichotomous partitioning of freedom and necessity, and the corresponding dichotomous organization of human experience.

LIBERATION OF OR LIBERATION FROM WORK?

There is considerable disagreement among writers on what precisely people will do or should do once liberation has occurred. In Gorz's view they will engage in 'optional, gratuitous, or superfluous activities' (1985: 57). According to writers influenced by Arendt's distinction between work and labour they will create, make, and engage in a quest for potency. However, all writers agree that it is necessity from which humanity must strive to be liberated, and that freedom is above all the freedom to chose. Freely chosen human activity is free in the sense of being outside the realm of necessity and its various compulsive constraints. What is of interest here is the oppositional character of free and necessary, i.e. the very phenomenon of polarity and contrast. The burning core of the question of work therefore lies in the dividing line itself, and not on one or other side of the gap. Both sides together are only fragments of a 'fractured whole' (Adorno 1974).

In the following I want to give two examples of writers whose ideas at first glance seem to have nothing or very little in common, but who nevertheless present different aspects, and different formulations, of very similar attitudes. I chose those two writers, Hannah Arendt and Andre Gorz, as representative for several reasons. They wrote in two different periods: Gorz during a time when the development of technology had already attained its current allure, Arendt during a time where this issue had not become a major item on the social and economic agenda. Gorz writes within the Marxist sociological tradition, Arendt as an heir to and proponent of classical philosophy. In addition, both of them formulate more sharply and poignantly what appears only as a tendency in other writers, and they make explicit what are otherwise only implicit assumptions and social attitudes.

Gorz's vision of a future paradise is a society which has to a large part been liberated from work (1985: 58):

> It [social or industrial production] minimises the sphere of necessity and the work which goes with it, leaving each individual free to define and produce in his or her own way all that is optional and inessential.

The meaning of Gorz's concept of necessity can only be understood in relation to his concept of work. For Gorz, work exists only within the sphere of industrial production, which he – like Marx – considers the only true realm of *social production*. The meaning of 'social' deserves some attention here, particularly as it entails, in fact lives on, a – however implicit – oppositional relationship to 'natural'. Gorz here works with notions and ideas which are derived from original Marxist positions. In Marx, 'social production', 'socially necessary labour', 'the socialisation of production', etc. are all aligned with a certain concept of rationality, which, in turn, is based on a certain form of (capitalist) rational organization of labour. This is the 'routinised, calculated administration within continuously functioning enterprises' (Giddens in Weber 1958: 3). In this sense, the social organization of the capitalist enterprise structures the relationship of the individual participants (workers, supervisors, managers) to each other in a mechanical way where each is assigned a certain function in the overall system, organized according to principles of rational control and efficiency. The workers are integrated into an organized production process, and their co-operation is equally administered from the outside (or from above) rather than created intentionally or inter-subjectively. Marx (1972: 66) criticizes the alienating character of such a social production where individuals remain 'indifferent to one another', and which exists outside, and therefore independent from their own will and intentions. However, in Marx's view, this is a necessary stage because it is the very condition for a final release of individuals from socially necessary labour through the development of science and technology, and the latter's application to the production process (Marx 1972: 85–6).

Gorz shares with Marx the belief in a kind of qualitative rupture between alienating social production relations where the worker is a mere function in the general production process, and an appendix to the machine, and the liberating new social relations once the worker's function has been completely taken over by machines.

Herein lies the origin of the Marxist concept of freedom: freedom is believed to reside mainly in the collective control over the common life (Taylor 1979: 175), but this control is embodied by the technological development of the productive forces. Control here implies not only control over the production process as a whole, but also control over the forces of nature, i.e. over necessity. Only then has the social individual become 'a subject controlling all the forces of nature in the production process' (Marx 1972: 124). Consequently, and quite logically, labour ceases to exist as a separate notion since it is so closely aligned with necessity. Whatever work the free individual performs is therefore in no way related to production of the means of daily subsistence. Marx (1972: 85–6, my emphasis) himself speaks of 'a full development of *activity*, in which the necessity has disappeared in a direct form, since the place of natural needs has been taken by needs that are historically produced'. This view is more fully expressed in Marx's famous passage on work in communist society (1963: 110–11):

> In Communist society, where nobody has one exclusive sphere of activity but each can become accomplished in any branch he wishes, production as a whole is regulated by society, thus making it possible for me to do one thing today and another tomorrow, to hunt in the morning, fish in the afternoon, rear cattle in the evening, criticise after dinner, in accordance with my inclinations, without ever becoming hunter, fisherman, shepherd, or 'critic'.

It is difficult to resists the image of the country gentleman conveyed in this passage, and to round out mentally the picture with servants, maids, and above all a wife who supervises the preparation of the dinner and the raising of children. Gorz's description (1985: 57) of a future Utopia reveals a similar upper-class or aristocratic touch:

> Free-time activities, insofar as they are productive, will be concerned with autoproduction of all that is optional, gratuitous, superfluous, or all, in short, which is not necessary, which gives life its spice and value: as *useless* as life itself, yet exalting life as the one end which gives all others their meaning.

Marx already reveals a certain élitist bias by indirectly denigrating the production and accumulation of knowledge, skill and expertise that go into activities like rearing cattle and shepherding. It is difficult to imagine how such knowledge could be produced or come about outside a context of at least some usefulness rather than of merely pleasurable pastime or individual enrichment. In Gorz's writings this bias is heightened to the élitism of shunning usefulness altogether. Usefulness is, of course, a close relative of necessity, and the one-sided celebration of uselessness Gorz displays is inseparable from a contempt for certain kinds of labour, especially labour tied to the sphere of necessity, and, by implication, of those who are associated with that kind of work. Marx and Gorz reveal their own social position through their imagery which is peculiarly close to images of a self-gratifying, consumption-oriented leisure existence of the rich. For somebody who does not share such a position, or does not identify with the privileges represented by it, such a 'Utopia' is quite unattractive, since it does not contain any notion of a truly alternative way of life, which would mean a different way of treating human beings and nature.

Gorz's world is a totally industrialized one where wage work is the only recognized form of work, and where *all* necessity can be bought by the wages paid. Gorz does consider unpaid work, but it is structurally not different from waged work because the goods produced by it could presumably all be bought (1985: 57). On the whole, however, the phenomenon of unpaid work is considered to be dismissably small because 'almost everyone in industrialised societies purchases almost everything that is necessary (and many things which are not necessary) with the wages from heteronomous work.' Gorz defines 'heteronomous work' as 'work whose form and objectives are externally determined by the organisation of production on a national or continental scale'. In other words, Gorz is talking exclusively about the formal national and international economy. By default, any kind of non-waged labour, especially any form of subsistence labour, either does not exist at all in Gorz's interpretation of reality, or if it does exist, it can only lie outside the sphere of the social or the cultural because it is apparently irrelevant for the discussion of work or liberation from work.

The mystification of wage labour (and the industrial sphere), and the closely related, indeed inseparable belief in the continuous progress of science and technology is, of course, not a Marxist prerogative. The Marxist focus on industrial labour, and on a mechanistic, instrumental concept of the social, as well as the resultant vision of a scientific–technological liberation from labour, come entirely out of the Western tradition to view necessity as something to be controlled and ultimately surpassed by expurgating it from social life and civilization altogether.

In Gorz's view, such a purge makes it possible to have a 'life'. Gorz is an unequivocal camp-follower of those who draw clear distinctions between living and making a living. Because of the convergence of meaning of work and necessity, life is the direct opposite of work. Only where work ends can life begin. 'Life' is thus doubly removed from issues of immediate survival. First, it banishes work which is linked to necessity, a definite survival issue, but necessity is itself already of a second order, removed from biological or physical necessity, since Gorz talks about social and cultural rather than biological or physical (or 'basic') needs. In Gorz's words, 'the necessary is ... the object of needs which all social individuals have in common'. 'In essence, what is necessary is what we need as social individuals to live in the socio-cultural context of our own civilization' (1985: 57–8). In the absence of any recognition whatsoever that social and cultural needs are inherently tied to our physical or biological foundation, the previously criticized trend for biologists to depict basic needs as entirely asocial here finds its (necessary) counterpart in a total neglect of the physical underside of human existence or life. Both views fail to produce a dialectical concept of need, and hence of work oriented towards satisfying needs, which takes into consideration the fact that human beings have physical bodies *within* a socio-cultural and historical context, i.e. a concept that 'we can use to acknowledge the way biology and nature influence general and anthropological conditions, without our view becoming ahistorical and static' (Bennholdt-Thomsen 1984: 258).

Marx never denied the relationship of work and production to nature and to biological/physiological survival. In fact, as Arendt (1958: 88) points out, Marx saw the chief function of labour in the *production of life itself* where human beings and nature engage in a process of 'metabolic exchange'. Work is therefore a process which always brings the human being into a certain relation to nature, i.e. a process in which both, human being and nature, participate. As expressed in the following quote, this is itself not a natural or biological act but full of social and historical implications:

> Man opposes himself to nature as one of her own forces, setting in motion arms and legs, head and hands, the natural forces of his body, in order to appropriate nature's production

> in a form adapted to his own wants. By thus acting on the external world and changing it, he at the same time changes his own nature.
>
> (Marx 1967: 177)

Although the metabolic exchange with nature is the material foundation of all human action, dictated by the necessity to survive, the concrete form such exchange assumes depends on historically changing circumstances which are expressed in different social and economic arrangements. Marx's concept is, in principle, quite useful for a discussion of work and productivity because it is inherently dialectical, taking into account the interplay of biological and social dimensions of human existence. However, the above-mentioned quote excludes something which has shaped the entire discussion of work, labour, and productivity. And, as I want to add, this exclusion must also be held responsible for the potent and tenacious equation of technological with social progress.

According to Marx, in the process of the development of the forces of production, the function and capacities of arms, legs, and hands are refined, their power magnified (as well as objectified) into technical aids like tools, later into machinery, i.e. in the application of science in technology. The capacity of the head is symbolically expressed in accumulated social knowledge, particularly scientific knowledge (see Marx 1972: 135). However, Marx's human being is (presumably) sexually undifferentiated. As soon as we take sexuality and, consequently, sexual difference into account and substitute the 'he' of Marx's quote with a 'she', we have to add to the 'natural forces' of the body the capacity to bear and to nurse children. This is a capacity on which the woman works as much as on other 'natural forces' in the form of conscious interaction and appropriation.[2]

THE NATURALIZATION OF LABOUR

Ironically, but not surprisingly, the biological assumptions inherent in the Marxist concept of labour are not only shared, but brought into sharp relief by one of his staunchest critics, Hannah Arendt. In *The Human Condition* (1958) Arendt heavily criticizes Marx's glorification of labour. However, there is a peculiar historical eclipse in her critique, which is in accordance with her overall ahistorical treatment of the issue of work and labour. The Marxist biologistic bias is expressed mainly in a total blindness against the social, and hence historical implications of a kind of productivity represented by a specifically female labour capacity. In Arendt it finds its explicit expression. She makes a division between the biological–anthropological aspect of labour as producing the means of subsistence, or producing life, and the concrete social-historical forms such production always assumes. She fully separates the biological, or 'life', from the social. Her critique of Marx therefore misses the point because she does not, cannot, recognize that the concrete form of labour Marx discusses in his economic theory is, in actuality, far removed from, indeed itself dependent on and living off, production for life. Marx glorifies labour (i.e. wage labour) precisely because it is assumed to contribute to a development that will ultimately rid humankind from necessity altogether. Marx's vision is an old one, rooted in the Bible's Genesis: the liberation *from* not *of* labour. Arendt obviously does not believe that this is possible, but the structure of her entire argument, her conceptual apparatus, and especially her main distinctions between 'labour' and 'work' point in exactly the same direction: towards a preferably total emancipation from the 'urgencies of the life process' which are seen as antithetical to a truly human or free existence.

Marx's emphasis on a totally socialized human existence where nature and biology are confined and controlled by science and technology, and thus themselves 'socialized', finds its logical counterpart in Arendt's explicitly biologistic concept of labour, and in her description of activities subsumed under that category. Arendt contrasts labour with work, where work refers to the human act of creating a permanent object. Work is an integral aspect of the human world, and an activity which directly contributes to the creation of this world. Labour, on the other hand, is part of the ongoing natural cycle of birth and decay, never resulting in permanence, and therefore ultimately futile. Furthermore, labour is so utterly subservient to nature that it seems to be a direct part of nature herself, and hence a mindless, unconscious activity:

> The only experience which corresponds strictly to the experience of worldlessness, or rather to the loss of world that occurs in pain, is labouring, where the human body, its activity notwithstanding, is also thrown back upon itself, concentrates upon nothing but its own being alive, and remains imprisoned

> in its metabolism with nature without ever transcending or freeing itself from the recurring cycle of its own functioning.
> (Arendt 1958: 115)

Arendt looks upon life and the activities associated with maintaining and nourishing life with a kind of horror. The world has to be protected and preserved against these 'processes of growth and decay through which nature forever invades the human artifice, threatening the durability of the world and its fitness for human use' (ibid. 100). In fact, the labouring activity itself has a 'destructive, devouring aspect' to it, and – a point where she claims to part ways with Marx – is therefore far from being creative or productive. 'Necessity', 'futility', and 'shame' are all bedfellows of life, and of activities associated with giving and maintaining life. Although she never concretely describes any of these activities, she nevertheless mentions the two areas where they are located: tilling the soil, where the labourers 'with their bodies minister to the [bodily] needs of life' (quoting Aristotle, *Politics*), and giving birth, where the labourers 'with their bodies guarantee the physical survival of the species' (Arendt 1958: 72). In both cases, the human being is entirely subjected to, indeed 'urged and driven' by the life process itself (ibid. 115), only obeying 'the orders of immediate bodily needs' (ibid. 100).

I am here quoting Arendt somewhat extensively because she expresses in a rather pure form a deep-seated cultural attitude towards life and nature, as well as towards those human beings who are traditionally associated with the work of sustaining life. We can find this attitude expressed – in however many different guises – throughout the literature on work and the future of work. Arendt's description of the life processes as threatening, devouring, and as constantly intruding in the human world represents a powerful ideological inversion of the truth, an inversion which for centuries has helped to sanction and to justify precisely the opposite in the name of progress and civilization: the destruction, devouring, and vampirizing of forms of production which are directly oriented towards subsistence, i.e. towards creating, maintaining and improving life, rather than to the accumulation of capital and the creation of profit. The very structure of her argument reveals the basic relationship enacted in the many distinctions and demarcations of concepts typical not only of Arendt but of many writers on the subject. It is the relationship of power and control, of mastery and dominion over nature, and, consequently, over those who are considered part of or close to nature.

As I mentioned earlier, if freedom is considered the antithesis to necessity, the major emphasis of the concept is placed on choice. Thus, once necessity has been 'abolished', choice assumes an absolute character. Gorz, for instance, carries this unilateral emphasis only to its logical extreme when he talks about the 'gratuitous' and the 'superfluous' in connection with a 'life' freed from necessity. Such freedom assumes a free-floating, abstract and unconditioned character. In Arendt, who sees necessity as an inevitable part of the human condition, the absolutist moment of unconditioned freedom is carried to its logical conclusion: because of the close affinity of necessity with life, or with giving and sustaining life, and because of the direct association of life with coercion and compulsion, the ultimate expression of freedom lies in the power to kill. As Arendt maintains, the one who 'conducts himself as lord and master of the whole earth' (1958: 139) is he who is 'free to produce, free to destroy' (ibid. 144). According to Arendt, *homo faber* surpasses the *animal* (sic) *labourans*, and taming is replaced by 'tearing' the material out of nature (1958: 140). In her words (ibid. 140), '... the experience of this violence is the most elemental experience of human strength and, therefore, the very opposite of the painful, exhausting effort experienced in sheer labor'.

This, of course, looks very much like the 'man the hunter' syndrome, the staple of traditional anthropological thinking and research, where the cradle of civilization is claimed to lie in the killing act of the hunter rather than in the taming and cultivating act of the horticulturist (see Mies 1986, Shiva 1989). It is also a staple of our cultural heritage that the glory of killing is greater than the glory of giving and sustaining life, and, consequently, that strength and superiority are directly defined, as well as portrayed in omnipresent images and messages, as the greater power to destroy. For example, in his account of the origin of male domination the French anthropologist Maurice Godelier (1981: 2) writes that hunting had 'a higher value, in so far as it involved greater risk of losing one's life and greater glory in taking life'. Killing or hunting are visible and dramatic activities, as compared to the invisible, quiet, and unspectacular work of women taking care of daily life. As Shiva writes (1989: 44–5), 'such work and wealth are "invisible" because they are decentered, local, and in harmony with local ecosystems and needs', whereas 'the visibility of dramatic breaks and ruptures is posited as "progress"'. Moreover, the power to kill is the core of *patriarchal* power, and, as Mies (1986) convincingly argues, an inherently patriarchal way of appropriating nature, and of benefiting from the fruits of human productivity through the use of violence. The glorification of death is therefore fully linked with the division between masculinity and feminity. In fact, precisely because the obsession with death is at the very core of patriarchal power, an unravelling of its origin and nature will lead us to an understanding of the power relationship between men and women. As Hartsock (1983: 301) observes:

> The preoccupation with death instead of life appears as well in the argument that it is the ability to kill (and for centuries, the practice) which sets human above animals. Even Simone de Beauvoir has accepted that 'it is not in giving life but in risking life that man is raised above the animal: that is why superiority has been accorded in humanity not to the sex that brings forth but to that which kills!'

We have now reached the heart of the matter where not only apparent differences among writers like Marx, Gorz, and Arendt disappear, but where blindnesses, silences, and empty spots along with a whole system of evaluation which produced them, become visible and explicable.

NATURE VERSUS SOCIETY

The freedom to destroy directly presupposes a relationship of dominance. Since necessity is the mortal enemy of freedom, only those who master necessity are truly free. Such mastery may take the form of slavery or of a self-regulatory, automated technology. The dream, the vision of a total emancipation from necessity, and therefore the overall attitude of dominance and control, are the same. However, the assumption that a relationship of dominance is enacted only if the participants are human, while the use of machines or robots is not only free from such a stigma but is actually morally desirable has been questioned repeatedly in this chapter. Technology represents more than dead instruments or neutral tools for human use. Rather, it is inserted in and itself reflects a symbolic context of human purposes and intentions. In other words basic human relationships enter into 'technology' as into any other manifestations of human will and effort.

I am, of course, not the first one to point out that the natural sciences, and their application through technology, enact as well as structure a certain relationship to nature or to the world of natural objects.[3] If we tie this evident insight more closely to the discussion of necessity or necessary labour, and to the belief in a total emancipation from nature through science and technology, the issue becomes less clear cut. Returning to the point made above that the structure of the underlying relationship is one of dominance, we need to specify this assertion.

The relationship encapsulated in and itself structuring science and technology, in the last analysis arises out of the impetus to control and to master. The scientific revolution marked the beginning of a fundamental process of reconceptualizing the world. In the scientific mind the world came to be perceived as rationally understandable, and as a world which could be calculated, predicted, and controlled. At the end of a long process of 'mechanical reconstruction of the cosmos' (Merchant 1983: 125) 'man' had entirely distanced himself from nature.

Previous images of nature as a live organism or a nurturing mother had functioned as social constraints on possible human treatment of nature. These images were now replaced by those of control and dominion which bore a direct appeal to 'man' to become the lord and master of nature. As an object of rational knowledge (itself construed in terms of dominance), nature had to be seen as infinitely 'malleable' and 'tractable' matter (Lloyd 1984: 16). This presupposed, indeed necessitated, an undialectical separation of the human being from nature. Man (in the presumed generic, but more adequately in the sexual sense) thus became the measure of all things on earth. As Jay (1973: 260) succinctly stated in his summary of the ideas of Horkheimer and Adorno: 'At the root of Enlightenment's program of domination was a secularized version of the religious belief that God controlled the world. As a result, the human subject confronted the natural object as an inferior, external other'.[4]

Such hypostatization of the distinction between 'man' and nature has become one of the most important components of the overall self-definition of Western culture and civilization, and particularly of the notion of rational knowledge. As Lloyd (1984: 2) observes, 'rational knowledge has become construed as a transcending, transformation or control of natural forces', and 'it was the relationship of master to slave ... that provided the metaphors of dominance in terms of which the Greeks articulated their understanding of knowledge. But this Platonic theme recurs throughout the subsequent history of Western thought' (ibid. 5).

Lloyd herself traces the 'symbolism of dominance and subordination' mainly in terms of the relationship between male and female, but because of the recurring association of the female with nature in varying forms and guises, her discussion of the male–female dualism is fully interwoven with the articulation of the culture–nature relationship.[5]

In the course of the scientific revolution knowledge itself became construed in terms of a domination of nature (Lloyd 1984: 7), i.e. 'itself as an instrument of control of Nature' (ibid. 10). The father of modern science, Francis Bacon, used metaphors and images which clearly expresss the social implications of considering nature as a field for human manipulation and exploitation. He portrays nature as a female to be tortured by mechanical inventions in order to 'wrest her secrets from her' (Merchant 1983: 168).

Keller (1985) reveals, however, that Bacon's metaphors played with a sexual dialectic which was much more subtle than Merchant's descriptions portray. It is a dialectic which combines the scientist's 'feminine' receptivity and submission to nature, necessitated by his 'masculine' desire to dominate. In her interpretation of Bacon's writings, Keller (1985: 37) describes Bacon's own puzzlement over the fact that 'Nature is commanded by being obeyed, revealed by being enslaved, hounded and vexed'. In the continued history of modern science, however, this dialectic gave way to an unequivocal domination of nature by man (ibid. 45).

It may seem that my argument is moving in the direction of mystifying nature into a separate, living creature, to be left alone, untouched, and therefore uncontrolled by science and technology. The thought of viewing nature as a being endowed with a subjectivity of her own, and hence as possessing an integrity which human beings should not violate, is certainly intriguing.[6] At present, however, I am mainly concerned about the way the dominance-relationship to nature translates into a dominance-relationship between human beings. The question I want to pursue is: How do the two combine?

As Lloyd (1984) describes, the history of the distinction between nature and culture (or between 'natural' and 'social') has always been caught up in a master–slave symbolism, and has therefore always been based on an actual, concrete separation of one kind of human being from another. The categories 'natural' and 'social' therefore divide the true representatives of culture or society from those who are denied full social membership because of their alleged greater proximity to nature (as in the case of women) or because of an alleged lack of an essential human principle (as in the case of Aristotle's slave, or the European colonialist's savage).

Mastery over necessity inevitably seems to translate into mastery over those who take care of the necessities of the life process. The very division between 'mastery' on the one hand, and 'labour' on the other, contains the seed for concomitant social divisions and hierarchies. It is the old Platonic distinction between those who know and those who act, and the corresponding 'identification of knowledge with command and rulership and of action with obedience and execution' (Arendt 1958: 225) which criss-crosses with the culture/nature distinction.

CONCLUSIONS

Behind the profusion of scenarios, interpretations and vocabularies that characterize the discussions of work and the future of work, there lies a common core of values and attitudes. Once we see through the myriad definitions and interpretations of work to its very material foundations, the problem of work presents itself quite differently: it is no longer a matter of 'choosing from a menu of options', or of sufficiently clarifying the definitions, but it literally becomes a matter of life and death. As I tried to show, work is ultimately tied to the question of necessity, or to the physical foundation of our existence, and hence to our dependency on nature. How we perceive necessity, how we value and deal with it largely determines our social attitude towards (inner and outer) nature, and thus to ourselves and to each other.

I argued that the notion of labour *includes* the notion of necessity. Labour either has to take care of 'the urgencies of the life process', or it is itself considered an expression of necessity. In both cases the (proposed or actual) 'solution' to the presumably compulsory and therefore undesirable dimension of the human condition is a split, a separation between control and mastery over necessity, or labour, and the actual execution of what is considered necessary, or necessary labour. The triumph over necessity always takes the form of mastery: over slaves, over women, over nature. In the merging of the Judaeo-Christian theology with Greek philosophy such mastery came to include control over one's own inner nature, one's spontaneity and sensuality, culminating in the asceticism of the work ethic (Weber 1958). The 'economic man' of the capitalist era had to fully internalize the enslavement of nature. In the ascetic premises of the work ethic 'the fate of nature became man's own' (Jay 1973: 266): 'The new conception of the natural world as a field for human manipulation and control, ... corresponded to a similar notion of man himself as an object of domination' (Horkheimer in Jay 1973: 257).

We can expand the individual–psychological scope of meaning of the term 'repression' by acknowledging its larger dimension: the socially and culturally sanctioned and permanently reinforced repression of the fact that we are dependent on and ourselves part of nature, and the consequent glorification of death and destruction. The privilege of the ancient sovereign to decide over life and death of his subjects lives on in the current general hubris of man to decide over the fate of nature and of humankind in the name of technological and economic progress.

Many philosophical and sociological questions are at issue here and would have to be addressed if we want to claim to understand fully our cultural obsession with death. At this point it is sufficient to say that the social and cultural attitude towards life is highly problematic and contradictory. Any critical and meaningful discussion of work must therefore include the ultimate question: what does life mean for us, and what value does it have? And, in the light of this question we would also have to ask what we expect from our economy, what we consider its purposes, and thus what we consider truly human and truly productive forms of work. We would have to call into question the death-worship of a society that sees its highest expression in objects or things, in 'congealed' or 'dead' labour which was extracted from the living in the past. In other words, we would have to call into question the overall orientation of our economy towards the accumulation needs of capital rather than towards the satisfaction of human needs. Consequently, the hierarchy of social evaluations of different kinds of work, and different forms of production would have to be radically called into question as well. Work oriented towards life, and towards the production and sustenance of living things, itself a live, non-mechanical process, would then cease to be considered at the bottom of the social hierarchy, as worthless, devalued (and unpaid). Its potential for a truly autonomous, life enhancing form of production, based on a cooperative attitude with nature and necessity could then be released.

Clearly, not only the relationship between work and education, but also the very nature and explicit purposes of education would have to be reconsidered in the wake of a changed concept and ideal of productive work. It is not surprising that the content, organization, concerns, issues, and the overall purposes of education bear essential structural similarities with the content, organization and overall purpose of work and production in our society. As discussed in Part II, the dichotomies and divisions, as well as the valuations and social priorities that characterize the world of work are in many ways reflected in the domain of education. The underlying mode of rationality that allows for a glorification of technology (presumably triumphing over necessity) is expressed in a continuous trend towards technocratization and standardization of education – a process which is closely related to the currently tightening bond between work and education. The continuous process of devaluation of human labour, and therefore of productivity, has its parallels in education. For instance, in the predominance of 'skill', conceptualized entirely in terms of an instrumental rationality, as the paradigm for knowledge considered valuable and useful we can see a general social preoccupation with frozen, congealed and 'dead' forms of knowledge that bears great similarities to the high social value placed on dead labour or commodities. Skills, like commodities, are bought and sold, indeed make sense only in reference to a market-place. On the other hand, the concept of education as a form of self-actualization is bound to a hollow consumerism if simply presented as an option fulfilling different needs of a different clientele. Such a view only reinforces an already divided and stratified curriculum where the masses of people need to update their skills or acquire basic, literacy, or even leisure skills, whereas the more fortunate have the opportunity to expand their horizon, to self-actualize, or to develop professionally.

Part IV

SKILLS AND KNOWLEDGE

8

THE RECONCEPTUALIZATION OF SKILLS

KNOWLEDGE WORK

In the preceding chapter I discussed the origin of the prevailing patriarchal–industrial concept of labour and its intimate alignment with the idea of a technologically defined progress. Today, the pinnacle of this progress is 'the smart machine' (Zuboff 1988), that is, the computer, with all its possibilities and forms of application. The computer presumably not only incorporates the (current) ultimate of human ingenuity and inventiveness, but also tends to be considered altogether smarter than humans. At least, that is the current perception, and it lies at the heart of an apparently growing cult of computer worship. As regards the computer's relationship to the world of work, it should have become clear throughout the preceding discussions that the various uses of the computer in the world of work are not themselves responsible for current social and economic changes and developments. Nor can the computer be considered a panacea for the ills and problems which are accompanying these changes, although the introduction of the new micro-electronic technology into the workplace has, in many instances, altered the content and relations of work.

As Zuboff (1988) describes in great detail, how the particular potential of the computer is realized depends in large measure on the surrounding social and organizational conditions. The potential of 'the smart machine', and its possible effects on the workplace are, however, circumscribed by the specific rationality inherent in the computer and the kind of human intelligence it represents and magnifies. According to Zuboff (1988), the computer's potential is determined by the two possibilities of 'automating' or 'informating' the workplace. In the former case, people's jobs will become monotonous and undemanding in terms of skills or intellectual effort although demanding in terms of stress and responsibility. In the latter case, work will require considerable conceptual abilities. One can look at this difference as one of location and concentration of knowledge (and the power that comes with it): knowledge is either a monopoly of management, which guards the knowledge and power contained in the smart machine or which reserves its right to greater access and use of this knowledge, or it is more widely dispersed throughout the layers of the organization. In other words, it is a question of control and addresses the underlying social relations of the workplace or organization rather than the potential of the computer itself.

However, the theme of power and control that is acted out in the drama of restructuring the workplace, and which Zuboff so vividly describes, is inherently related to the potential of the smart machine itself. The many possibilities of use and application of new technology all point in the same direction: towards the effective and efficient control and manipulation of the (social and physical) environment. I believe that it is these seemingly limitless possibilities for control which lie behind the enchantment with the computer, and behind its addiction-inducing as well as fear-provoking power. Although the computer has been heralded as ushering in a new age and as being responsible for 'revolutionary changes', its celebration reverberates with century-old social assumptions, valuations, and beliefs. An old canon of themes is reactivated and in many ways expressed more poignantly than ever in our history and culture: dominion over nature and the associated dichotomies of nature and culture, body and mind, freedom and necessity, culminating in the dream of a total emancipation from nature through technology.

These themes also cluster around the notion of 'knowledge work' which promises to be clean and intellectually demanding, one of the *leitmotifs* in the literature dealing with the future of work. The considerable allure of the idea of knowledge work as the work of the future is nourished by the same fertile ground of hopes, beliefs, and practices which charge technology and technological progress with the task of liberating us from the limitations of nature, from our own, as well as from the nature that carries and surrounds us. It is a dream of absolute power captured by the glamorous images of many science fiction movies: men (and possibly a few women) working in the clean and glittering central computer station where the fate of entire galaxies is decided. Reality enters this sterile environment only in its symbolic representations, and has ceased to be the unwieldy, cluttered, and certainly unclean stuff of concrete life and reality 'out there'. In this image, power and knowledge have merged to a degree which makes them almost indistinguishable. Knowledge has become power, and power has assumed the form of 'pure' knowledge, purged from any embarassing corporeal vestiges, and spared the necessity of asserting itself in the unpredictable and potentially emotionally disturbing medium of human encounters.

The notion, or myth, that (computer-mediated) knowledge work requires a superior form of knowledge and higher skills than work which comes in direct contact with and directly *acts on* the material world is suffused with the allure of power and control. It is the kind of knowledge which marks Arendt's 'lord and master', who is 'free to create, and free to destroy' (1958: 144). The fascination of video games undoubtedly feeds on the seductive power to kill discussed earlier. The greater this power, the greater the fascination, and the higher the prestige of the skills and knowledge that exercise this power.

Related to the promise of engaging higher forms of human intelligence, and of participating in the power knowledge work represents, is the promise of work stripped of physical exertion or effort. Knowledge work today functions as an ideal for work which has been 'freed' from the drudgery, dirt and grease associated with physical labour. However, not everybody despises the idea or the reality of working with one's body. As some of the workers Zuboff interviews in her book *In the Age of the Smart Machine* (1988) describe, apart from suffering from the noise and (industrial) dirt, they appreciated and enjoyed that part of their work which demanded a physical engagement with the work materials, and the intimate (or 'bodily') knowledge of this material was a source of pride and personal power. Writers who facilely indulge in a vision of future work requiring no physical effort further mistake the current conditions of work, particularly the social division between manual and mental labour, and its brutal consequences for physical labour as an ahistorical given of the human condition. The very concept of 'physical labour' makes sense only with respect to the specific historical circumstances of work under capitalism. Zuboff (1988), for instance, reveals a similar bias when she speaks of the 'century-old dilemma' of the role of 'the body' in work, evoking, of course, the dichotomy of freedom and necessity.[1]

Irrespective of its actual or projected empirical occurrence, knowledge work serves as an ideal and therefore wields considerable power over our conception of good work.[2] It contains a view of the relationship between work and cognition, and between thought and action which greatly contributes to the ongoing impoverishment of the reality and experience of work. In particular, it is an essential factor in the current reconceptualization of all work-related skills along the contours of instrumental rationality, leading to the loss or erosion of abilities, competence, and ways of knowing which draw on a more comprehensive and substantive human intelligence, and which contain a morality which transcends the imperative of control and the maximization of private interests.

In the following I want to discuss what has been described as a fundamental, far-reaching alteration of 'the intrinsic character of work' (Zuboff 1988: 11) through the introduction of new technology, leading to a redefinition of work-related skills. However, this claim of a qualitative rupture between previous notions and experiences of work and current ones is true only on a certain level of analysis. Underneath this level we not only find a historical continuity but also an increased poignancy of themes, interests and concerns. What Marxist economic theory says about the 'economic underside' of society rising to the surface under capitalism is, in related terms, true for the experience of work as well: it is the underside of instrumental rationality which is now emerging most clearly in computer-determined work ('automated' or 'informated'). It is this issue which will be the focus of the following historical sketch.

SKILLED WORK AND SCIENTIFIC MANAGEMENT

The traditional notion of skilled work (in industrial production) is derived from skilled trades or crafts and therefore exhibits similar characteristics and relationships between cognition and action. The most important feature of such skilled work is the traditional and personal nature of knowledge. Knowledge of procedures, methods, materials, and processes is accumulated over a period of time, through active, concrete involvement with the materials and requirements of the craft and such knowledge therefore resides in the individual worker him/herself. In other words, this knowledge is an 'embodied' one. In reference to the skills of the craftsman, Zuboff (1988: 40) writes: 'It was knowledge that accrues to the laboring body – in hands, fingertips, wrists, feet, nose, eyes, ears, skin, muscles, shoulders, arms, and legs – as surely as it was inscribed in the brain.'

Or, in the words of another writer (Braverman 1974: 109), 'the worker combined, in mind and body, the concepts and physical dexterities of the specialty'. Because knowledge reposed in the individual worker, and revealed itself only in the act of work and production, knowledge and practical action were fully intertwined. Just as such knowledge was gained only through prolonged involvement or experience with the materials and processes of the particular craft, it was taught in a similar way, where the pupil (or apprentice) learned the 'know-how' of the craft through direct practical involvement over a lengthy period of time.

It is important to stress that this model of knowledge and skills represents a certain unity of mind and body, of distance from the material or substance by way of critical judgment and control as well as 'mimetic' nearness through developing a 'feel' for the unique qualities and possibilities inherent in the subject matter. What Polanyi (1964: 59) writes with respect to the use of tools is true for the relationship of the craftsperson to his or her materials as well: 'We pour ourselves out into them and assimilate them as parts of our own existence. We accept them existentially by dwelling in them.' The mimetic aspects of the craft can be described as 'an effort to submit to reality' (ibid. 63) in the very process of active involvement and 'acting-on' (Zuboff) which alone yields the intimate knowledge the skilled craftsperson has of her or his trade. It is precisely this dialectical unity of control and mimesis, of acting on and reflecting, of sensual touch and thoughtful distance which makes for the implicit, tacit and generally unspecifiable character of this kind of knowledge and of corresponding skills.

The implicit and personal nature of skills that had grown out of the experience of the crafts also meant that power which emanated from such knowledge likewise resided in the individual worker. In the process of industrialization this posed a problem for the capitalist who needed to rein in such power in order to control the labour process. For this purpose, knowledge and skills had first to be made *explicit* before they could be appropriated by the factory owner or manager.

The figure of Frederick Taylor looms large in the history of attempts to wrest from the workers the knowledge they embodied and which was lodged in their experience, to concentrate it in the hands of the rulers or 'captains of industry', and make it largely inaccessible to the actual producers. Zuboff (1988: 43) summarizes this process in the following way:

> Taylorism meant that the body as the source of skill was to be the object of inquiry in order that the body as the source of effort could become the object of more exacting control. Once explicated, the worker's know-how was expropriated to the ranks of management, where it became management's prerogative to reorganize that knowledge according to its own interests, needs, and motives. The growth of the management hierarchy depended in part upon this transfer of knowledge from the private sentience of the worker's active body to the systematic lists, flowcharts, and measurements of the planner's office.

Braverman (1974) describes how Taylorism was based on three major principles: first, 'the dissociation of the labor process from the skills of the workers .... where the labor process is to be rendered independent of craft, tradition, and the worker's knowledge. Henceforth it is to depend not at all upon the abilities of workers, but entirely upon the practices of management'(ibid. 113). Second, 'the separation of conception from execution', where, in Taylor's own words, 'all possible brain work should be removed from the shop and centered in the planning or laying out department' (ibid. 113); and third, 'the use of this monopoly over knowledge to control each step of the labor process and its mode of execution' (ibid. 119).

In this description, and more so in Zuboff's interpretation of the rise of Taylorism, a number of troublesome questions arise, concerning major assumptions about the scientific or objective nature of the process of inquiry into the 'laboring body', as well as the kind of knowledge thus produced and stored outside the workers. For instance, how is it possible to make explicit what has been described as *intrinsically* tacit, inexplicable or unspecifiable? What is the nature of this inquiry process, what are the assumptions built into its methods and procedures, and how do they affect the results, or the knowledge thus extracted? How is this new, distilled knowledge different from its previous, embodied and implicit state?

In her critique of sociology, Smith (1987) discusses the main epistemological positions that structure the conceptual practices of this field. Her analysis has considerable bearing on the current discussion because the same epistemological presuppositions that shape the social–scientific inquiry process determine the restructuring of work-related knowledge and skills in the wake of Taylorism. Her critique therefore helps to illuminate the precise nature, as well as consequences, of this transformation process.

Employing Alfred Schutz's descriptions of 'the finite provinces of meaning' (Schutz 1962), Smith (1987: 70) writes that 'entry into the world of scientific theory organizes consciousness into a mode detached from the everyday world of working'. To be scientific, or to 'do' science 'involves attention to a domain constituted separately from the particular and immediate interests and concerns of the individual located in her body' (ibid.) The social scientist who locates herself at a point external to the particularities of subjective, lived experience is confronted with the paradox that it is precisely these lived realities out of which 'the cognitive domain of sociology has to be organized' (ibid. 71). This dilemma is caused by the particular relationship that the sociologist establishes between herself and the object of the knowing process: the requirement of scientific inquiry to be objective, that is to be impersonal, detached and impartial, is fulfilled by creating a relationship of distance and control between the knower and the known (Smith 1987: 73). In Smith's words, these are the 'extralocal relations of ruling' (ibid. 78).

Although in sociology the social relations of ruling are veiled by the symbolic medium of discourse, they are quite apparent in the relations between workers and management. However, they recur as well in the structure and conceptual framework within which inquiry into the knowledge of the worker takes place. The abstract mode of (social) scientific inquiry *a priori* conceptually organizes the knowledge of the worker in a way which makes it possible to articulate this knowledge for the interest and task of ruling and control. In other words, this model of scientific inquiry perceives as well as extracts the element of control from the previous intricate blend of power over the work material and submission to its intrinsic characteristics and possibilities. This is the ideological core of the proclaimed superiority and objective 'purity' of the new knowledge. It leaves behind, of course, the subjectivity of the workers, including their unique and specific modes of knowing that are associated with their subjectivity, and that are rooted in their experience. Subjectivity is left behind, or discarded precisely because it does not lend itself to scientific investigation and control. From the perspective of the 'scientific manager', it is a surplus that is quite useless.

What I discussed in the previous chapter with respect to the hierarchical relationship between subsistence and commodity production is repeated here on the level of knowledge and skills. The proclaimed objectivity and impartiality of science bolsters the superiority of 'scientific management'. The very idea that scientific inquiry is capable of explicating the essence of the knowledge and skills stored in the individual workers implies that this knowledge is 'pre-scientific', and thus in a state of underdevelopment, parallel with the 'pre-capitalist' modes of production discussed in previous chapters. By declaring experience-based knowledge and corresponding skills as simply 'pre-scientific', the idea of the labourers as unintelligent, and the interpretation of the implict character of their knowledge as an inability of the worker to articulate it are reinforced. In the last analysis, the extraction and explicit articulation of the worker's knowledge becomes a sign of civilization and progress which appears to emanate directly from science and technology itself. In other words, the transformation and appropriation of the worker's knowledge and skills is represented as a scientific–technological rather than social, normative process. Its character as such a social process, and the social relations of class divisions, exploitation and control in which this process is embedded, are hidden or denied.

Before examining further the nature and consequences of this denial, I want to describe briefly the transformation of skills in computer-related work.

COMPUTERS AND SKILLS

The computer's main functions are to store and to process information, which are continuations of two different lines of 'technolgical descent':

> *Storing* data connects the computer with the job of record keeping; it dates back to the ledgers and filing cabinets which electronic data banks are now replacing. In this capacity, the computer mimics the faculty of memory. *Processing* data, on the other hand, represents a different line of technolgical descent. Here the computer dates back to the adding machine, and in this capacity, it mimics the power of human reason.
>
> (Roszak 1986: 109)

It is the latter quality, the mimicking of the 'power of human reason', which is of interest for the discussion of skills. Not only has this power entered the machine itself, but it has to be matched by the abilities of the human being who wants to exploit the full potential of the machine's power. The skills that are necessary for this task 'combine abstraction, explicit inference, and procedural reasoning' (Zuboff 1988: 75). As such, they are, of course, not new, although they are applied to and within a medium which is itself constructed by, and represents, the same rationality that its use or application calls for. It is this interplay between the 'smartness' of the machine, itself of human origin, and the smartness of the person who works with it which allows for new combinations and dimensions of the old human logical–mathematical intelligence and which is thereby enhanced or magnified by the machine.

From the perspective of the ongoing rationalization of work, the computer represents continuity through a new or different application of essentially the same rationality that previously extracted certain aspects of the workers' knowledge. From the perspective of the workers' relationship to the material aspects of their work or production, and thus of the actual experience of their work, we can speak of discontinuity. As Zuboff (1988) so vividly describes, the material aspect of work, the process of direct, immediate engagement and production, be it of things or relationships, is translated into its symbolic representations. The worker literally loses *touch* with the concrete material of her work. In a way, this rupture is so dramatic that we cannot simply speak of a transformation process. Rather, it is a process where the sensuous involvement in production is discarded, and the particular kind of knowledge and mode of knowing such involvement represented.[3] As Zuboff (1988: 72) writes with respect to her case study of a paper mill,

> ... where operators relied upon action-centered skill, management must convince the operator to leave behind a world in which things were immediately known, comprehensively sensed, and able to be acted upon directly, in order to embrace a world that is dominated by objective data, is removed from the action context, and requires a qualitatively different kind of response.

To use Zuboff's terminology, 'action-centered skills' are either seized altogether by the smart machine, or replaced by (rather than transformed into) 'intellective skills'. In the former case the workplace is 'automated' or de-skilled (in every respect), in the latter case the workplace is 'informated', requiring the worker to apply or develop intellectual abilities like inference, abstract thought, or procedural reasoning.

The concerns that need to be raised go beyond the question of skills, and of either de- or re-skilling the workplace, especially as these questions are generally conceived of entirely within the confines of what I would call 'encircled thinking'. This sees the solution to the problems caused by the introduction of new technology within the very same technology, and only there. Inevitably, it screens out realities, experiences, and problems surrounding the issue of work and production which are of a normative, non-technological nature, and which I will now address.

Through computer-related technologies, the experience and reality of work have been altered because computer-dominated work reorganizes the worker's sense of what is real, and restructures her relationship to reality. It further poses a different relationship between knowledge and reality, and, consequently, changes the worker's view of where knowledge is located or where it comes from. Zuboff (1988) describes how this process is in most cases accompanied by considerable distrust, anguish, fear, and often also physical pain, particularly in cases where the new work requires physical immobility which the workers experience as a form of 'interior confinement' (Zuboff 1988: 142). Because the workers lose touch with the concrete, material, but also contextual and personal aspects of their work, they feel disoriented and disempowered. In Zuboff's words, they suffer from a 'disruption of identity' (ibid. 185).

THE DETACHMENT FROM REALITY

One of the recurrent complaints voiced by workers whose workplaces had been restructured was the difficulty of learning to 'trust' the machine (Zuboff 1988). Because the workers (and, to a certain extent, management), were 'cut off from the action-context' (ibid. 83) of their work, and no longer saw, heard, touched, or spoke to the things, objects, or people they had previously been working with (or 'acting on'), they lost an important avenue for regular 'reality checks', and therefore a sense of direct control. This is one in a cluster of complex experiences resulting in behaviour which is frequently stigmatized as 'fear of change' or 'resistance to change'. Such stigmatization reveals a kind of thinking which from the outset closes off the possibility of examining the potentially rational ground for such resistance, or its potentially progressive elements.

The notion of 'resistance to change' (in the specific context of restructuring the workplace) is held together by themes and beliefs which are worth looking at in some detail. Above all, it resonates with the themes of 'backwardness' and 'progress', so familiar in Western history. The idea of learning to trust the machine, to surrender one's sensuous involvement with reality to one's disembodied manipulation of its abstract, truncated 'data version', implies that there is really nothing to mind or to worry about, and that nothing important or worthwhile is lost. Such thinking is obviously behind a statement like the following:

> With the growing realization that working through the computer could be physically easier than anything they had ever known, many of the older workers were finally weaned away from their attachment to concrete objects. *Many of the younger ones were persuaded that direct knowledge of a tangible reality was not, after all, crucial.*
>
> (Zuboff 1988: 92, my emphasis)

The question is, of course, crucial for what? We are here dealing with two separate but highly interrelated issues: a process of *detachment* from 'tangible reality', and a process of *attachment* to a new, highly abstract reality that lends itself to symbolic manipulation and control. It is a reality which has been worked over twice. First, in the form of the concrete materials and substances and second, in the form of actual people, tangible reality was transformed into simple economic 'inputs'. In an earlier chapter I discussed how this transformation process required a perception of people as part of 'nature', (a nature which had already come to be perceived as dead and endlessly malleable matter), to be counted among the 'things' which were to be consumed by economic processes.[4]

In the recent phase of computer-mediated reality, matter has been transformed further into manipulable data. In a peculiar paradox, this is the source of fear and anguish mentioned above, but also, eventually, the source of a feeling of omnipotence after psychological adjustments have been made. Once the workers are socialized into the new mindset not only do they no longer worry about their detachment from reality, they come to appreciate and enjoy it. This is not surprising.

Psychologically speaking, the manipulation of reality in the worked-over and highly abstracted form of data is infinitely easier than a manipulation of the multi-layered, multi-dimensional, constantly moving, shifting, and resisting stuff of corporeal reality. The data version of reality promises total control because it represents a closed, and internally perfect logical system, whose occasional glitches and bugs are considered mere signs of momentary, fixable imperfections.

As Roszak (1986: 110) describes, the aura of superiority which surrounds the data representation of knowledge and reality (and of knowledge *of* reality) derives from the old ideal of pure, 'unaided reason, fashioned from the logical structure of the mind itself'. Rozsak further describes that in the history of philosophy, mathematics and mathematical ideas frequently served as a model for '*a priori* knowledge, knowledge which supposedly has no connection with sensory experience, with the data of observation and measurement'. (ibid. 110). Although this view of knowledge, dating back to Plato's idealization of geometry as the only reliable knowledge, has been criticized, its mystique dispelled, 'a trust in the clarity of numbers and of mathematical logic ... lingers on in modern science and ... survives in cybernetics and information theory. Plato's mysticism may have been banished from these new sciences, but the spell of geometrical certainty remains' (ibid. 110–11).

It survives especially in the reactivation of the dichotomy between body and mind. 'Knowledge work' lives off the old attraction of 'head work', which carries higher intellectual as well as social appeal than 'body work'. Computer-mediated work is superior because 'it all occurs in your mind now' (a worker quoted by Zuboff 1988: 75) which, according to an argument that is constructed entirely out of the mind/body dichotomy, leads to a freeing of 'the production process from the organic limits of the body' (ibid. 30). The ultimate dream is, of course, to develop a machine which has absorbed even the disembodied presence of the worker altogether. Roszak (1986: 112) quotes from Robert Jastrow's study of 'mind in the universe' where this dream is expressed in vivid terms:

> When the brain sciences reach this point, a bold scientist will be able to tap the contents of his mind and transfer them into the metallic lattices of a computer. Because mind is the essence of being, it can be said that this scientist has entered the computer, and that he now dwells in it.

> At last the human brain, ensconced in a computer, has been liberated from the weakness of the mortal flesh.... It is in control of its own destiny. The machine is its body; it is the machine's mind ...
>
> (Zuboff 1988: 29)

This dream promises nothing less than an escape from the fear of death, because death 'reminds the living of the ultimate uncontrollability of the body'

THE DIALECTICS OF DEPENDENCE AND CONTROL

We have come full circle with the themes of control and denial mentioned ealier in the chapter. In the last analysis, the presumed superiority of the machine, and the posited superiority of scientific or technological knowledge are firmly rooted in the rationality of control. This rationality is tied to a thinking, and to an epistemology, which perceives and therefore structures reality primarily in terms of its (actual or potential) controllability, and which therefore neglects, discards, or denies all those aspects of reality which resist or escape the confines of its parameters. The existence of a separate, closed reality which is intrinsically controllable and manipulable greatly assists in creating the idea of superiority of instrumental rationality, and that it is the only form of rationality which deserves this name. This idea contributes to the illusion that all of reality, like all of nature, is potentially controllable.

In a political (rather than psychoanalytical) sense, denial assumes a three-fold form: in an epistemological sense, it denies the importance, or even the possibility, of other kinds of rationality which could organize our ways of seeing and knowing the world, and which could structure our experience of work and production (an issue which will be addressed in the final two chapters); in an ideological sense, it feeds into the illusion of a technological independence from 'the organic limits of the body', from the 'weakness of the mortal flesh', i.e. from nature; in a material sense, it represses the violence that has accompanied the progressive rationalization of the production process. It is the last two points I want to focus on in the remainder of this chapter.

In the self-enclosed, seemingly omnipotent world of data reality, just as in the 'finite province' of scientific thought, the concrete, bodily reality of animate and inanimate objects vanishes from view, becomes unimportant or not crucial, and in a way therefore ceases to exist. 'Reality' becomes its data version. We cannot consider this situation separately from the social division of labour which provides the very conditions for the suppression of bodily reality.

The scientist, like the knowledge worker, assumes a specific position within the social division that separates and brings into a hierarchical relationship thinking and doing, or 'mental' and 'manual' labour; they are its product, and this division organizes their experience and the particulars of their work. As described above, to the extent to which they assume the 'superior position' in this hierarchical division they do the work of ruling, and this experience of ruling gives rise to a certain form of ideological consciousness. In Smith's words (1987: 80):

> Ideological forms of consciousness are definite practices of thinking about society that reflect the experience of ruling. From the standpoint of the ruling, the actual practices, the labor, and the organization of labor, which makes the existence of a ruling class and their ruling possible, are invisible.

Just as bodies with their organic limits continue to exist, and human beings continue to exist within their bodies, work oriented towards satisfying corresponding needs will continue to be necessary. Thus, while ideologically displaced by the social division of labour, this work 'depends upon a world known immediately and directly in the bodily mode' (Smith 1987: 81).

We are once again reminded of the division between subsistence and commodity production, and of the concomitant idea that commodity production is not only the higher and more advanced form of production, but also independent from subsistence production. In reality, the reverse is true, just as both the scientist and the knowledge worker are dependent on those who work on, help to sustain, and produce the conditions which make their separate existence possible in the first place. As discussed in Part I of this book, it is women, and Third World producers (men and women) both inside and outside the industrialized countries who do this work, who will continue to do it, and whose overall devalued status will make it possible to suppress society's dependence on their labour.

Suppression here refers to a false or ideological form of consciousness which arises out of the experience of ruling. As discussed above, control seizes certain aspects of reality and discards others. This process is not a simple, neutral, or peaceful one because reality does not lend itself easily or voluntarily to control and manipulation (see also Chapter 10). Once it has reached the sterile, air-conditioned environment of the computer laboratory, it has left behind all that has been used up and discarded: broken bodies and spirits, including those who were the producers of new technology, unimaginable heaps of garbage, and the wasteland of a fouled environment which is the main mark of our unstoppable progress. In short, the dream of total control, and of total emancipation from nature turns out to be a nightmare made out of the stuff of dispossession, destruction, violence, alienation, and of the enforced silence of those who do not participate in the work of ruling (Smith 1987: 57).

A thinking which glorifies technology, and work which deals primarily with the technological representations of reality, in the last analysis participates in this violence, and in an erosion of the very basis of survival. This includes educational paradigms and responses to the issue or the future of work which move within the magnetic field of this kind of false thinking. Such thinking prevents the examination of themes, interests, and concerns as regards the origin and social context of technology, the ultimate meaning and purpose of work and production, and of a useful knowledge. It also contributes to the formation of a consciousness which has lost the ability to reflect critically on these themes and issues, and to organize experience based on a reality which is understood and reflected upon. In the following chapter I will look more closely at the problem of skills which have now been conceptualized in entirely instrumental terms. The prime focus will be on the loss of the dimension of critique and of critical reflection which accompanies the absolute rule of instrumental rationality. In the last part of the book I will focus on the relationship of action and cognition contained in older or alternative notions of skill and knowledge. Here the focus will be on Utopian possibilities for work and production as represented by these conceptions. These possibilities do not evolve exclusively out of the rational potential of the smart machine, but out of the potential of a more comprehensive and substantive human intelligence.

9

THE TRIUMPH OF INSTRUMENTAL RATIONALITY

INSTRUMENTAL AND COMMUNICATIVE RATIONALITY

In the preceding chapter I discussed how work-related skills and knowledge have been reconceptualized along the lines of a strictly instrumental rationality. In Part II I addressed two related phenomena: the shrinkage of the idea of a liberal education and of highly complex social and economic issues to questions of skills and skill deficits, illustrating the narrow boundaries within which work-related educational questions are permitted to be raised. Within these boundaries, educational concerns are conceived of in strict relation to economic growth and profit maximization. As the primary purpose of work-related education, all educational activities are therefore essentially strategies oriented towards reaching this end.

In this chapter I will look at the 'deep structure' of strategic thinking, and investigate more closely its particular mode of rationality. I will contrast this rationality with one which is not based on instrumental means-ends relationships. For this purpose I will borrow Juergen Habermas' distinction between instrumental and communicative rationality. These distinctions are useful for a number of reasons. First, they challenge the idea that science and technology provide the only model for true rationality. As Habermas describes, the realm of social action, and thus of questions relating to norms and values, provides a different, more comprehensive model where instrumental rationality is only a *partial* aspect. He calls this form of rationality 'communicative' because it is located in the normative basis of human speech. Second, Habermas's distinctions allow an examination of confusions, misplaced importances, and false hierarchies between these two modes of rationality. Above all, they help to investigate situations where instrumental reason has usurped experiences which are of a communicative rather than an instrumental nature.

Habermas first draws the distinctions between 'purposive–rational' and 'communicative action' in his 'Technology and science as "ideology"' (1970). They appear as primary distinctions in most of his later writings. Purposive–rational action is further divided into 'instrumental' and 'strategic' action and corresponding modes of rationality.

Instrumental rationality refers to the rationality of *technical means*, requiring 'technically utilizable, empirical knowledge' (Habermas 1979: 117). To be rational therefore means to use the appropriate technical means to reach a certain end. Baking a cake, for instance, requires using the right ingredients and following the correct procedures for working with them (including the proper sequence and way of mixing ingredients, choosing the right temperature for baking, deciding on the right amount of time allowed for baking, etc.). To be rational here means to select and organize means in the most efficient and economical way in order to reach the desired result. Choosing the wrong kind of means, or organizing them inappropriately, leads to failure and therefore indicates incompetence.

Strategic rationality refers to the rationality of *decisions*, requiring 'the explication and inner consistency of value systems and decision maxims, as well as the correct derivation of acts of choice' (Habermas 1979: 117). Similarly to instrumental action, criteria for what is rational include efficiency and appropriateness of means, but also the availability of adequate information, and the logic and consistency of decision-making procedures. From the perspective of strategic action, irrational behaviour is incompetent, employing faulty decision-making procedures based, perhaps, on insufficient or the wrong kind of information, violating the rules of deductive logic, or operating on the basis of inconsistent values. Such behaviour will therefore result in failure.

Some of the major preoccupations of the adult education enterprise move within the orbit of strategic thinking. For instance, the emphasis on serving the needs of 'adult clients' is one of the primary 'decision maxims' in adult education, determining needs assessment strategies and programme developments where a close 'fit' between the needs of the 'clients' and the 'educational product' is aspired. Of similar importance are strategies to increase administrative and organizational efficiency. The backdrop of behaviourist psychology to many of the adult learning theories further testifies to the predominance of strategic thinking in adult education.

Instrumental as well as strategic actions are characterized by an objectifying attitude, where a detached observer is looking at 'the' external world. Technically or strategically useful knowledge is knowledge about 'what is the case', i.e. what is accepted as true or a fact. Its application may lead to technological progress or to improvements in decision-making procedures (McCarthy 1981).

In contrast with purposive–rational action, communicative action is characterized by a relationship of complementarity and mutuality among the participants, and it is oriented towards mutual understanding rather than effective control. Here behaviour is not governed by technical rules or strategies, based on correct calculations or rational choices of means, but instead by socially sanctioned norms concerning right or wrong, proper or improper behaviour. These norms establish an *intersubjective* structure of interaction where people anticipate and therefore understand each other's intentions (Habermas 1984). This reciprocal structure is characterized by the following dynamics: I expect that you know what is proper or right in certain situations, but I can also rely upon you knowing that I know that you know what is right (and vice versa). It is such reciprocity of anticipation which is captured by the term *intersubjectivity*. Behaviour-guiding norms are therefore grounded in intersubjectivity, and intersubjectivity is constituted by norms which define reciprocal behaviour expectations.

The kind of knowledge involved in this process is 'moral-practical knowledge, or knowledge about 'what is right' (or wrong). This term is borrowed from Habermas (1984). It refers to knowledge about the norms and customs prevailing in a particular society, the ability to act according to those norms, and also the ability to reflect critically on their validity. Moral–practical knowledge is manifested in social institutions, in cultural products, in world-views, and in social value and belief systems. All of these expressions contain the norms that prevail in a particular society at a particular point in history.

On the most immediate level, behaviour is rational if it follows established rules of right and wrong, of proper and improper. We can speak of 'existing' norms only to the extent to which they actually have the force to guide social conduct or to define proper action. According to Habermas, the ultimate source of the power of norms to guide and regulate behaviour lies in their 'validity claim'. This is the inherent claim of norms to be *justifiably* valid, or to deserve to be followed (Habermas 1984). Habermas (1979: 96) calls this ever-present implication of the existence of norms the 'gentle but obstinate', 'the never silent although seldom redeemed claim to reason.' In principle we can always interrupt a process of communication and move to its meta-level by focusing on that claim explicitly. We can therefore at any time be pressed to give *good reasons* for why we think something is right or wrong, or why we follow certain norms and not others. Ordinarily we simply assume that our behaviour is rational, and that we follow norms which we could defend by enlisting good reasons or by bringing forth persuasive arguments.

NORMS AND CRITIQUE

If we define the particular rationality of communication as one that presupposes that we have *good reasons* for our behaviour and moral–practical decisions we have to ask 'What are good reasons?' To put it simply: good reasons are those to which all people affected by a particular norm can agree. To say this is not a sudden leap into the cloudy realms of unattainable ideals but rather a step into the 'deep structure' of communicative action because the idea that we could – if pressed to do so – provide mutually acceptable reasons makes communication possible in the first place. During ordinary conversations we assume that the other person is accountable, reasonable, and responsible, i.e. rational in the sense of being potentially able to persuasively justify her actions and behaviour. We further believe that the other party in the conversation thinks the same of us. In short, our communication is based on these shared assumptions. In the absence of such a belief in the basic accountability of the other we can no longer speak of truly human communication. We are either engaged in a therapeutic situation, where the other person is not held fully accountable for her actions, or in a (covert or overt) manipulative and thus strategically structured situation, where one or both parties to the communication is concerned primarily with their own private gains. However, covert manipulation, like lying, can be successful only because it directly relies on the assumption of a consensus (Habermas 1973).

If lying is one possibility allowed by the consensual structure of speech, so is its opposite: to come to a rational agreement about acceptable norms, and to make consensus itself the explicit goal of communication.

As described by Habermas (1973), consensual decision-making requires the absence of any kind of coercion in order to allow for non-hierarchical, 'symmetrical' relations, the primary conditions for reaching a true consensus. Consequently, 'good', 'rational', or 'mutually acceptable reasons' are likewise those that are expressed under power-free conditions. Thus, an authentic consensus is one where 'no force except that of the better argument' prevails, precluding the force or power of any one group or individual to impose their beliefs on others (Habermas 1975: 108).

By stipulating that a process of rational decision-making be free of dominance relations of any kind, Habermas establishes a close link between communicative rationality and critique. In the process of justifying the validity of norms (or of normative systems like entire ideologies), the participants scrutinize the social consensus about acceptable norms thus far taken-for-granted so it can be seen where this consensus may be held together by false claims, threats, or other kinds of coercion. The tacitly accepted reasons legitimizing certain norms may likewise emerge as quite unacceptable to those most affected by them. Critique therefore means to name (or, in Habermas's terminology, to 'thematize') social norms and to question their validity. Only in such a way can a presumed social consensus be recognized as a false one.

In the sense established here, critique aims at a dissolution of external and internal power structures. Its very mode of existence is to indict the deceiving effect of power to create a false consensus, based on covert or overt social hierarchies and dominance relations. The slogan 'What is good for GM is good for America' is an illustration of such an alleged consensus where the interests of a private group are presented as the interests of all. Critique therefore refers to a process where false claims of universal acceptability of norms are challenged. By implication, critique is also a process where truly common interests are discovered or shaped. Habermas's theory therefore not only points to the ideal of power-free communication and social relations, but also to the fundamentally communal structure of truth-seeking and norm-shaping. Both aspects are important for education.

THE CONTAINMENT OF CRITIQUE

In the light of the preceding discussion, the recent emphasis on 'critical reasoning skills', and on suggestions for critical reflectivity in the workplace, is a dubious one. It is both promising and frustrating. It is promising because adult education generally suffers from a lack of emphasis on critical thinking. It is frustrating because critical reflectivity is normally allowed to take place within well-defined boundaries, rarely leaving the safety zone of an unquestioned acceptance of the status quo. Such acceptance relies, first of all, on the powerful ideology of continuous and unlimited economic growth, which appears eminently self-evident, thus pre-empting the need to raise questions concerning its validity. A number of important issues therefore remain undiscussed and uncriticized. The ideology of growth, as any other ideology, 'pretends', as it were, that its inherent 'validity claims' have already been justified and approved by all, i.e. it has a *built-in* consent.[1] This makes it possible to propose educational procedures whose purpose it is to foster critical reflectivity without directly clashing with the power-bound organization of work. However, as described in the preceding section, critique comes into its own only when it thematizes rather than suppresses the issue of power. We are therefore dealing with a truncated version of critique where relations of dominance, the actual object of critique, remain systematically suppressed.

Marsick's book *Learning in the Workplace* (1987b) is a case in point. Marsick speaks of a 'paradigm revolution' which makes it necessary to go beyond the narrow thinking of technical skills or expertise associated primarily with a behaviourist paradigm of workplace learning. She presents a number of theories which offer different ways of looking at the issue of workplace learning. Despite their differences in terms of approach, conceptual frameworks and vocabularies, Marsick proposes that these theories all work with a notion of critical reflectivity. Her interpretation of these theories proceeds, however, within certain pre-established limits (partly reflecting the limits of these theories themselves, partly reflecting her own interpretation) which precisely mirror those I indicated in the above discussion.

Most importantly, the overall organizational, and thus socio-economic context of work is entirely taken for granted. Thus, the overall structure of her argument in which her plea for critical reflectivity is embedded, is a decidedly strategic one. First of all, the need for critical reflectivity is justified by pointing to current changes which make the old paradigm dysfunctional. To a certain extent critical reflectivity is therefore part of an overall *adjustment strategy*. Second, and relatedly, critical reflectivity is fully tethered to the primary end of economic growth and productivity, and it therefore constitutes a process which starts and ends with the pre-defined goals of 'the organization'. Consequently, the contexts Marsick and the other contributors to her book *Learning in the Workplace* (1987) describe are inherently hierarchical, where management *allows* employees to be critically reflective. The following quote captures this inevitable combination of hierarchical and strategic assumptions:

> The organization provides a clear picture of its perception of desired outcomes, but training is not a lock-step process inculcating these pre-defined objectives. Individuals are encouraged to develop a habit of reflectivity in both formal and informal learning modes in which ... they continually probe their experience to determine why they are or are not effective and how they can learn to become so.
>
> (Marsick 1987a: 24)

This description is reminiscent of the potential of new technology to self-diagnose its own problems rather than having an expert examine these problems from the outside. In both cases, the underlying framework for thought and action remains the same.

Marsick draws on a number of quite diverse theories and conceptual frameworks whose ramifications actually conflict with the economic growth and productivity model. But because Marsick does not unfold these implications, she can proceed as if these theories can be placed rather unproblematically within an overall strategic context. For instance, Mezirow's ideas on a critical adult education from which Marsick heavily borrows contain a critical potential which ultimately explodes the strategic thinking pradigm, but this potential remains safely ensconced in bottom line thinking.[2] Thus, when Marsick (1987a: 18) talks about examining 'internalized norms' relating to the notions of femininity and masculinity she opens up the issue of male-female power relations. She writes (ibid.), that allowing male managers to develop 'feminine' skills like empathy, and a female manager 'masculine' skills like assertiveness, 'might not lead to deeper reflection on masculine or feminine identity that could lead to a perspective transformation'. However, the problem is presented in a sufficiently vague manner as to avoid some troublesome questions – all of which would be raised by an uncircumscribed process of critique. These questions concern the sexual division of labour as the hidden foundation of the unequal and segregated employment structure, and they point to material rather than merely psychological limitations to equality.

To contain the power of critique by censoring the most important questions results in binding critique to a strategic context of action. As described above, however, critique is rooted in communicative action. In order to engage in critique one has to step outside a strategic action context and focus explicitly on its 'social boundary conditions' (Habermas 1979: 121). Instrumental and strategic action, for instance in the form of lists of skills or proposed procedures, do not carry their own justification with them like a snail carries its house. These justifications have to be developed in a context specifically created for that purpose, and involving a process of discursive reasoning. Instrumental reason cannot reflect on itself, on its own social context, and on the interests that are contained in it.

It is important to note that the distinction between communicative and strategic (or instrumental) action is not simply a distinction between action governed by norms, and that governed by technical or procedural rules. All action, including strategic action, is social in the sense of being embedded in a social context. This context determines the scope and nature of one's action, the practical effects it can have, and how it is perceived and interpreted by others.

For example, an 'interpersonal skill' such as 'controlling the impulse of anger and hostility' (Klemp 1982) contains a host of normative assumptions. To say that such a skill is effective does not automatically justify the rightness of underlying norms (nor does it signify a universal acceptance of those norms). We could ask, for instance, effective for whom? Within what kind of context? Under which circumstances? We can further question the whole idea that 'efficiency' is a valid norm for regulating human interaction. We can therefore also look at the overall social context in which 'impulses' like anger arise, in order to understand fully their nature and origin, and in order to be able to assert that controlling these impulses is a good idea. It may well be the case that feelings of anger and hostility are perfectly rational responses, and their expression (in a yet to be determined form) may serve the collective interest of those whose anger is aroused. Anger would therefore also cease to be a mere 'impulse', but a feeling whose cause is recognized as justified, and whose expression may therefore be allowed in a form that is appropriate to the goals and interests of those who feel offended. In a hierarchical situation of subordinates and supervisors, i.e. of an unequal distribution of power, such 'impulse control' is demanded by the interests of those in power since it makes for a smoother functioning daily operation. For the subordinates it may serve the short-term interests of individual self-protection, but it may also lead to stomach ulcers, and to feelings of helplessness and defeat.

The example given above raises other questions as well. Attitudinal skills such as 'suppressing hostility' contain normative assumptions and expectations and therefore prescribe *normative* rather than *technical* or *strategic* behaviour. In terms of the categories borrowed from Habermas, these kinds of skills represent – in whatever distorted or congealed form – inherently communicative experiences which are, however, inserted in a decidedly strategic context of action. As I shall discuss below, this affects their internal structure as well.

THE DESTRUCTION OF INTERSUBJECTIVITY

I want to turn to an example that is particularly illustrative since it addresses the concept of communication directly. In fact, so-called 'communication skills', sometimes subsumed under the larger heading of 'interpersonal skills', have recently taken centre stage in discussions concerning future work-related skills. They include not only the old 'basic skills' like reading, writing and speaking/listening, but also the motivational dimension of interaction, indicated, for instance, by such 'skills' as 'positive regard for others' or 'accurate empathy' (Klemp 1982).

Employing the categories discussed earlier, speaking and listening, regarding others positively, or empathizing with others are all expressions for human interaction or communication. These experiences therefore imply mutuality and reciprocity of intentions and are oriented towards mutual understanding. Thus, to empathize with someone involves an effort to 'understand' someone's feelings and motivations on one's own level of feelings and motivations, to *feel with* someone. The parties to the communication establish a definite 'we', are (or become) part of a *shared* world. The overall intersubjective structure of the situation is therefore inherently *dialogical*.

To clarify further the dialogical nature of experiences like respect or empathy, two interrelated dimensions have to be addressed. First, empathy or respect signify an affirmation of the other's unique individuality. If this affirmation is tied to some 'ulterior motive', such as 'making the other feel good about herself' in the hope of increasing her productivity level, it ceases to be communicative in nature. In fact, it ceases to be a true affirmation of individuality, because what matters in the whole interactive process is productivity rather than individuality. Second, to be respectful and emphathetic is a form of participation in the other's world of experience, including the meanings and intepretations the other gives to her experience. This is different from 'psyching' someone 'out', from learning what makes others 'tick', in order to 'manage' more successfully, i.e. manipulate their behaviour according to the dictates of one's own private goals.[3] The basis of participating in another's frame of reference is based on the motivation to *understand* – nothing more, but also nothing less. As soon as elements of control, of private schemes aimed at realizing unilaterally determined purposes enter into the situation, the underlying communicative structure is transformed from a dialogical into a monological one.[4]

A process of understanding involves first of all moral–practical rather than technical or analytical knowledge. This knowledge represents a complicated web of assumptions, convictions, beliefs, and values. It therefore includes cognitive as well as motivational elements, where the particulars of individual experiences intermingle with the general patterns of socially pre-given value and belief systems. Rather than being schematically or strategically applied according to certain rules, various elements of this knowledge are spontaneously 'activated' into a specific configuration, dependent on the specifics of the communication situation itself, and as called for by the unique individuality of the participants. Thus, an action like empathizing is a form of *social practice* which signifies the versatile and, above all, reflective (rather than mechanical) use of one's own experience and moral–practical knowledge. 'Reflective' here refers to the conscious recognition of the moral–practical content and requirements of a particular situation, and on action that grows out of or is adjusted according to this recognition. In other words, empathy is a moral ability or *virtue*, which includes being able to recognize when and where empathy is called for. Such an ability cannot be broken down into its behavioural components which can then be taught and acquired bit by bit. Rather, like any other virtue, it needs an appropriate normative context, or a moral ecology which allows and nurtures it.

In contrast, the predominant emphasis on skills constitutes a moral ecology which precisely prohibits the free and spontaneous unfolding of action primarily oriented towards mutual understanding. Instead, an emphasis on skills orients all action and interaction primarily towards success in the sense of an *effective control of people and their environment*, thus destroying the basic morality of an ability like emphathy. Significantly, from the perspective of skills, empathy has to be 'accurate' because as an integral element of a means–ends relationship it ceases to be a form of human communication and becomes one of the 'factors of success', and one more strategy in the 'effective performer's' arsenal of behavioural options (Klemp 1982). Likewise, to 'make' others 'feel that they are themselves understood' is part and parcel of the overall purpose of employing one's interpersonal skills 'to promote feelings of efficacy in another person' (Klemp 1982: 68). Efficacy, like efficiency, control, and success are what Habermas calls 'decision procedures' or 'preference rules' (1984) that are squarely located within the parameters of strategic action.

The procedural regulation of interpersonal skills creates an intersubjective structure which is inherently *monological*. The proprietor of a skill like 'accurate empathy' or 'impulse control' makes unilateral decisions about when and where to employ these skills. Such decisions are based on a correct assessment of the situation and on a rational choice of one among several possible strategies or behaviours (for instance, to express one's anger or to control the impulse). Instead of moving within the spontaneous and fluid medium of communicative experience, this form of rational, strategic behaviour can be procedurally regulated, be broken down into sub-units and ordered into logical sequences of steps. Klemp (1982: 68), for instance, proposes to first 'diagnose a human concern', followed by an attempt to find an 'appropriate response to the needs of the person' (ibid.). This example illustrates that regardless of the nature of the experience subsumed under a particular skill (technical or interpersonal), all skills are similarly conceived of as pre-defined ends. Once these skills have been defined, or their absence diagnosed, the only task remaining is to find the best possible ways to teach or acquire them. The latter task becomes easier the more the skills can be broken down into discrete bits and pieces, into 'sub-skills' and minute behavioural descriptions, organized into logical sequences, or ordered into hierarchies of simpler and more complex skills (see, for instance, Conger and Mullen 1982).

FEELINGS – A NEW RESOURCE

We are now in a better position to evaluate the current interest in workers' feelings. This interest was fuelled by the report *Work in America* (1973) (issued by the Department of Health, Education, and Welfare), which spoke of increasing worker alienation, dissatisfaction, and, consequently, lower productivity (see Apple 1980). Various plans for job enrichment, job enlargement, worker self-management, worker co-management and so on ensued as a partial response to this situation (ibid. 54). Today, the 'touchy-feely' approach which characterized the various plans of the 1970s (including the Quality of Work Life movement, see Parker 1985), has been replaced in the 1980s with a more hard-nosed and, above all, more thoroughly calculated approach. As Parker and Slaughter describe (1988), the most modern version can be found in the 'team approach' practised mainly in the car manufacturing industries, but setting models for other industries as well.

These new management approaches have been heralded as a new 'humanistic' shift in management theory and practice. They are presented as a new vision of cooperation and harmony, of dignity and respect for the workers (Parker and Slaughter 1988), and of 'trust' and 'commitment' (Howard 1986: 100). They are further described as presenting new opportunities for education to assist management in the training of a workforce which is capable of performing under these new and challenging conditions (see Marsick 1987b).

In the light of the discussions presented in this book, it is difficult to embrace these new trends as unequivocally positive. When one considers the larger social and economic context of these new 'paradigm shifts' in management theory and practice, and looks more closely at the actual structures established by these new approaches, the picture becomes quite complex as well as somewhat troublesome.

As described in the previous chapter, management's historically new interest in workers' feelings, or in the worker as a 'whole person' comes at a time of increasing rationalization of work and workplace design, and an increasing rather than lessening emphasis on control. As Howard (1986: 99) describes, 'this contradiction has given birth to an extraordinary irony':

> Precisely at the moment when the workplace is becoming more rationalized, more technologically intensive, more automated and more controlled, managers are turning their attention to the irrational side of working life and making the ineffable realm of human values and motivations the conspicuous object of their concern.

However, these contradictions are only of a superficial kind. Instead of being rejected in these new management paradigms, the logic of instrumental rationality is actually extended into the realm of human values and motivation. In many ways, these new approaches represent the latest, more refined, and more intimate form of controlling every single aspect of the worker and the workplace. In other words, the new interest in the worker as a whole person is fuelled by the need to control the whole person, leading to a highly effective recentralization of management (ibid. 66).

We must not forget that the current push for greater worker self-management takes place against the background of extensive purges of the ranks of middle management, historically the layer of employees responsible for direct supervision. To a large extent this purge has been the result of cost-cutting demands, but it has also been made possible by the supervisory potential of new technology itself. Thus, the two main features which distinguish the new forms of management control from earlier ones are the sophisticated use of technology to supervise in an inconspicuous, indirect fashion, and (or in combination with) psychological strategies which stress self-discipline as a form of internalized supervision.

A number of writers have investigated the psychological consequences of the modern organization of work and production. People construct a sense of self, and an identity which is as 'monological' as the interpersonal relationships that characterize the workplace. Howard (ibid. 123) discusses this issue in terms of 'crafting the corporate self', where instrumental rationality is extended into the realm of the human personality. This may take the form of greater internalized control (especially among workers at the lower level of the corporate hierarchy), but also of minutely calculated behavioural strategies aiming at 'self-actualization' and 'personal growth'. In a similar vein, Hayes (1989: 37) makes a connection with the loss of social cohesiveness and the increased emphasis on self-control and self-sufficiency. He describes how especially in a context of high employment insecurity and turnover workers acquire a kind of 'mobile solitude' where they are learning not to mind any more the constant disruption of social relations (1986: 39). In an interesting twist, Parker and Slaughter (1988) describe how this kind of isolation may be more bearable than the pressure towards mutual policing, and the resulting constant fear of losing peer acceptance that characterize the team approach in the car manufacturing industry.

As Parker and Slaughter (1988) further report, the possibilities for helping each other out, an essential part of an authentic, self-determined workers' code of ethics, are often systematically eliminated – a situation which flies directly in the face of 'cooperation' and 'harmony'. In fact, the kind of cooperation demanded by the so-called 'team approach' can be used explicitly to undermine or prevent any worker-determined form of cooperation. The most important strategy is to isolate the motivational elements of co-operation from their context of interaction and turn them into explicit objects of manipulation. Pierce (1987: 31), for instance, bluntly states that addressing workers' 'achievement, affiliative and growth needs' is an effective means for avoiding the 'threat' of unionization. Such psychological co-optation is necessary because of high job insecurity, and because deteriorating social relations at the workplace have created a psychological vacuum. Combined with the requirement for greater self-supervision on the part of the workers, extensive efforts are necessary to create a sense of loyalty to the overall goals of the company. In some workplaces highly aggressive methods of 'psychotechnologies' are therefore used to adapt employee motivation to company needs (R. Lindsay 1987, 'Gurus hired to motivate workers are raising fears of "mind control"', *The New York Times*, 17 April 1987 p. 8). In efforts like these, the main goal is to 'manage' employees in a way which makes them feel good (see Howard 1986: 6, Parker and Slaughter 1988: 189). In other words, feelings are directly put in the service of a strictly instrumental means-ends relationship.

CONCLUSIONS

Educational practices that move entirely within the narrow confines of instrumental reason, and which consider instrumental reason their only standard, lose their critical and therefore truly educational potential. They contribute to the ongoing erosion of forms of human action and interaction which are based on the rationality of egalitarian and reciprocal relationships and forms of organization. In fact, as I shall discuss in the following chapter, these practices reinforce a form of consciousness which 'reifies' social relations, interests, purposes, etc. into quasi-natural phenomena which appear to follow their own laws of development, beyond human interference or control. The idea of progress as unstoppable, for instance, reflects this kind of thinking. Such thinking is anchored in a form of consciousness which can no longer transcend its own boundaries because it has lost its capacity for social imagination, the most important prerequisite for engaging in emancipatory action.

In terms of the social experience of work, such educational thinking trains people explicitly for an uncritical acceptance of the current oppressive reality of work under the banner of progress and realism, and at the threat of becoming or staying marginalized within society as a whole. It contributes to the fear, and ultimately to the inability of even *conceiving* of work and production differently, let alone taking action to create different work and production relations. Because work assumes such a promiment position in individual and social life, such education ultimately contributes to the impoverishment of everyday experience.

10

THE MISEDUCATIVE EXPERIENCE OF WORK

WORK AND KNOWLEDGE

The progressive rationalization of the workplace discussed in Chapter 8 has been described as a process of stripping live, concrete experience of work and production more and more from its subjective and bodily vestiges. The skills and knowledge which are required for this work have been shaped by an experience of work which posits static opposites between body and mind, or thought and action. It therefore also poses a static, oppositional relationship between knowledge (cognition) and the self, or, in more specifically work-related terms, between individual worker and skills. It is especially the latter relationship which holds some of the most important educational questions, as its nature determines the kind, the quality, or the very possibility of learning.

The question concerning the relationship between learning and experience has been addressed extensively and with much insight by the philosopher John Dewey. His analyses of the pedagogical value of experience are particularly relevant because they help to identify the structure, and the main elements of an experience of work which is truly educative, because it involves the worker in a continuous, cumulative learning process. In the following I will start my discussion of the experience of work based on Dewey's notion of experience, but later go beyond some of his analyses. In my view, despite his sharp critique of the organization of industrial work, and his concern that education collaborates with the leaders of industry in preparing the workers for meaningless, mindless labour, Dewey considered industrial work as the main model of productive work. He proposed that its conditions, and the economic arrangements within which it takes place needed to be reformed, but his view was closed towards considering other realms and modes of work as containing democratic and educative potential. I will address this issue in the final two chapters.

In his many analyses of the value of experience for education, Dewey repeatedly stresses the importance of interaction between the student's own, inner reality and the external conditions in which she finds herself, and considers this interaction one of the prime relations which make an experience potentially educative. Learning takes place when the student actively draws on both these poles of reality, where her subjectivity, her own desires and purposes become part of a process of reflecting and acting on the objective world. 'The world' here becomes a medium encompassing, and flowing through the learner and her external surroundings, a medium which is full of possibilities as well as limitations which are themselves changing as they are recognized, shaped, or created in the process of learning.

Another, and instrinsically related, characteristic of an experience which is educative is therefore continuity. Continuity refers to the ongoing movement between the 'before and after' of limitations which become possibilities, which, once realized, become the ground on which new possibilities and limitations grow, where the 'before' eventually becomes the 'after', opening up the view to a new 'before'. It is a situation where 'the past absorbed into the present carries on; it presses forward' (Dewey in McDermott 1973: 540). This makes experience not only continuous but also cumulative.

Continuity, and a sense of unity, despite the multitude and diversity of individual experiences, are guaranteed by the active involvement of the learner who brings about changes not only in the objective conditions of her experience, but also in herself. In other words, she shapes the world around her as well as her own inner world, but this is possible only if this inner world, her own interests, desires, and purposes are fully involved in the experience, in fact, co-structure the experience itself. Interests, purposes, or desires are, however, anchored in, and only live in the concrete actuality, the here and now of the learner's bodily existence. As Dewey (1966) describes, to bring the educative potential of a situation to fruition requires the involvement of the learner's concrete actuality, her thinking as well as sensuous capacities.

One of the recurring concerns in Dewey's writings, particularly with respect to traditional education, is the severance of the senses, and of a sensuous involvement with the world from 'the head'. In his view, such a split inevitably freezes the fluidity of live interaction between the learner and her object of learning, and reduces her to a passive receptacle of knowledge which itself has turned to stone. Because experience is not only, or not even primarily, a cognitive affair, Dewey repeatedly stresses the importance of the senses in fruitful educational experiences because the very aspect of purposeful activity, of active involvement versus passive undergoing, depends on a participation of the senses. He considered the senses 'the sentinels of immediate thought and outposts of action, and not, ..., mere pathways along which material is gathered to be stored away for a delayed and remote possibility' (Dewey 1958: 19). He criticized traditional education for its neglect, if not hostility towards the senses, which extinguished the active dimension of learning, and thus the possibility for knowledge creation. The following quote was written in the context of a critique of traditional education. It reverberates, however, with the themes and issues discussed in the preceding chapters:

> [In traditional education] the very word pupil has almost come to mean one who is engaged not in having fruitful experiences but in absorbing knowledge directly. Something which is called mind or consciousness is severed from the physical organs of activity. The former is then thought to be purely intellectual and cognitive; the latter to be an irrelevant and intruding physical factor. The intimate union of activity and undergoing its consequences which leads to recognition of meaning is broken; instead we have two fragments: mere bodily action on one side, and meaning directly grasped by 'spiritual' activity on the other.
>
> (Dewey 1966: 140–1)

This quote, written in relation to traditional education, captures the separation of 'intellective' and 'action-oriented' (Zuboff 1988) skills discussed in an earlier chapter, and of work which is mindless and requires mainly physical or psychological effort, and work which requires mainly intellectual effort (of a certain kind). Both signify the separation of the relationship between thinking and acting, reflecting and sensing, and between the subjective and objective conditions of experience. According to Dewey, the educative (or miseducative) potential of an experience is precisely determined by the nature of this relationship. Only if this relationship is one of *live interaction* rather than static opposition can we speak of an experience in the full meaning of the word, and can this experience unfold its educative potential.

Within the parameters of the skills paradigm, where skills are conceptualized in terms of a strategic, means–ends rationality, the dimension of live interaction between the various poles of experience has been fractured. In many ways, the world of work becomes a fixed and finished world, where nothing really new is created, because this world lacks the vitality of live interaction between the worker and the object of her work, where she shapes her own subjective reality as much as she produces an object. The relationship between the worker and the skills/knowledge associated with her work is one of the most problematic relationships, but also of particular relevance to education. It contains questions concerning the origin of knowledge, the process of its creation, and its relationship to the worker/learner. Within the confines of the skills paradigm, knowledge, and skills as derivatives of knowledge, confront the learner as pre-given, external, as well as finished entities, very similar to the pre-given bodies of conserved knowledge which confront the pupil in traditional education.[1]

What needs to be learnt – and how – is determined independently from the worker's own interests and purposes. Thus, management may decide to keep workers from acquiring certain skills; it may coerce them into learning different skills for different jobs (as is the case in multi-skilling schemes); or it may decide what kind of skills are needed, how they are to be acquired, and who is permitted to learn. In all cases the control over any of these aspects does not lie with the workers themselves. Stored knowledge, and accumulated experience are here not placed in a live context of challenge and suspense that arises from the self-determined, purposeful activity of the worker who meets her task, applies and tests her knowledge, not mechanically, but in close contact with the specific and changing objective as well as subjective conditions of her work.

Such a situation would require, above all, an overall context of worker self-determination and worker control over workplace design, production conditions, and work relations. As discussed in the previous chapter, in the absence of such a context, even skills which on the surface appear to involve the worker's subjectivity and to bring her into a relationship of live interaction with the people and circumstances of her work, freeze into static attributes or mechanical procedures. Their conception (and proposed application) disallows a truly interactive, *dialogical* situation, involving the worker's full participation. Thus, these skills reflect internally the external circumstances of their construction: they are 'the skills employers want' (the subtitle of *Workplace Basics*, Carnevale *et al.* 1988), meeting the workers as pre-determined entities.

So-called knowledge work, the prototype of the work of the future, and the major theme in work-related adult education literature, poses particular problems for the question at issue here. These problems are not dissimilar to the ones Dewey discussed in the context of traditional education.

In my definition of knowledge work I want to exclude the work and expertise of computer scientists and other highly trained experts, although questions concerning their particular knowledge and skills, their relationship to knowledge and the process of knowledge creation deserves to be studied as well (see Hayes 1989, and Roszak 1986 for an interesting discussion of some of these issues). I have already discussed (see Chapter 5) how the concept of knowledge work is a rather abstract as well as largely ideological construct. My definition therefore includes work with and on new technology, and with the symbolic representations of reality, without indicating any particular level of skill or expertise.[2]

Earlier, live interaction, bodily location and active involvement of the senses were described as primary conditions for a truly educative experience. Seen in the light of these conditions, knowledge work represents an extreme separation of mind and body, of 'intellective' and 'action-oriented' skills. 'Extreme' is here measured in terms of distance to the material dimension of production, the concrete object which is worked upon, shaped and created, but which the knowledge worker no longer sees, hears, or touches. In its data version, this material world has died a double death, and the knowledge which is used in the processing and manipulation of its symbolic representation is likewise dead. Thus, it no longer deals with the idiosyncratic, recalcitrant, and unpredictable stuff of concrete, live reality. In a peculiar way, this work does not produce anything really new, only different, perhaps more and more complex versions of the same. The notion of a 'knowledge explosion', where knowledge begets knowledge all by itself, captures this kind of non-production remarkably well.

I am here, of course, operating with a different notion of production or productivity, one which does not sever the relationship between body and mind, between the material or physical and the human–intellectual world. Furthermore, and more importantly, this notion of productivity is also not separated from its true purpose: the sustenance and improvement of life. In a way, a production which is oriented solely towards profit maximization, and calculated in the abstract categories of input and output, should be more appropriately considered a kind of non- or even anti-production. It is a form of anti-production because rather than creating life, and the optimal conditions for life, it continues to eat away at the substance of natural as well as human resources, reflected not only in the environmental and human destruction that marks the path of production, but also in the immense heaps of useless, trashy, or downright damaging products pouring from our production sites and accumulating on our growing garbage dumps.

The adoration of endlessly multiplying data, envisioned as an independent, self-moving process, is based on a view of knowledge which equates the mere factual existence of discrete bits and pieces of data with truth itself, no longer adulterated by its involvement in concrete reality. The knowledge contained in the computer brings variables into a multitude of relations to each other by applying procedural reasoning skills. This knowledge moves in a different realm than truth. To establish the truth of things means to draw on and examine ideas, for instance those which underly the computer program, and which have governed the focus and selection of research into the multitude of phenomena which are captured and transformed into data or pieces of information. In a chapter titled 'Of ideas and data', Roszak (1986: 119–20) criticizes the delusions of a thinking which is incapable of examining ideas, because it has fallen victim to a 'mathematical mystique'. He writes (ibid.):

> It is only when we strike a clear distinction between ideas and information that we can recognize that these are radically different levels of discourse requiring different levels of evaluation. In most cases, we may be able to assess the data that flow through the program as either 'right' or 'wrong,' a question of fact that yields to standard research methods. But the ideas that govern the data are *not* information; nor are they sacrosanct matters of mathematical logic. They are philosophical commitments, the outgrowth of experience, insight, metaphysical conviction, which must be assessed as wise or foolish, childlike or mature, realistic or fantastic, moral or wicked.

The truth is neither born, nor simply represented by the self-enclosed, synthetic world of data and information which is based on omissions and denials, but by a thinking which reaches backward to illuminate the practical and epistemological origin of knowledge, data, or information, and forward to assess not only their applicability, but also the practical consequences of their use. Rather than submitting to their mystification, such thinking involves asking questions about the context, quality and usefulness of the information which is being processed and does not submit to a mystification of the actual origin of data or information. Such thinking cannot shun contact with concrete reality, but seeks it because it receives its major impetus, its nourishment from active involvement in it.

In many ways, the glorification of knowledge work, and the one-sided description of a certain kind of intelligence with generally higher reasoning and problem-solving skills must be looked at from the perspective of a tremendous loss. Lost are those skills, knowledges, and abilities which have been shaped by, and which can only survive through active involvement in and productive transformation of material reality. These skills are lost not only because they are no longer practised, but also because they are socially devalued.

As Noble (1984) reports, the translation of a real production process into a computer program has to abstract from so many 'irregular' human and social processes, that it frequently causes more problems than it delivers gains. He (ibid. 343) describes the problems and difficulties that arise from the attempt to translate the complex and highly unpredictable nature of material reality and human social processes into the uniformity of 'formal descriptions, standardized procedures, and algorithmic regularity', and lays bare the fundamental irrationality behind the idea that computerized processes are *inherently* superior. In reference to the metal-cutting industry, Noble writes (ibid. 344) that these irregularities make it difficult to comprehend fully the manufacturing process, 'a major stumbling block in computer-integrated manufacturing', and that

> ... this difficulty is compounded by the limited formalized knowledge of the metal-cutting process, despite nearly a century of engineering effort since Frederick Taylor. There is still no guaranteed 'scientific' way of accounting for and fully anticipating variations in tool wear, the 'machinability' of

> various materials, actual machine performance, or changing conditions. Of course, such contingencies are readily and routinely dealt with by machinists and machine operators, relying upon their skills and accumulated experience with just such challenges.

Noble (1984: 344–6) quotes at great length a machinist who describes these difficulties, and the tremendous bureaucracy that is established to deal with them in a way which does not allow the workers themselves to assume control over the production process by using or applying their special skills and knowledge.[3] Those skills, in many ways superior, because more subtle, more flexible and attuned to change, and therefore also involving different kinds of 'intelligencies' (Gardner 1983), will over time atrophy and be permanently lost.

To avoid misunderstanding, some qualifications need to be made. Above all, I want to stress that I do not intend to reverse the false dichotomy of technological superiority/human inferiority into the equally false dichotomy of human superiority/technological inferiority. I want to question the very relationship of polarity that exists between the two, but also the association of 'inferior' with genuinely non-technological capacities. This association leads to insensitivity towards the actual or potential loss of vital human capacities, thus directly contributing to their loss. False polarity further mystifies the relations of power which produced such dichotomous thinking in the first place. The machinist's account is therefore primarily an indictment of the overall social relations in which the duality of technological superiority/human inferiority arises, rather than an indictment of imperfect technology. He ultimately describes the fundamental irrationality of a production process where the concern for hierarchy and control overrides common sense, and even such sacrosanct principles as efficiency and productivity.[4] It is not technology itself which is responsible for the devaluation and eventual loss of non-technological capacities, but the many social and technical divisions of labour which determine that knowledge is fragmented and dispersed, and that conception and execution have to be separated:

> Most of the thinking is supposed to be taken care of in programming. The operator is just supposed to clamp the part in the machine and press a button and start up. The philosophy behind it is that the operator's the least smart person. So if you

> let the operator go messing around with anything, he's gonna screw the part up.
>
> In practice the problem when you have the tape machine, is that you end up with such a bureaucracy. You have one group of people making the fixture that the machine is going to be on, tooling, then you have somebody that is programming the part. The people in tooling use machine tools to a certain extent but they don't have any knowledge of production machines. The engineers who design the fixtures have probably never worked in machine shops. The programmers are usually people who have a lot of computer experience but not people who've ever worked in a machine shop.
>
> (quoted in Noble 1984: 344–6)

Some products, especially those representing complex engineering systems (like aeroplanes) require systematization and standardization. Also, automation may lead to greater and faster output. This still leaves the question concerning issues of quality, but also, more importantly, of purpose and usefulness of these products and of the overall system of production. What is being criticized here is not that much (if not most) work can be mechanized, automated, or computerized, but that mechanization, automation, and computerization by definition constitute a more highly evolved, more efficient, and more productive kind of work, and that it should be technologically transformed wherever and whenever feasible (or profitable). As the example of the Green Revolution shows, a fully technologized agricultural production process was entirely feasible, as well as extremely profitable, but it resulted in large-scale environmental destruction and impoverishment of people (Shiva 1989). Whereas chemicals and machines helped agribusiness to reap abundant profits, 'chemicals and machines can[not] replace the life in food and the life of the soil' (Shiva 1989: 117).

NO SENSE OF TIME, NO SENSE OF PLACE

We can analyse the miseducative experience of work from yet another angle. Tied to the problematic relationship between the worker and her knowledge/skills are questions concerning the spatio-temporal relations contained in the experience of work. The particular structure of time as well as space greatly determines the quality of experience, and therefore also the quality of learning which can arise from it. Some dimensions of this question have already appeared in the preceding section. For example, to characterize experience as continuous and cumulative signifies a particular temporal structure; or to speak of experience being anchored in the bodily actuality of the individual learner (or worker) signifies its dependence on a concrete, specific location in space.

Turning to the issue of time, learning requires a historical continuum of past, present, and future, and an experience which is structured qualitatively rather than quantitatively. How time unfolds, what rhythm it assumes, depends on the quality of experience itself. Many experiences ideally require such qualitative structuring of time, although, in reality, it seems that practically all our experiences are rearranged under the spell of quantitative, objective time, no longer allowing us to linger or simply move along with the task, and to assume a stance of 'it takes as long as it takes', instead of being forced into an externally determined time frame.

This is certainly true for the experience of work. The history of industrial work is a history of progressive regimentation of qualitative time structures, accompanied by tremendous efforts to socialize or re-socialize a workforce which not only submits to this structure but which has internalized it as much as possible (Thompson 1967). Taylorism in particular transformed the concrete, qualitative organization of time of crafts production into an organization where time has been segmented into individual and identical 'time-pieces', which are then serially ordered and strung together into consistent sequences. This is the prototype of the industrial time scheme. It still provides the main model for a *rational* use of time, leading to the belief that all useful and productive activity must be organized in that way. The history of schooling shows many parallels, where a similarly industrial time discipline was established in schools, and where the workplace became the major metaphor for educational research and practices (see Marshall 1988; see also Thompson 1967, and Bowles and Gintis 1976).

Where the organization of time is objectively given, time and experience are not organically connected. Within the industrial time structure, time is either experienced as a standstill because every time-unit that passes is identical with the one that came before and the one that follows. This is the case in highly repetitive work. Or time is experienced as a race, as, for instance in the case of 'busy schedules', where too many tasks have to be accomplished in a short period or have to be completed at high speed.

Many indicators point in the direction of an overall intensification or speed-up of the pace of work in many workplaces as diverse as the check-out counter in a supermarket, and the 'work team' in a car manufacturing plant (Garson 1989, Parker and Slaughter 1988). In fact, the team approach to work, heralded as contributing to the worker's autonomy and 'ownership' of their work and work-related problems, has appropriately been called management-by-stress (Parker and Slaughter 1988). Among other pressures, this approach works with a new version of work speed-up that makes Taylor's scientific management look amateurish.

I don't have to cite scientific studies to prove that most people suffer tremendous stress from this situation, and experience numerous health problems. Seminars and workshops teaching 'stress-management' and 'time-management' strategies, and skills for 'absorbing' rather than eliminating stress (Carnevale *et al.* 1988), all aimed at countering the problems and ill-effects of such experience of time, in their own way contribute to self-alienation and self-repression. They teach people to *cope* with inorganic time, by arranging their experience in more 'efficient' and refined ways in accordance with this time structure. It is not surprising that people who successfully deal with such situations very often display highly compulsive behaviour.[5]

Inorganic, quantitative time liquidates the historical dimension of experience, human memory and remembrance. The monotony of repetitive work turns time into a series of ever-present moments, where nothing needs to be remembered, as nothing needs to be anticipated. Because time loses its qualitative, ever-changing and flowing character, it freezes into space, and the worker is no longer an active participant, but a passive spectator with little or no influence on the event in which she participates. In its latest version of computer-mediated work, monotonous labour has been robbed of the last small route of escape even highly repetitive industrial work often still allows. Work on the assembly line, for instance, requiring routine physical movements and often a minimum of attention, has traditionally left space for daydreaming or indulging in reveries, and has therefore allowed for a certain amount of emotional or psychological detachment. This makes it possible for the worker to temporarily 'forget' time, and to be relieved of the torture of time creeping only very slowly. Now, computer-mediated work frequently requires a high level of total concentration and continuous attention if serious mistakes are to be avoided, although the actual knowledge content of the work is minimal (Zuboff 1988: 132–3). Thus, work can be excruciatingly boring, but never allow the worker to mentally fade out. Howard (1986: 69–81) describes the anguish and physical suffering caused by these 'high demands for mental engagement' despite the workers' emotional detachment from their work. Workers experience time as simultaneously racing, as they very often work under a rigid quota system, and as standing still by being glued to the ongoing immediacy and sameness of the task. In a similar manner 'slack time' has been rationalized away under management-by-stress schemes (see Garson 1989, but also Parker and Slaughter 1988). In addition to a thoroughly calculated production design, other psychological or social pressures are placed on the individual worker. As described by Parker and Slaughter (1988), for instance, the *andon* principle allows an instantaneous display of a particular worker's mistake (e.g. in the form of slowing down or skipping a particular sequence), putting tremendous pressure on the worker to keep up. This pressure is increased by an extremely tight organization of production (including 'just-in-time' inventory systems), where an individual worker's mistake immediately affects the rest of the production sequence.

While automated work does not require the active use of memory, in fact has extinguished all concrete aspects which could trigger memory (Zuboff 1988: 131), the 'frantic juggling of too many tasks' (Howard 1986: 70–1) which characterizes the 'busy schedule' draws only on the simplest, and least human, aspect of memory: to 'keep in mind' the list of tasks and activities that need to be done, or more precisely, that need to *have been done* or finished by the end of the day, next week, in a year. The future does not appear in the form of its vague and vast possibilites, its hoped-for promises or feared forebodings, but in terms of what will have been accomplished, or completed. In such anticipated and highly specified completion the future is closed, not really a future at all, because it is a direct continuation of the present, replicates the present in its very same packaged and measured time frame. Within this context, memory refers merely to the ability of mechanical recall of pre-specified details, individual bits and pieces of information in exactly the way they were stored. In contrast, human memory appears irrational and unpredictable, because it is firmly lodged in the uniqueness of individual experience, and often 'below the level of awareness and articulation' (Roszak 1986: 97). But it is precisely there where the live interaction of past, present, and future is still intact, where human memory can unfold its unique creative and imaginative potential. Human memory does not resemble a storehouse of well-organized, well-ordered packages of data or information, which we recall in full and equal clarity. Rather, it is the place where

> the recollections we retain are mysteriously selected, enigmatically patterned in memory. There are hot bright spots filled with rich and potent associations; there are shadowed corners which may only emerge vividly in dreams or hallucinations; there are odd, quirky zones that delight to fill up with seemingly useless, chaotic remnants...
>
> (Roszak 1986: 97)

As this quote so vividly describes, human memory is endlessly creative in combining the elements of our experience in imaginative and unpredictable ways, where past, present and future constantly flow in and out of one another in fluid and ever changing constellations. Human memory is a quality of lived experience, or, more precisely, 'the shape of memory is quite simply the shape of our lives' (Roszak 1986: 98).

In work which is organized in accordance with a quantitative, inorganic time frame, this human quality is liquidated as irrational surplus. Lacking an outlet for the creative, imaginative power of memory, experience becomes sterile, unproductive. Moreover, the structure of individual consciousness begins to resemble the fragmentation of time – it becomes fragmented itself, lacking the unifying, adhesive force of continuous, overlapping, interactive individual experiences.

More complex, intellectually demanding computer-mediated work in its own way creates a sense of timelessness, but also placelessness. The experience of having tremendous amounts of data at one's disposal in an instant, data which furthermore 'travel' over great distances, extinguishes a sense of time, history, as well as memory. In Zuboff's words (1988: 179–80):

> The electronic text exists independently of space and time. When text is confined to concrete objects, such as books or pieces of paper, it generates pressures for centralization (you must go to the text if you want to read it) or for possession (you can own the book or maintain your own files). The electronic text is the result of an even more radical

> centralization: a wide range of information can be gathered and codified in a single computer system. However, this radical centralization enables an equally radical decentralization: in principle, the text can be constituted at any time from any place.

The computer's capacity for processing information at high speed adds another dimension to the experience of timelessness and spacelessness. In his book called *Time Wars: The Primary Conflict in Human History* (1987), Jeremy Rifkin describes how the computer's measurement of time, the nano-second (or billionth of a second) organizes speed beyond the realm of consciousness and experience. He points out that this not only contributes to a sense of human inadequacy in the face of such a tremendous capacity for speed (and a corresponding disdain for 'merely' human capacities), but also makes people less capable of appreciating experiences which are tied to a qualitative or biological rhythm of time. If we add the previously discussed structural distance of knowledge work from the material underside of production to this phenomenon, we can see how such an experience of work contributes in practically every respect to a heightened sense of alienation from everything living or natural. In many ways, the electronic text repeats on a microstructural level what is happening in the larger social arena. In Chapter 5 I discussed the problematic assumptions behind the present emphasis on flexibility and mobility, culminating in the idea of the generic worker whose skills are immune to obsolescence, and who can therefore be placed anywhere at any time.[6] Marx's notion of abstract labour seems to have found its point of completion in the generic worker. In addition to the universal applicability of generic skills, the worker is expected to be geographically mobile as well. The notion of flexibility of skills stresses independence from time, because skills are no longer developed or accumulated over time in concrete, specific contexts, nor are they dependent on experience. The notion of mobility translates into an independence from space, and from ties to specific, concrete places and communities. In the light of the reality of employment and job loss, flexibility and mobility appear as euphemistic terms for the throw-away nature of skills and for the total disposability of individual workers.

THE PRODUCTION OF A DEPOSITORY CONSCIOUSNESS

The experience of work which is organized mostly or entirely by an objectively given, non-qualitative structure of time should be of prime concern for educational theory because it contributes to the formation of a sealed-off, ahistorical consciousness whose capacity for critical reflection, and for autonomous production of knowledge about self, others, and society has been seriously weakened.

A critique of consciousness, or of forms of thought and experience which have been shaped by alienating conditions of work, or by oppressive relations, is relatively rare in educational theory. Educators influenced by Marxist theory have taken up this theme, borrowing from analyses of Marx, Lukacs, Gramsci, and writers of the Frankfurt School (see, for instance, Aronowitz and Giroux 1985). These theorists investigate the problem of consciousness from the perspective of the influence of the market, and of the capitalist mode of production on forms of thought and action. Feminist theoreticians have discussed the issue of consciousness from the perspective of patriarchy's denial or misrepresentation of women's experience leading to an internal and external 'eclipsing' of women's interests and knowledge of themselves (Smith 1987).

Within the realm of adult education proper, it is Paolo Freire (1970) who has concerned himself with the problem of forms of consciousness which make true learning impossible. He attributes the problems of uncritical, 'naive thinking' to the hierarchical, oppressive social relations between peasant and feudal lord which keep the peasant's mind fixated on a static, 'normalized today'. His programme of conscientization constitutes a rigorous procedure to open up these confines, and to 'temporalize space' by allowing thought to immerse itself 'in temporality without fear of the risk involved' (Freire 1970: 81). It is important to note that although suppressed by the oppressive social relations of the feudal system, Freire's students still have the capacity for theoretical-reflective consciousness. Freire does not discuss the source of this continued capacity, but I believe we must locate it in the general context of the peasants' experience which allows spaces for autonomous production and organization despite the overall oppressive situation, spaces which can become pockets of resistance and independent thought. In particular, the peasants' experience of work and production is rich with history, and draws on knowledge which has been accumulated and stored over time and which has to be applied according to the fluctuating and changing conditions which characterize working on the land. In other words, the peasants' own work makes for experiences which are inherently educative (in the sense established by Dewey).

Freire himself does not discuss this situation in these terms. In fact, it was only feminist theoreticians who saw parallels between women's work, especially mothering, and working on the land as containing Utopian possibilities for non-alienating, non-exploitative work and production relations, and who developed corresponding epistemologies which may prove useful for education. Shiva in particular has articulated this thought in connection with her study of Indian peasant and tribal women, ecological principles, and 'maldevelopment'. She writes (1989: 46):

> In contemporary times, Third World women, whose minds have not yet been dispossesed or colonised, are in a privileged position to make visible the invisible oppositional categories that they are the custodians of. It is not only as victims, but also as leaders in creating new intellectual ecological paradigms, that women are central in arresting and overcoming ecological crises. Just as ecological recovery begins from centres of natural diversity which are gene pools, Third World women, and those tribals and peasants who have been left out of the process of maldevelopment, are today acting as the intellectual gene pools of ecological categories of thought and action.

The situation is entirely different for work under current industrial, highly technologized conditions. Above all, the logic of the market and of capitalist production has not only thoroughly structured all aspects of work (epistemological, social, or psychological), it has usurped every sphere of life, and permeates every experience, not only the experience of work. Whereas the peasants' consciousness can be considered as merely beleaguered, the principles and strategies of the market have reached into our very psyches and our consciousness, because all spheres of life have become an object of market interests and exploitation. The German sociologist Knödler-Bunte (1975) speaks of forms of 'secondary exploitation', where spheres of life which are not directly part of the world of work, as for instance human sensuality, are more and more integrated into the 'industrial mode of production', and where the 'basic conditions of human life become the object of a packaged system of exploitation' (ibid. 72). As discussed in the previous chapter, the current interest in the workers' feelings and motivational life can likewise be interpreted as a way of management reaching into and exploiting hitherto untouched realms of experience.

Although all these writings (and others) are highly relevant and pose specific challenges for education, within the context of the present discussion it may suffice to summarize some major points, particularly as they relate to the experience of work and production. I want to point out once more that work cannot be seen as clearly separate from life, and as unrelated to the questions, issues, or concerns of other spheres of life and experience. Work is not only embedded in a larger social and cultural context which therefore colors the experience of work, but its own structure and networks of relations mirror the main norms, assumptions and beliefs that underly this overall context. The main elements of the experience of work discussed so far are: the predominance of instrumental rationality; the polarity of thinking and acting; the finished, external character of skills or knowledge; the fetishization of technology into an independent entity obscuring underlying divisions of class and labour; the quantitative, objective structuring of time. All contribute to a form of consciousness which is glued to immediacy, and which loses its capacity to transcend such immediacy by binding together the manifold situations and experiences into coherent, analytical insight. In education this consciousness is encountered in the form of a fixation upon the concrete, the visual, and the literate, characterized by 'an inability to penetrate the most superficial levels of sensory experience, to associate and dissociate concepts, or to engage in systematic debunking and depth analysis' (Scott 1986: 109). It is a 'depository consciousness' (Freire 1970) which resembles a storehouse of disconnected fragments of experiences, pieces of information and facts. Such consciousness has difficulty grasping the meaning of individual or social experience as complex but coherent totalities, as both become mere accumulations of unconnected situations. Such a consciousness does not allow for a production of true knowledge, nor does it allow true self-knowledge – a situation which should be of prime concern to education.

Education is not an unproblematic given. How it is interpreted, and how these interpretations are translated into actions or programmes, depends on specific historical and material circumstances. Because consciousness, like experience, is a historical product, education must be able to recognize the historical, and hence social and political determinants of the material it is working on or with. The primacy of the skills paradigm, and of instrumental rationality, has institutionalized a form of thought which today colonizes all modes of experience and production, and which organizes all forms of interaction (with self, others, the environment) according to its reductionist and alienating dynamics. This form of thought constitutes a kind of consciousness which is incapable of reflecting upon itself, or on the historical context and genesis of individual and social life and experience. The loss of such historical consciousness is accompanied by a loss of critically reflective and Utopian modes of thinking, as it blocks the view towards modes of experience, interaction, and production which are not appropriating, power-bound, or exploitative, but which are non-possessive, reciprocal, reconciliatory and preserving. It is to these possibilities, and the impetus they could provide for education, I want to turn to in the last part of the book.

Part V

WORKING AND EDUCATING FOR LIFE

11

PRODUCTIVE WORK

THE PRODUCTION OF LIFE

Feminist theoreticians have for some time explored the reality of women's work, not only in the negative terms of its economic exploitation, social devaluation or ideological mystification, but also in the positive terms of its special quality and contribution to individual and social well-being. These analyses have been as varied as the individual writers' unique outlooks, moving on different levels of description and critique, and illuminating different aspects or facets. Overall, in writings which explore the unique qualities of women's work rather than the oppression under which it takes place, it is the maintaining, caring, nurturing, or generally relational aspects which are presented as the core of women's unique work capacity and experience. In other words, it is the work women perform as housewives and mothers which is central to these descriptions and analyses.

In Parts I and III I presented some theories which push this concept of women's work a bit further by asking questions concerning the ultimate reasons behind the devaluation of 'women's work', or, more precisely, of work which is delegated to or associated mostly with women. As discussed in Chapter 7 in particular, behind the devaluation of women's work lies the rejection of necessity and of all experiences that bind us to the physical, bodily, or natural conditions of our existence, as antithetical to freedom, which is presumed to be the truly human or social realm. It is this horror of organic or natural life processes which enters into the degradation of women's work. As a low status group, women have therefore been burdened disproportionately with some of the major tasks and responsibilities of sustaining the everyday fabric of life: bearing and raising children, and providing a large number of (paid or unpaid) personal services directly relating to other people's physical and mental well-being. In other words, as a group women are expected to produce and take care of life.

However, if we look at women's work from a wider perspective, we can see that it is not only women whose work is oriented towards the immediate sustenance of life, but all those who produce for immediate use or subsistence. Although this work may not appear in the form of mothering or housework, it shares some fundamental characteristics with it. As discussed in Parts I and III of this book, in addition to women, many Third World people (men and women), particularly peasants and tribal people perform subsistence work, although, just like the housewife, always in some form of combination with waged work, and, under conditions of extreme poverty, often in the form of production for immediate survival.

In keeping with earlier discussions, I want to use the term 'subsistence labour' to summarize some of the commonalities of the different realities of work oriented towards immediate use and sustenance, especially since the term connotes 'necessity' and 'life'. All forms of subsistence labour share an orientation towards maintaining or improving life, and towards use rather than exchange. All subsistence work comes in contact with quality, uniqueness, and concreteness, and, by its very nature, it acknowledges rather than denies the natural foundation of human existence. As described in Chapter 6, such an acknowledgement does not always assume the form of voluntary, positive affirmation, but is frequently forced upon the producers as the only way of staying alive. Thus, an inhabitant of a Brazilian *favella* who builds her dwelling from the scraps of discarded materials does not joyously embrace necessity, but her action nevertheless illustrates the ultimate purpose of human work, and thus makes it meaningful. As subsistence work, her work is meaningful, but it also expresses the absolute separation of freedom and necessity.

However, this is more than a philosophical issue. Within the context of the world capitalist system, the quiet and invisible work of women and other subsistence producers has been considered unproductive and unprofitable. As Shiva (1989: 43–4) describes, work which produces sustenance and life is useless when looked at 'from the dominant view of the productivity of labour as defined for the process of capital accumulation'. And, she writes (1989: 4):

> The assumptions are evident: nature is unproductive; organic agriculture based on nature's cycles of renewability spells poverty; women and tribal and peasant societies embedded in nature are similarly unproductive, not because it has been demonstrated that in cooperation they produce *less* goods and services for needs, but because it is assumed that 'production' takes place only when mediated by technologies for commodity production, even when such technologies destroy life.

Today, subsistence labour is marked with scars and damages, and much of its substance has been eroded (see Chapter 5). It is important not to lose sight of this reality. It is equally important not to idealize the reality of actual subsistence work as it has taken place over the centuries, in many different parts of the world, and under many different circumstances, which were often quite harsh. I will now make an attempt to describe some basic features of subsistence work of an ideal-type, providing 'new categories of thought and exploratory directions' (Shiva 1989: 47). With its overall orientation towards use and life, and with its preserving rather than destructive attitude, subsistence labour can serve as a model for a truly human vision of work and life. Rather than idealize the reality of subsistence producers (past or present), I want to acknowledge, like Shiva, that they 'have the holistic and ecological knowledge of what the production and protection of life is all about' (Shiva 1989: 47), and that with the help of this knowledge we can construct a vision of work and life which is both life-enhancing and progressive.

By describing some of these 'new categories of thought and exploratory directions' (Shiva 1989: 47), I am proposing a counter-concept to the prevailing industrial–patriarchal notion of work. My purpose in doing this is threefold: first, to provide a critical counterweight to the ideological notion that work with and for new technology is a genuinely superior form of work which is at the 'cutting edge' of progress; second, to describe fundamental human qualities and forms of interaction which are of vital importance in the construction of a truly human society; third, to argue that education can itself be conceptualized as a productive process containing the major elements of subsistence production. In the following section I will list the main characteristics of subsistence work, which can serve as important themes for an education for life. In the next chapter I will discuss the epistemological implications of these themes, and their relevance for education.

THE UTOPIAN POTENTIAL OF SUBSISTENCE WORK

Subsistence work is based on a conscious and positive acknowledgement of the ultimate purpose of work and production: to maintain and improve *life*. Only such an acknowledgement keeps the link between work, life, and necessity intact. To place the production of life rather than of things at the core of an alternative concept of work consequently affects the vision of work-related experience, and of the relations contained in this experience, because the production of life follows a fundamentally different rationality. Above all, because such a notion does not place the realm of freedom in antithetical opposition to the realm of necessity, it does not set up all the other dichotomous partitions that characterize the rationality of patriarchal–industrial work and production. As we have seen, the desire to keep necessity at bay, to isolate it from any association with freedom inevitably results in divisions of labour and in corresponding dominance relations among human beings, because to control necessity is inseparable from controlling those who have to take care of necessity. By dissolving the rigid opposition between freedom and necessity work emerges as an experience which contains the elements of burden as well as enjoyment in an inseparable dialectical unity. These elements remain integral to the experience of work itself, and they are neither sectioned off into the sterile opposites of leisure and work, nor do they become the basis for hierarchical divisions of labour (Mies 1986: 216).

The dialectical unity of freedom and necessity contradicts the perversity of a view which considers exchange primary, not use (Hartsock 1983). In production which is oriented towards use rather than towards exchange work retains its character of being useful and necessary, and results in equally useful and necessary products (Mies 1986: 218). This aspect is usually neglected in discussions about creating meaningful work. In these discussions responsibility, and an intellectually challenging content of work is emphasized without regard to what is actually being produced, and without regard to the usefulness of the product.

A primary orientation towards use also abolishes the distance between production and consumption, where alienated work is complemented by alienated consumption. Not only do things appear in shapes and forms which are entirely stripped of any traces of their origin or the context of their production, but they are also acquired in ways which are separated from the way they are used (Fromm 1966: 120). Objects are often bought for the sole purpose of 'having' them rather than using them, where having signals success, prestige, or simply purchasing power. Moreover, many people seem to further reduce the experience of consumption to the abstract activity of buying or shopping *per se*, often without any idea of what they are looking for (see Hayes 1989).

In *The Sane Society* Fromm (1966: 123) attributes this kind of addictive behaviour to the fact that the individual's only connection with the things she buys is their consumption or manipulation. And, because a connection with her real needs is lacking, she can never attain true satisfaction and is driven to repeat the behaviour in the futile search for fulfilment. On the other hand, where objects are appreciated for their intrinsic value, for instance their beauty or their usefulness, a non-alienated relationship between person and object is established, opening up the possibility for true satisfaction and fulfilment.

A conscious acknowledgement of the natural foundation of human life, of the need for effort, or work, to produce and maintain it, leaves no room for the dualistic opposition between the natural and social world. As discussed in Part III, such a dichotomous division underlies the various existing divisions of labour, and results in the degradation, invisibility or naturalization of work and workers who are considered closer to or part of nature, not yet fully socialized or civilized. In the absence of such a dichotomy, nature is not considered simply dead matter or an assemblage of various natural resources to be used and exploited, but is placed on a continuum which includes rather than sets apart human life. Because the duality of natural and human life is embedded in a greater unity, the intricate and complex interrelationships between all living beings are respected.

Within such a context work assumes the character of conscious interaction and of a partnership with the natural forces and conditions of human existence, drawing out their inherent potential, but also accepting and respecting their limits. In the experience of pregnancy and childbirth, for instance, a woman can consciously and intelligently *act upon* and influence the natural forces of this event and closely interact with them. She can fully comprehend these forces in relation to her own unique experience and capacities, thus making them her own. In the medicalized model of childbirth, on the other hand, the woman is confronted with an institutionalized body of knowledge in whose construction she has had no part, and which is entirely monopolized by experts who assume total control over this process. Undergirding this emphasis on control is a view of childbirth as a disease which needs to be cured. The natural forces of pregnancy and childbirth are consequently experienced as hostile, to be mastered with the help of an elaborate technological apparatus. Many women not only feel that they are helplessly dependent on the medical profession, but also that they have been robbed of a major experience in their lives.

An egalitarian, interactive relationship between human beings and nature accords the latter its own integrity and inviolability, thus setting limits to human use and interference. This contradicts the Western patriarchal–industrial view of limitless technological development, and an equally limitless economic growth as the prime insignia of progress. It also contradicts the idea that constant and essentially undirected and abstract change are more progressive than steadiness and stability. Such a view is oblivious to the destruction and violence which accompanies such change; it ignores the quiet and invisible human effort as well as the wealth of accumulated knowledge and wisdom which is needed for maintaining life, and which can only grow within a context of stability. As Shiva (1989: 36) writes, for instance:

> ... contemporary women's ecological struggles are new attempts to establish that steadiness and stability are not stagnation, and balance with nature's essential ecological processes is not technological backwardness but technological sophistication. At a time when a quarter of the world's population is threatened by starvation due to erosion of soil, water and genetic diversity of living resources, chasing the mirage of unending growth, by spreading resource destructive technologies, becomes a major source of genocide.

Where work remains (or becomes) direct and sensual interaction with nature, it provides opportunity for self-expression and enjoyment (Mies 1986: 218). The asssociation of work involving the body with drudgery and toil does not testify to the tyranny of 'necessity', but to the construction of all activities relating to life and necessity 'in ways which systematically degrade and destroy the minds and bodies of those who perform them' (Hartsock 1983: 302). Although it involves the body and is in close contact with material reality, all elements of freedom have been extracted from this work, leaving little room for sensuous enjoyment, self-expression or creativity. Likewise, the cult of the computer, and the glorification of computer-mediated work destroys productive human power, an understanding of nature, and the capacity for sensual enjoyment (Mies 1986: 218). Computer-mediated work which does not involve any physical activity, and which uses the senses 'not as organic participants ... but as external inlets and outlets of mind' (Dewey 1966: 142) causes considerable physical distress. In a paradoxical way, the attempt to banish necessity in the form of the body from the activity of work flips over into an entirely negative reassertion of the body in the form of pain, distress, and sickness. Such distress is testimony for the destructive consequences of the freedom/necessity dichotomy, of rending apart what belongs together, and of entirely disregarding fundamental aspects of human reality as irrelevant. This form of violence is similar to the environmental violence of reducing the intricate, live complexity of ecosystems into dead matter, to be sold on the market. For example, Shiva (1989: 63) describes how the rise of 'scientific forestry' in India ignored 'the complex relationship within the forest community and between plant life and other resources like soil and water', and reduces 'the diversity of life to the dead product, wood, and wood in turn to commercially valuable wood only', in the process leading to the destruction of the entire ecosystem itself.

An interactive relationship with the material conditions of work also signifies a close and continuous contact with quality, and a corresponding ability to deal with 'concrete, many-qualitied, changing material processes' (Hartsock 1983: 292). These abilities, and the knowledge gained in intimate encounters with these material processes, with objects, and also with human beings, are of vital importance for the quality of social and cultural life. Erich Fromm (1966: 106) describes the loss of this ability under the auspices of the commodity form of thinking and relating. He writes that the prime importance of an object's exchange value, or the (visible or invisible) price tag attached to it, structures an abstract relationship between person and object. The object is not encountered or experienced in its full concreteness, where all its unique, specific qualities are recognized. Rather, it is perceived in a way which emphasizes only qualities common to all other objects of the same genus, accentuating only some, ignoring all others. He further points out that if everything is perceived first of all in terms of its market value, everything is potentially expendable, i.e can be sold.

This attitude extends to the human realm as well, where people likewise experience or classify themselves (and each other) in terms of commodities, 'assets' who 'invest' in themselves in order to be more marketable or less expendable. Fromm (1966: 109) points out that such thinking eventually dissolves any concrete frame of reference in the process of life.[1]

Another important dimension has to be added, however. Work which allows an involvement in qualities, in concrete and changing processes, cannot follow the dictates of abstract, quantitative time. As discussed in an earlier chapter, the rhythm of time would be determined by the specifics and requirements of the task itself. Very similar to the relationship of burden and enjoyment, work and rest would alternate or be interspersed without being assigned to entirely different, mutually exclusive spheres or experiences (Mies 1986: 217).

In earlier chapters I discussed the issue of the worker's relationship to the object of her production in terms of the knowledge and skills that enter into this relationship. We can see that a primary concern for the object's use would structure this relationship in ways which reflect this orientation. How knowledge about the object is gained, the way it is known, and how this knowledge enters the process of work and production is likewise structured in ways which reflect the primary orientation towards use. In other words, we are here dealing with a different kind of epistemology than the one criticized in the preceding chapters. Because questions concerning knowledge, ways of knowing, and ways of gaining or creating knowledge are intrinsic to educational concerns it is worthwhile summarizing some of the basic features of this epistemology. I believe that an understanding of an epistemology which arises out of non-possessive and non-dominating organization of work is crucial for developing different questions not only about work but also about educational approaches, programmes, and methods based on egalitarian concerns and forms of interaction.

12

SUBSISTENCE KNOWING

THE EPISTEMOLOGY OF MOTHERING

In Chapter 8 the relationship of the artisan to the object of his or her production was characterized as combining a critical distance to the material, allowing for control and judgement, with a mimetic nearness, allowing for an intimate feel for its unique qualities and possibilities. I believe that it is precisely this movement between critical distance and mimetic nearness, where both mutually influence and enhance rather than exclude each other, which is at the heart of an epistemology which does not reflect dominance relations, but rather relations characterized by equality and reciprocity. Only such a dialectical unity can prevent the creation of power relations and, most importantly for education, can keep the bond between work, knowledge and experience intact.

The work of mothering is a form of subsistence labour which lends itself particularly well to an illustration of non-hierarchical, interactive work relations, and a non-dualist epistemology that arises from its practice. I believe that the raising of children, if blessed by social and individual circumstances which acknowledge the importance of nourishing new life, provides numerous parallels for an educational process which is likewise life-oriented. If motherhood is conceptualized as a labour process, a number of dialectical relationships emerge which contradict the static, oppositional dichotomies structured by industrial–patriarchal production. As I shall discuss below, the multi-faceted, complex tasks that comprise the practice of mothering intricately combine intellectual and emotional demands which cannot be neatly separated, thus undermining the usual divison between reason and emotion that characterizes masculinist epistemologies. Furthermore, because of the inherent dimension of biological necessity, the activities of mothering do not permit a clear separation between caring for the body and caring for the mind, and between attending to 'the natural' and attending to 'the cultural'. Because of the bodily dimension of mothering, which may include the productive capacity of the biological mother's body itself, motherwork can therefore also be profoundly sensuous and pleasurable. Furthermore, there are probably few productive experiences which so intimately combine the element of enjoyment and burden.

Recent feminist writings have explored the experience of mothering in terms which can serve as a model for alternative conceptions of work and as a foundation for a feminist epistemology. Although not all of these writers look at mothering as a labour process, when seen together, their analyses yield descriptions which can serve as the foundation of alternative models of work, based on a non-instrumental rationality, and calling for a different, non-dualistic epistemology. Feminist writers have approached this issue from many different perspectives employing different conceptual frameworks and emphasizing different aspects. Hartsock (1983) and Rose (1986), for instance, develop their perspectives and proposals for a different epistemology based on an analysis of the material reality of women's work under capitalism without stressing mothering *per se.* Other writers (Gilligan 1982, Noddings 1984, Tronto 1989, Lauritzen 1989) single out the dimension of caring or care, mainly within the context of discussing alternative ethical theories. In a similar manner, Held (1987) looks upon mothering primarily as a model for moral relations, although she talks about the fact that 'mothers and mothering persons ... produce and create human culture' (1987: 115). However, she does not pursue the idea of production, nor does she conceptualize mothering explicitly as a form of work. Ruddick (1984, 1989) takes up the issue of mothering directly and investigates the intellectual and mental attitudes which comprise 'maternal thinking'.

In the following I have gathered together what could be considered the main features of mothering conceptualized as a productive process. My description therefore presents an ideal-type, abstracting from the tremendous variety of actual practices and experiences of mothering in different historical, social, or cultural contexts. My suggestions will have to prove themselves, be re-thought and described again in the light of the multiple possibilities that exist for the forms the work of mothering may assume. Despite these varieties, however, the constellation of growing, immature child and mature adult, of yet-to-be realized potential, and potential already realized remains a constant element. It is this constellation which contains the most important questions for education, and which allows one to see the work of mothering as a form of production, no matter under which cultural circumstances it is performed. My discussion is also meant to contribute to the demystification and 'de-naturalization' of women's work which is based on the assumption that it does not require specially learnt skills and demands, 'only love, not labour' (Rose 1986: 178).

PARTICULARITY AND GENERALITY

The relationship between the particular and the general is the first important relationship contained in the work of mothering. Raising a child can be seen as a process of actualizing the latent potential of the not-yet-developed person, and of performing this work in a context of established social norms and expectations concerning a future fully socialized adult. This may take the form of an individual mother's conscious concern with her child's 'acceptability' (Ruddick 1984). Such a concern seems to be strongly related to the experience of relatively isolated mothering under the conditions of the White middle class nuclear family. The notion of acceptability may take on a very different meaning when the child is a member of a low-status or marginal social group, which makes her by definition less acceptable or perhaps even unacceptable altogether. Her very existence therefore clashes with the hierarchy of worthiness whose underlying norms cannot simply serve as a guide for raising an acceptable child. If we look at the problem of acceptability from the margin rather than the centre of established White masculinist norms, this task would be better defined as one of raising the child *against* these norms, teaching her about their power, but also about their built-in injustice. Whatever the context, in one form or other the mother (or mothering persons) will have to negotiate between the child's latent but developing *particular* qualities and the normative context within which the child is being raised. This may assume many different forms, and one or the other pole – unique individuality or social expectations and membership in a community – may be emphasized. I believe, however, that a truly communal, non-repressive social context presupposes fully individuated people whose individuality has been nourished and shaped by the communal context in which they were raised. Here mothering can be seen as a dialectical process of letting a child grow according to its potential, but which is, to a large extent, defined by the ability to engage in egalitarian forms of interaction.

Mothering is therefore also an interactive kind of labour, dependent on the labour of many others, not only in terms of material and psychological support, but also in terms of producing a fully individuated child. For such a child to be fully herself, but also to be many others who are not like her, requires a communal situation very different from the restricted and homogenous situation of the White, middle class, heterosexual family.[1]

The moments of particularity and generality appear in another dimension as well. Because the child follows general patterns of biological, emotional, and cognitive maturation, knowledge about the general stages and phases of this process may assist the mother to interpret properly and respond to her child's behaviour. At the same time, this knowledge can only truly come to fruition by moulding it along the contours of the individual difference and uniqueness of the child, which also necessitates constant expansion, revision, and, most likely, also rejection of this general knowledge based on the mother's specific knowledge about her particular child.[2] This movement between the general and the particular is reminiscent of Fromm's description of a 'full and productive relatedness to an object'. He (1966: 106) describes this relatedness as a way of perceiving the object 'in its uniqueness, and at the same time in its generality; in its concreteness, and at the same time in its abstractness'.

To arrive at an intimate knowledge of uniqueness and concreteness requires an existential dwelling in the object (Polanyi 1964: 63), a form of submitting to the intrinsic qualities of the child on the part of the mother in the process of interaction and active involvement in her child's life. The word 'caring', frequently associated with the work of mothering, implies this ability of actively submitting to the object of knowledge, with an attentiveness to particularity, i.e. to the concrete, specific needs of the person cared for (Tronto 1989). Furthermore, caring signifies interaction as well as emotional involvement or love.

ENGAGEMENT IN REALITY

The capability for mimetic nearness, for an existential dwelling in the object of work or cognition is founded on a fundamental respect for empirical reality. In other words, a close contact with reality is sought rather than shunned, as it is in technologized work (see Chapter 8). It is only through such a contact that valuable knowledge about reality can be gained, and that the various phenomena of this reality – objects, organic materials or living organisms – are respected in their own right, may even be considered 'co-equals' in the labour process (Bookchin 1982: 233). In his descriptions of work and production in 'organic societies' Bookchin provides us with many examples from anthropological studies which illustrate this co-equal relationship between the worker and the object of her or his labour. He summarizes his descriptions in the following way:

> Concrete labor thus confronted concrete substance, and labour merely participated in fashioning a reality that was either present or latent in natural phenomena. Both labor and the materials on which it 'worked' were *coequally* creative, innovative, and most assuredly artistic.
>
> (Bookchin 1982: 233)

He further writes that 'work was distinguished by its capacity to discover the "voice" of substance, not simply to fashion an inert "natural resource" into desired objects' (ibid. 233).[3] Bookchin's descriptions often refer to a mythical-sounding past, but can be read as a way to critique the epistemology of ruling which sharply divides the natural from the social world, and which structures an attitude of detachment and control. Although Bookchin makes frequent references to the experience of 'gestation and birth', the participation of *women*, i.e. of live, concrete agents in this process is never mentioned, and the productive processes of pregnancy and birth (not to speak of raising the child) serve as analogies rather than as direct, primary examples in his descriptions.

For instance, Bookchin talks about *active* matter, which 'strives to realize itself, its latent potentialities, through a nisus that finds fulfilment in wholeness', concluding with the thought that 'self-realization of matter finds its very exact analogy in the processes of gestation and birth' (ibid. 232). If we extend this process to the work of actually raising the child, the aspect of *activity* of the 'matter' striving towards self-realization becomes even more apparent (although remains invisible to Boockchin's male vision). It is precisely children's indomitable desire for self-realization, their unbounded activity and liveliness which makes mothering such strenuous work, particularly while the child is young, and her efforts are not matched by her physical or cognitive development. This situation therefore calls on the mother's ability to judge and control.

In Chapter 8 the work of the artisan was characterized as an intricate blend of power over the material and submission to its intrinsic characteristics and possibilities where the element of control was not extracted as a separate and dominant reality. Likewise, in the process of mothering the need for control is contained by the mother's respect for the child's independent reality, and by her concern for its growing autonomy. The mother has to monitor her child's as well as her own responses constantly if she does not want to stifle her child's efforts or sense of independence, without entirely giving up her authority as the mature adult. In the productive work of the mother, control can therefore never assume the absolute dimensions that characterize the technological model of work which relies upon total control over the material conditions of production, and on a sharp division between the labour process and its results. In addition, because the child's autonomy is continuously growing and developing, the work of mothering requires a gradual relinquishing of control altogether (Hartsock 1983: 293).

PROVISIONAL AND AMBIGUOUS KNOWLEDGE

To acknowledge the child's uniqueness as well as its independent, unfolding reality not only places limits on the mother's authority, but also on the nature and importance of her knowledge. Because she is in contact with the continuously changing nature of her child, and, consequently of her task, the mother's knowledge can never be finished or be absolute, but must remain tentative and provisional.[4] It is a kind of knowledge that 'does not necessarily lead to general propositions' (Belenky *et al.* 1986: 201) because it is constantly affirmed or disaffirmed, created and recreated in accordance with the unique and constantly changing reality of the child. In Ruddick's words (1984: 218), 'innovation takes precedence over permanence, disclosure and responsiveness over clarity and certainty'. And, she continues (quoting Iris Murdoch, ibid. 218), 'the idea of "objective reality" itself "undergoes important modification when it is to be understood, not in relation to the world described by science, but in relation to the progressing life of a person"'.

Another dimension has to be added to the provisionality and ambiguity of the mother's knowledge. One can say that children and adults inhabit different worlds, similarly to the way humans and animals live in different worlds. An adult can never fully know what it means to experience the world from a two-year-old's perspective, or through the mind of a cat. I believe that Lugones' (1990) concept of 'playful "world"- travelling' is very useful for addressing this issue. Playful world travel refers to the ability to travel to the world of the child and to get a glimpse of it without imperialistically occupying or appropriating it. Tronto (1989) draws attention to two other important dimensions that characterize the dynamics and relations of knowing in the act of caring (which, as I would claim, is included but not exhausted by the work of mothering). First of all, the caring person, or mother, constructs her knowledge to a large extent from sources other than her own. She is dependent on the knowledge she has inherited from other mothers or caregivers, or which she seeks from knowledgeable others, including information from books and other written documents. Second, and more importantly, in the act of caring a kind of knowledge comes into play that is 'completely peculiar to the particular person being cared for' if that person's needs are to be truly recognized and met (Tronto 1989: 177). We can see how a different epistemology implies different ethical relationships, because to acknowledge the importance of recognizing and knowing others' needs undermines the capitalist ethos of self-interest.

Furthermore, Tronto discusses an aspect which ties in with the above discussion of authority and control. She contrasts the epistemological notion of attentiveness towards others' unique needs with the liberal view of the self as the best judge of one's true interests. Giving the example of the child asking for junk food, Tronto (1989: 177) states that in the caring relationship the person being cared for may not be the most knowledgeable person as regards the child's true needs or interests, and 'genuine attentiveness would presumably allow the care-taker to see through these pseudo-needs and come to appreciate what the other really needs'. In a way, this problem recasts the previous one of combining judgement, or critical distance with mimetic nearness or responsiveness. It also brings into focus the importance of self-knowledge. As Tronto (ibid.) writes, 'if a care-taker has deficient self-knowledge about his or her own needs, then there is no way to guarantee that those needs have been removed in looking to see what the other's needs are'.[5]

We can see how knowledge, and the act of knowing are intricately woven into the relational matrix of mother, child, and society. Knowledge does not come from one single source, and is not monopolized, owned or guarded by one particular individual or institution. Rather, knowledge has multiple sources, combines in manifold ways, forever attuned to the particulars of the situation. It is knowledge that is alive, contracts and expands, alternately adjusts to the contours of its object, and, flowing outwards, assumes the form of its own internal dynamics, separate from the original context, but ready to meet a new context, and new tasks. It is knowledge which is constantly created and recreated. Furthermore, to know requires an attitude which does not recoil from concrete substance, but ignites in a close encounter with it. This attitude provokes a thinking which does not thrive on the hubris of certainty and omnipotence whose primary gesture is one of ruling and appropriating. Rather, this kind of thinking endures ambiguity and provisionality, and its primary gesture is therefore acknowledgement and respect for the endless complexities of reality, but also relentless, ongoing doubtfulness.

To summarize, the epistemology that can be developed out of the experience of mothering is characterized by non-dichotomous relationships between the knower and the object of knowing, between the natural and the social, between critical judgement and empathetic intuition, between reason and emotion, and between the subjective and the objective. It does not reduce the particular or unique to a mere specimen which can be exchanged with any other by subsuming it under the general, but respects and acknowledges it. Because of this respectful, preserving attitude I have called this way of knowing 'subsistence knowing'. Such subsistence knowing also stresses complexity and change rather than linearity and stasis, and it implies and structures non-dominating forms of interaction.

Numerous implications exist for an education which takes as its starting point a model of work which is oriented towards the production, sustenance and improvement of life, and which can therefore be called productive. To start from such a concept of work would lead to entirely new and alternative educational paradigms. It would affect theory and practice, point to different educational principles and premises, and therefore alter processes as well as contents. Those (proposed) changes can be examined on two different levels. The first concerns educational programmes and approaches directly relating to work. Here the assumption of a different starting point, based on an alternative concept of work, leads to entirely new questions and concerns. The second level concerns the idea that education is itself a productive process which can be organized according to the principles inherent in productive work. If the relations that are structured by the predominant educational paradigms repeat in however complex and contradictory ways the alienating, power-bound relations of industrial–patriarchal production, it must also be possible to establish educational processes and procedures which mirror the reciprocal, non-appropriating relations of alternative modes of production. In the following section I will address this point, and discuss larger theoretical and practical programmatic implications in the conclusions of this book.

THE PRODUCTIVE PROCESS OF EDUCATION

In the most general terms, education can be considered a process which produces (or helps to produce) the capacity for speech and action, or the ability to participate in the human community as an autonomous, critical, and active member. More specifically, autonomy, critical ability, and capacity for competent action imply the individual's capacity for experience itself, where active participation in reality and critical judgement about the consequences of one's action are fully intertwined. In other words, education helps to produce the capacity for having 'fruitful experiences' in the sense Dewey described. This means not only that the individual learner must be able to recognize and actualize the educative potential contained in experience, but also be able to organize her experiences in such a way that they are or become educative. The capacity for experience therefore indicates a practical and critically reflective involvement in social reality from the centre of one's own subjectivity. The latter likewise has to be reflected upon and understood in a process of a critical and creative engagement with one's own inner nature.

Some of the components of this education may look familiar: to learn from and through experience, and to organize educational experiences in ways that are conducive to this learning. These are not only cherished principles of adult education, but also the basis of the 'experiential learning theory' which was developed by Kolb (1974), based on Lewis' 'action theory', Dewey's model of learning, and Piaget's theory of cognitive development. However, from the perspective of production for life, we need to go beyond this theory. Although experiential learning theory stresses the primacy of experience, it lacks essential elements when looked at from a comprehensive critical perspective. Instead of dialectical unity it poses polar relationships between thinking and acting, or experiencing and reflecting; it provides no impetus or vehicle for a critical examination of power relations as, in fact, it lacks a comprehensive notion of critique; it therefore has no future-oriented, Utopian dimension. Finally, experiential learning theory remains entirely within the confines of individualistic thinking. Because a communal orientation is entirely absent, by implication the relationship of self and others is stated in terms of the primacy of the former. Interaction or communication, reciprocity or mutuality are therefore not integral elements of experiential learning theory, as they must be for an education for life.

The points I am raising in this chapter do not only bear similarity to experiential learning theory, but also to many suggestions and ideas presented in the emerging field of a feminist pedagogy.[6] Despite similarities and points of agreement, and a grounding of ideas in female experience, none of the proposed theories and methods of a feminist pedagogy have been systematically developed out of a theory of women's productive work and of a corresponding epistemoloy. Furthermore, no connection has been made between a feminist pedagogy and epistemology from the larger, more encompassing perspective of subsistence production.

When looking at education as a productive process, modelled after the rationality of production for life, one can see many important parallels with the work and epistemology of mothering. In fact, the basic premises underlying mothering also structure education for life. At the centre of a productive educational process lies the same dialectical unity of the particular and the general, of mimesis and reflection, or of attending to the concrete and assuming the critical distance of judgement which characterizes the work of the mother. From this basic relationship all others flow, and it recurs in different forms and guises in all other important educational relationships. This is the same as saying that education for life does not allow for creating *articifial dichotomies* in any of its basic relationships, be it between the role of teacher and the role of student, between authority and obedience, process and content, thought and emotion, self and others, subjectivity and objectivity, empathy and critique, caring and judgement, knowledge and knowledge acquisition, and transforming and submitting to reality. While these pairs represent different poles of a relationship, they never assume the character of static opposites, ordered into hierarchies. Each of the individual elements may occur as a distinct moment in the educational process. However, they never crystallize into separate entities but constantly interweave and interlace within a context of live interaction.

VALIDATION OF SUBJECTIVITY

In the educational process 'mimetic nearness' refers, above all, to the validation of the individual learner's subjectivity. Within an explicitly educational context, the acknowledgement of another's unique individuality is a deliberate, purposeful activity based on the assumption that true learning is dependent on such an acknowledgement. It can therefore not simply be a formal gesture in the sense of a statement like 'I grant you the right to be your own person' but has to be expressed in action, above all in the willingness and deliberate attempt to know the individual learner as a unique human being. Knowing the learner here has two components: understanding the learner's reality as much as possible from her perspective, and knowing her in the sense of being attuned to, 'dwelling in' the unique qualities of her person. The latter form of knowing can be described as empathy, the former as a way of consciously participating in the learner's reality in order to understand it, and the meaning she herself gives to it. We can see how acknowledging the learner's experience and individuality implies a movement between attentiveness and empathy, and drawing conclusions and making judgements. Because it is not possible to simply 'crawl into another person's mind and meaning' by separating 'our interpretations from connections with our own hermeneutical situation' (Habermas 1983: 11), to understand someone else's experience always implies, however subtly, to judge.

To understand means to recognize the other's reasons for her opinions, interpretations and actions, and to recognize someone's reasons is impossible without reasoning oneself, i.e. without assuming an evaluative stance: we inevitably agree or disagree with the other person's reasons, or we deliberately withhold judgement, for which we likewise must be able to give reasons. Thus, to take the other's perspective, or to at least partially identify with her means both to 'feel with' the other, and to participate in the other's reason- ableness (or unreasonableness), to become aware of the rational-emotional ground of the other's behaviour and self-identity. Because empathetic understanding and judgement are so intricately intertwined, we can speak of a form of 'rational love' which neither signifies symbiotic merging nor indiscriminate acceptance.

Here the overwhelming importance of self-knowledge that was emphasized in connection with mothering or caring, emerges again. Although we cannot slip out of our own hermeneutical situation, our own assumptions about and interpretations of reality, we can nevertheless critically examine them if we do not want to run the risk of projecting our own judgements and interpretations onto the other person. In other words, as educators and co-learners we need to be (or become) critically aware of the various bases for our judgements and evaluations, requiring ongoing self-reflection. The non-cognitive elements of empathy, where a person's unique qualities are 'known' in a sensing, intuitive way are therefore always interlaced with moments of evaluative summaries of the other person's experience as well as with ongoing self-observation and self-criticism. In the context of adult learners, this is a requirement which extends to all participants of the educational situation.

From the perspective of a productive educational process, validating subjective experience and engaging in a relationship of empathy are not simply abstract moral imperatives, but structural requirements for the educational process to be successful, i.e. indeed to contribute to the individual learner's capacity to speak and act autonomously and in concert with others, and to the ability to organize her experience in ways that make it fruitful or educative. The learner's own 'hermeneutical situation', the meanings and interpretations that structure her reality, as well as her unique personal and biographical characteristics and circumstances all enter and become part and parcel of the educational situation. Because it is this 'material' which is being worked on in the educational process, it needs to be understood and be consciously integrated into the educational process, in order for it to unfold and develop its potential.

ACKNOWLEDGING DIFFERENCE

A stress on individuality and uniqueness implies respect for, and a creative use of diversity and difference. At the same time, diversity and difference, like individuality, have a decidedly social dimension which may be founded on and arise out of social divisions and hierarchies. Unique individual differences will always combine with socially defined ones, where difference ceases to be politically neutral, but becomes translated into inequality. Thus, differences and diversities that emanate from the different realities and experiences of age, class, race, sex, or sexual orientation are all fully tied to power-bound, hierarchical social valuations and institutions. They are therefore all imprinted with the mark of inequality, and these differences, and the experiences of dominance and injustice contained in them, will inevitably unfold their internal dynamics in education, distorting it from within. Only a profound understanding of social reality with all its divisions and hierarchies will make these dynamics visible and will allow educators and learners to separate authentic difference from artificially created ones, and to be realistic about the limits to equality and mutuality that can possibly be established in their educational setting (see Hart 1990a).

THE COMMUNAL DIMENSION OF EDUCATION

In a productive educational situation the learners (and educators) therefore pay tribute to and appreciate individuality, diversity, and uniqueness, but they are united by the common desire to reach mutual understanding through and with those differences. Such an education must therefore foster a theoretical consciousness which is capable of understanding and criticizing individual experience, as well as the wish and ability for mutual understanding. In other words, it must foster relations of solidarity among the participants of the educational situation (Hart 1990a). As I discussed elsewhere (Hart 1990b), an education which is oriented towards cooperative relations among the pariticipants needs to create moral environments which touch the deep structure of non-hierarchical, egalitarian relations. Such an environment would have to nurture 'progressive' needs or need structures, and corresponding identities which are free from the need to control (or be controlled). In other words, a moral ecology would have to be established which fosters virtues and ethical sensibilities needed for caring, egalitarian, communal relationships.

Educational theory is in dire need of a theory of community, and of educating for community, thus going beyond an analysis of educational practices which focus on transformative processes within the learner herself (see Hart 1990b, see also the conclusions reached in this book). It must also go beyond the strictly social realm. In the light of the main concerns of this book, education for life needs to pay attention to those competences and abilities which lead to a different attitude towards and relationship with nature, and with non-human living things. Thus, the ability for empathy and for caring is challenged as well in an attempt to understand, and at least partially to identify with and to attain 'mimetic nearness' with creatures with whom we cannot communicate in the medium of language. Thus far, no educational theory has systematically explored the skills and competences that would allow for such understanding and corresponding knowledge, and that would require intensive use of human intelligence and reason, a reason which has eliminated all traces of the pervasive need for hierarchy and control.

CREATING AND RECREATING KNOWLEDGE

Furthermore, productive education, like mothering, is attuned to development and change. One of its prime goals is to actualize the potential of the learners, to draw out latent possibilites, rather than to confront the learner with the completeness of certain predetermined or pre-defined knowledge or skills. The kind of knowledge that enters the educational process, and that is shaped and created by it, emerges as an ambiguous, provisional reality. Not only is knowledge constantly created and recreated in accordance with change and development, but it also has multiple sources: subjective and objective, social and individual, about self and about others. Since in principle all learners contribute equally to the process of truth-finding and knowledge-creating, in such an educational situation it cannot be determined from the outset who will learn from whom. Furthermore, the different sources of knowledge combine in an endless variety of ways, assuming the multiple shapes of a knowledge which has absorbed individuality and subjectivity, as well as the unique characteristics of a particular educational situation, without, however, losing its objective, generally valid core. This objective core is guaranteed by the shared or common medium of the social world in which educator and learners participate, and by their shared and common interest in critically examining and re-visioning this world. Thus, only a critical as well as Utopian dimension prevents the stress on individual difference, contextuality and multiple realities degenerating into an inconsequential and ultimately incapacitating, disempowering relativism.

Knowledge, skills and abilities which are shaped as well as presupposed by an education for life are as varied and complex as the educational process outlined above. They range from the intuition-based, non-cognitive 'feel' for and awareness of one's own as well as the other participants' individual uniqueness and difference to a relentless critical scrutiny of individual and social phenomena. Intuitive knowing, based on the positive act of respect and affirmation is therefore fully intertwined with the critical, evaluative stance of participating in the other's reality. It is such a stance which gives meaning to the requirement of taking the other seriously. Empathy and criticism or evaluation are therefore not separate, but only different moments in a combined, dialectical process. Both are embedded in the overall concern for power-free forms of interaction and communication which likewise encompasses the motivational as well as cognitive–critical realm of acting and learning, requiring both a desire for such social relations as well as the ability to recognize and criticize existing structures of dominance. The latter, in turn, involves substantive information and knowledge about social reality and therefore sets certain requirements for the *content* of education.

If the learners want to criticize society and arrive at a reflected-upon understanding of their own experience within society, they have to draw on a reliable body of knowledge, whose validity and reliability must, however, be drawn into the same overall process of criticism, and must be set in relation to their own experience. Neither externally given, objective knowledge, nor the knowledge contained in individual experience, are sufficient for arriving at the truth about the whole of society. The effort of truth-seeking is a profoundly transformative one, where knowledge about one's self and about the world is constantly recreated in view of a future society. This necessitates the shaping of a historical awareness, or an ability for historical thinking, where the present is examined in terms of its roots in a reflected-upon past, and of the possibilities and potentialities yet to be unfolded in the future. Freire's method of conscientization, and the method of consciousness-raising as developed by the women's movement are both examples for such a transformative process.

The abilities, skills, and knowledge which would be presupposed as well as acquired through a productive education, i.e. one that is based above all on an affirmation of life rather than an affirmation of 'the bottom line', are therefore fundamentally different from those we find in the list and catalogues of skills necessary for work of the future. Above all, these abilities move outside the orbit of technological control, and do not conform to the contours of hierarchical divisions as do the skills currently proposed and taught. They are based on, and in turn structure relationships or relational matrices which are reciprocal, egalitarian, and non-appropriating. To discuss, describe, and practise these abilities and skills, and to deliberately integrate them into educational theory and practice is a task that still awaits careful attention. It will have to be a collective, cooperative effort, addressing the issue from many different perspectives and experiential backgrounds, and drawing on many different existing critical analyses of education, work, and society.

13

SUMMARY AND CONCLUSIONS: RETHINKING WORK AND EDUCATION

CALLING ADULT EDUCATION TO ACCOUNT

Throughout this book I have criticized the prevailing industrial-patriarchal concept of work, its underlying assumptions, its surrounding cultural values, and its larger social and economic context. I have further criticized an educational enterprise which for the most part subscribes to these or similar assumptions, shares the same underlying ideology, and supports values and forms of consciousness which are shaped by patriarchal–industrial reality. I have criticized approaches to education, or to work and education, which are constructed on the basis of these same values, mirroring some of the same structures we find in the miseducative reality of work under patriarchal–industrial conditions. Those structures appear, for instance, in the subscription to the notion of individual success where isolated individuals are competing against each other for a limited offering of opportunities. I have further deplored the absence of values related to learning about life and work, values which connote a communal rather than individualistic orientation where a top-heavy, authoritarian structure is replaced by egalitarian forms of production and interaction. Furthermore, adult education responses to the current turbulence in the world of work have been criticized as assuming a one-dimensional view from above, pre-empting an understanding of the producers' concrete experience. Rather, this experience is frozen into the pin-head size reality of skills or skill deficits, and encapsulated in a curriculum which mirrors social divisions and hierarchies.

Within this framework, the training for skills is presented as a value-neutral, apolitical process, simply responding to the technical requirements of current and future jobs. Likewise, skills are themselves defined as value-free, technical as well as strictly individual attributes, a definition which disregards not only the social construction of skills and skill deficits, but also of jobs or job opportunities. This is made possible by a strong economistic interpretation of work, and work-related knowledge and competences, all of which are tethered to the unquestioned ideology of continuous and unlimited economic growth. The ideology of unlimited economic growth not only denies the tremendous social and environmental costs and the profound social and economic injustices which are associated with it, but fixates the learners to choices which do not provide real alternatives, either individually or socially. The adult education enterprise must therefore also be criticized for its profound lack of a critical and Utopian perspective, particularly with respect to the issue of work and production.

I believe that adult education needs to be called to account for its inabilty or unwillingness to provide more critical and creative responses to current crises surrounding the issues of work and employment. However, it must first of all let go of its fixation on merely 'building a quality workforce' which will contribute to competitiveness. Adult education would have to see the current troubled experience of work, accompanied by doubts, problems, dissatisfactions and sufferings as an opportunity for asking critical questions, and for opening up at least the conception of new possibilities for living and working. To feel the pulse of these kinds of changes, to be a midwife to these unborn ideas by helping to articulate them and give them a means of social expression which would make them conscious and actionable – this should be an educational task of primary importance.

If education is understood as a means of peaceful change, which rejects the individual as well as social status quo by drawing out latent possibilities, adult education cannot simply hide behind the mantle of alleged 'realism'. It is not realistic to support the current destructive forms of production and development, nor to try to adjust people to the unhealthy conditions of their work. Ultimately, it is eminently impractical to continue to see the crisis of our times in terms of an allegedly deficient 'human capital' rather than in terms of the shrinking conditions of our physical and psychological survival. Instead of simply adjusting people to the hierarchical and divided reality of work, adult educators need to ask the question of how we could and how we should work in a manner that contributes to the maintenance and improvement of life rather than profit.

The question of how we should work is also the question of how we should live. As described in this book, the insane separation of work and life impoverishes both, making the former deadly, and the latter empty. In fact, it destroys life.

In the preceding chapters I described in detail a kind of work which is bound to a life-giving and life-affirming productive process. I have repeatedly pointed out in this book that this is the only kind of work which can be called *productive* in the true sense of the word. As Shiva (1989: 5) stated in her book *Staying Alive*, this kind of 'productivity is a measure of producing life and sustenance'. And, she continues, 'that this kind of productivity has been rendered invisible does not reduce its centrality to survival – it merely reflects the domination of modern patriarchal economic categories which see only profit, not life' (ibid.).

An education which claims to be life-affirming would first of all have to acknowledge the centrality of subsistence work for human survival. Such an acknowledgement would signify a profound transformation in 'meaning perspective' (Mezirow 1990a, 1990b) with a number of far-reaching implications and consequences. It would lead to a questioning of accepted values and assumptions, to a re-thinking of existing programmes and research agendas, and to the formulation of new and different ones. Such a transformation in perspective would therefore have numerous consequences for existing as well still undeveloped educational programmes and approaches. It would affect their structure, their content, and the processes of teaching and learning enacted in these programmes. Such a changed perspective would translate into a multitude of tasks for adult educators to bring about or assist their students in unlearning old ways of perception, and in learning new ways of thinking and acting. Because work and life are not separated into two static and oppositional experiences, such a transformation of meaning perspective would affect educational endeavours in many different contexts.

In the light of such a new perspective, adult educators would constantly have to ask: What do we have to know? What do we have to learn? What do we have to do? These questions necessitate ongoing mutual and self-education of adult educators concerning information, knowledge, and competences which are part and parcel of such a new orientation, and will engage the educator in a collaborative process of learning with their students.

In the following I will list the main aspects of a changed meaning perspective as regards work and production and give a broad outline of their possible theoretical and practical implications. By looking at the issues, themes and questions which a new education would have to integrate into its programmes and approaches, I will thereby also recapitulate the main points made in this book. As a first attempt of this nature, these suggestions will remain rather general. There is a virtue in this generality, however, as every adult educator is allowed to examine her or his specific context, re-think its particular structure, content, and processes, and evaluate the possibilities as well as limitations for actual change. Furthermore, the reader will see that in the following the boundaries between education and other forms of social action, and between the responsibility of the educator as an educator or as a member of society, will at times become blurred. This is not surprising. After all, what I am proposing is to base educational endeavours on a changed *philosophy of life*. To try to delineate precisely where the responsibility of the educator ends and the responsibility of the human being begins would re-institute exactly the kinds of artificial divisions that characterize the existing value system. An education oriented towards life can neither afford narrow specializations nor the élitist and inevitably hierarchical requirements of so-called professionalism.

THE COURAGE TO KNOW

A transformed perspective alters one's location, the point from where one looks at reality. In earlier chapters, I criticized the rigid narrow-mindedness of a view from above, and the distorting effects of looking at the margin from the standpoint of the centre. This geography of seeing creates distances and separations between things that belong together. It makes large areas of reality look blurred or screens them out altogether. It is a static view, never leaving the point of its origination, never moving about in the frozen landscape it creates through its limited vision.

A transformed perspective on work and life not only changes location, but enables the seer to move about, to move 'from margin to center' (Hooks 1984), and outwards again, to assume the view from below, and to scrutinize the view from above. Such a view brings entirely new issues, questions, and problems to light. Above all, it makes visible 'the key phenomena of social and economic injustice' which are otherwise considered mere exceptions (Adorno

1974). For someone who is not herself placed at the margin, such a standpoint is difficult to assume. It is an ongoing achievement, and it requires considerable courage as it also makes visible where one participates in the injustice of the current order, and who pays for one's privileges. Thus, a changed perspective requires first of all *the courage to know*. It requires actively seeking out information which is generally withheld by mainstream media; it requires fresh analyses of old issues, and new theories about hitherto neglected ones. It cannot leave anything unquestioned. These are the general requirements.

In particular, a view which places the issue of life at the centre of concern must systematically unveil the real lines of dependency. The question of who is dependent on whom must start with the basic acknowledgment of human dependence on nature. This will establish a direct link between educational programmes and the ecology movement. Feminist ecological thought is particularly promising since it proposes a changed view of nature and of our relationship to nature, acknowledging her integrity as well as her ability to renew herself if treated in respectful and preserving ways (Shiva 1989).[1]

An acceptance of these ideas has a number of educational consequences. What would a population that is concerned about preserving the natural conditions of life have to know? What would it have to learn? In light of the level of ignorance, obliviousness, or outright denial, we are surely not short of educational challenges. Not only do we need to know how 'our' way of life, our technological progress and material wealth consume a grossly disproportionate amount of natural resources, and creates destruction and misery in other parts of the world. We also need to learn about ecological principles, and about ways to reduce waste and destruction.

Clearly, this requires a serious calling into question of our cherished notions of progress and development, and the idea that 'we' are entitled to a greater share of natural wealth, and to a way of life whose comforts and conveniences are dependent on hidden slave labour. Shiva (1989: 9) quotes Lovin as saying that

> the productivity of the western male compared to women or Third World peasants is not intrinsically superior; it is based on inequalities in the distribution of this 'slave labour'. The average inhabitant of the USA for example has about 250 times

> more 'slaves' than the average Nigerian. 'If Americans were short of 249 of those 'slaves', one wonders how efficient they would prove themselves to be?'

It is an ethical task of prime importance for everybody to trace the lines of dependency of her or his existence to these 'slaves'. In everyday terms, this means becoming aware how various divisions of labour operate in one's own life, above all the sexual divison of labour. Surely, a critical acknowledgement of this division in one's everyday life requires an immense learning process: critical analysis, self-criticism, and practical action based on newly gained insights. And it requires a supportive moral environment which questions the hiearchy of good and presumably 'dirty' work, and the workers which are associated with it. It needs to look at the division of tasks within each individual household. Thus far, these questions have been relegated to the netherworld of 'women's issues'. They have yet to become issues of general social concern, bearing important educational questions.

However, as discussed in Part I of this book, sexual and international divisions of labour are intimately related. To become cognizant of the latter requires, first of all, becoming aware of the extreme separation of production and consumption and asking questions not only about who produces our daily consumption goods, but also where they are produced, and under what conditions. Among other things, this includes technological devices as much as food or textiles. In my mind, a proper work-related education must make accessible the context within which things are produced. I believe such knowledge would have tremendous effects on our consumption patterns, and help us to evaluate the true usefulness (or uselessness) of things we produce, buy and consume.

THE CENTRALITY OF THE CHILDREN QUESTION

The divisions of tasks in the household includes the way responsibility for the raising of children is distributed. As discussed in Part I, the existing unequal distribution of this responsibility, and the view of child-raising as an individual choice rather than a social responsibility, constituting 'socially necessary labour', is one of the primary mechanisms that keep women from leading an autonomous existence. However, the 'children question' cannot be solved by demanding that fathers assume an equal share in the task of raising their children, or that more childcare facilities should be built. In many cases they are necessary and useful interim steps, in others they are irrelevant (especially where no father is around). In either case, these solutions do not even touch the core of the problem. They still consider waged work, and the production of commodities as central economic activites, relegating the raising of children to the private sphere of the family. In other words, these solutions do not consider the raising of the next generation as a form of productive labour which is central to social survival, and which should be cherished, supported, and protected.

Educational programmes could assist people to examine their respective workplaces (inside and outside the house), and to develop forms of organizing and distributing work which would reflect a new priority: to make the work of raising children the primary, and the work of producing commodities for the market the secondary one. Although such a new priority ultimately calls for revolutionary changes, many interim steps can be taken in existing contexts which could mark the beginning of a changed thinking and a changed practice. The most important question would be how the raising of children can be socially acknowledged and become fully integrated into a person's entire productive life.

Examples of these attempts already exist, from a law firm hiring women lawyers with children on a part-time basis, and distributing the work in ways which eliminate the typical lawyer's 12 or 15-hour days. Another example is a woman-led social service agency allowing its workers spontaneous 'flextime' for family needs as long as the work gets done (again, including job definitions which make such flexibility possible).[2] In cases like these a relationship of trust and partnership is created which enhances the employees' enjoyment of their work, and which guarantees a high degree of productivity.

At a recent conference on women and work in Chicago, Illinois, called 'If Women Mattered' (April 1990), the conference participants explored ways of creatively changing attitudes and structures in existing workplaces to educate co-workers about the primacy of childcare, and to find ways of supporting that work. Many suggestions were quite simple (e.g. to permit the scheduling of meetings only at times which could not possibly interfere with picking up children or making supper for them); others had more far-reaching implications (e.g. to design job descriptions which do not necessitate overtime or work on weekends). In general, however, the conference participants quickly realized that they were dismantling the male-defined notions of 'career' and 'success' which are built not only on unequal divisions of labour, primarily on the exploitation of women's work, but also on a considerable amount of (voluntary as well as externally imposed) self-exploitation. In the light of my critique in Chapter 4 we can speculate about what would happen to educational programmes if the conventional notion of success was systematically dismantled rather than solidified, and what would happen to the concept as well as content of a liberal'education that no longer ascribes to this idea.

BUILDING RELATIONS OF SUPPORT

The conference participants also pointed out that changes could only be instituted through cooperation based on solidarity among workers. I believe the current Greek chorus on looming crises and disasters (joined by many adult educators) because of alleged deficiencies in people's skills or competences has devastating effects: it makes people timid, isolates them from each other, pits them against each other, and generally fixates them to the status quo by robbing them in advance of the possibility of exploring existing (not to speak of future) avenues for change. In fact, as mentioned in an earlier chapter, we even find adult educators joining in the attempt on the side of management to prevent the formation of unions (see Pierce 1987).

As discussed in Chapter 9, current and developing forms of workplace organization in many instances destroy the last vestiges of a work-related social culture. Despite the emphasis on teams and other forms of collaborative work, these new forms are instituted from above, as well as highly regulated and controlled. They therefore impose structures of communication rather than letting them develop spontaneously and authentically. Furthermore, they affect only a thin layer of skilled workers. In many other workplaces, especially in employment situations where the use of microelectronic technology is prevalent the social fabric of work life becomes entirely destroyed (Zuboff 1988, Garson 1989).

Adult educators can explore together with their students ways of creating a work environment where individual workers can rely on mutual support and encouragement, thereby strengthening the attempts to shape this environment in accordance with worker-defined needs and interests. At the Lindemann Center in Chicago,

Illinois, adult educators assist in various forms of community organization. One could imagine a parallel assistance for developing forms of organization, task forces, and support groups which deal with employment-related issues of the nature described above.

BUILDING PARTNERSHIPS BETWEEN EDUCATION AND WORKERS

Although the importance of building a 'partnership between education and business' has been noted, written, and talked about, little has been suggested for a partnership between education and workers in their demands for self-determination and a humane work environment. While we have extensive lists of what business needs from the workers of the future, and equally extensive proposal for educators to prepare and train workers in accordance with these needs, we have not developed lists of concerns, problems, and demands as viewed by workers themselves. Where are the educational programmes that assume the workers' perspective and develop proposals for preparing and training business to respond to workers' needs? Where are the programmes that lend assistance and expertise to workers' attempts in identifying and articulating their demands, and in finding ways to have these demands met?

Isolated examples for these attempts exist, however. The Highlander Center in East Tennessee has a long tradition of placing its educational efforts within a broad context of social and economic justice while committed to concrete, practical changes on the local level. Among its current programmes are workshops which teach participants to research the 'economic impact of living in a toxic/polluted environment', and 'economic education work' in co-operation with a statewide organization helping people to develop long term economic alternatives' to plant closings in their community ('Highlander Program Updates' in *Highlander Reports*, Spring 1990: 6).

Another example is provided by Derber (1987). He reports how a team of faculty and graduate students from Boston College worked together with union leaders as well as rank and file in various manufacturing and service industries to develop an innovative labour education model. The project was based on the assumption of 'a *new partnership* between universities and labor federations committed to providing to labor many of the analytical tools and forms of information traditionally offered to managers' and on 'the need for a *new critical social curriculum* that would stretch labor's sense of its capacities and rights to chart its own economic destiny' (ibid. 50).[3] Another example is the Twin Streams Education Center in Chapel Hill, North Carolina which has been an agent in the worker-ownership movement, 'linking people, problems, and strategies' (see conference brochure, 'Building Friendship, Skills, Power,' of the Fourth North Carolina Worker-Ownership Conference, June 1984). In Chicago, Illinois, DePaul University and an independent community organization co-sponsored a conference on women and work, directly focusing on issues and demands voiced by women workers, and providing opportunities for the conference participants to develop strategies for putting these demands into practice.[4]

Apart from activities like the ones described above, others are possible as well. In his book *The Poor Cousin* (1979: 236–9) Michael Newman makes suggestions for 'survival learning', primarily for people who are without work. He lists possible educational activities which can prove useful not only for the unemployed, but also for people who want to examine the context of their work in order to find ways of changing it. Among other things, Newman proposes the 'training of professionals and activists', the formation of 'study groups and lecture series' in adult education centres, the provision of 'information on how to become self-employed', and lending assistance in forming 'nondirective support groups' (ibid.).

RESCUING THE SUBJECTIVE DIMENSION OF WORK

Activities and programmes like these are based on the actual knowledge and experience of the workers, and try to develop educational responses to some of their problems and concerns.

I believe that these problems and concerns and the educational questions as well as learning potential they contain could be a prime area for educational research. This would also mean contributing to the validation of the subjective dimension of work, i.e. of the producers' own knowledge about their work, a knowledge which encompasses immeasurably more than the various reasoning, problem-solving, or interpersonal skills listed as required for future jobs. It is knowledge about power, injustice, violence done to the body and soul of the worker, but also about the joy of creativity and productivity, relations of solidarity, and of an affirmation of self and life even under demeaning and destructive conditions. With his book *Working* (1974), Studs Terkel sets a unique example of bringing to light these experiences, and the knowledge about work and production contained in them. This was recognized by the Boston College labour education team as well. As Derber (1987: 55) writes:

> A primary lesson learned is that the union must play a role in the development of these innovative curricula. Workers themselves are the repository of much of the knowledge required to understand their changing industries and jobs and of the strategies required to save them. Worker education for 'economic literacy' not only means transmitting ideas and information from economics and other social science disciplines but it also means helping workers crystallize and pull together their own observations and insights about how their industry is being transformed, and it means facilitating their own process of developing options for themselves and their unions.

The innovative Master's Program at the School for New Learning (DePaul University, Chicago) is a model for work-related learning which allows for some of these explorations, although within the context of students' existing career paths or aspirations. The students (with diverse work-related backgrounds) stay together for the first year of the programme where they learn to communicate and interact with each other in egalitarian, non-competitive ways. This process, and the fact that it takes place outside the students' work environment, contributes to a sense of safety, where many issues which could never be expressed at the work site can be articulated and discussed. In their evaluations of the programme, the students generally see this experience as the most important one. This sheds some new light on the issue of partnerships between business and education, where the creation of such a safe space will most likely not be possible, since the knowledge and experience which are articulated in such safe spaces are inevitably subversive because they challenge the power-bound, hierarchical relations of work. From a perspective of an affirmation of usefulness and life, however, the really important questions are buried precisely in this knowledge.

REDEFINING COMPETENCE

As discussed in this book, the issue of relevant knowledge and skills is at the centre of discussions of the current and future reality of work. Related questions have been framed entirely within the confines of the status quo, from the perspective of a view from above, and based on a narrow definition of work as paid employment in primarily large bureaucratic organizations and entirely dependent on new technology. The overall structure of argumentation allowed by this framework eradicates most complexities by proposing a limited set of simple cause-effect relationships:

1 Change is affected by technological progress which is affecting the economy.
2 While the economy is thus 'technology-driven', economic growth is directly affected by education which is therefore called upon to produce adequately prepared 'human capital'.

The idea that work with and on new technology is of a higher order and requires higher skills than work which does not involve this technology, is part and parcel of this view.

In Chapters 5 and 8 I criticized this view as lacking a strong foundation in empirical reality, and as being rooted in a complex hierarchy of values surrounding the culturally prevailing notion of progress. The equation of work on high technology as work of a higher order emanates from a cultural definition of what constitutes higher skills, important knowledge, and methods of arriving at such knowledge. Likewise, this definition is responsible for the devaluation or invisibility of skills, knowledge, and modes of knowing which lie outside the orbit of technological or scientific thinking.

I believe that an education for life must pay systematic attention to such skills, competences, and modes of knowing. Similarly to my analysis of mothering as a productive process (Chapter 12), adult educators must study the many different productive experiences of other subsistence producers who have shaped and accumulated knowledge about life and nature which is in many ways superior for the task of guaranteeing human survival. Much of this knowledge has been destroyed already by scientific–technological 'progress', especially in the form of development projects which dispossess the original subsistence producers, disregard their knowledge, and impose allegedly superior production processes. In such a way, vital knowledge is forever lost.[5]

THE NEW SURVIVAL LEARNING

Within this context, 'survival learning' (Newman 1979) takes on a new meaning. If we want to survive, physically, psychologically, and spiritually, we need to learn new, alternative ways of dealing with nature, with each other, and with ourselves. While education can, of course, not be expected to bring about such transformations, it is nevertheless placed in a position of central importance. It can begin to introduce new themes into the discussion of work and productivity, and explore the educational implications of these themes. What would educational programmes and responses look like if they were oriented towards an affirmation of life rather than profit? towards preservation and renewal rather than limitless exploitation of nature? towards social responsibility and community rather than individual success? towards building relationships of love and care rather than control? towards work as a form of self-expression and sensuous enjoyment rather than a form of submission to technology and distance from material reality? What kinds of knowledge, skills, and abilities are needed to realize the vision contained in these themes?

The abilities, skills,and forms of knowledge implied by these new themes are infinitely more complex and challenging than the reasoning and problem-solving skills listed as required for jobs and careers. They cannot simply be relegated to a separate world of work but signify an entire way of life. Ultimately, they constitute more than 'skills' but signify a new morality. At the core of this new morality lies an acknowledgement of interdependence, and thus of constraints and limitations to personal freedom. In Elizabeth Cagan's words (1978), at the core of this new morality lies the deliberate cultivation of a 'collectivist' form of consciousness, with 'interdependence, cooperation, and concern for others' as the 'basic ingredients' (ibid. 236).

Adult education must therefore transcend the limitations of its individualistic and cognitive–psychological paradigm which dominates its theory, and which determines its research agenda. Cagan (1978: 230) describes the psychological and cultural dimension of individualism as having

> three distinct, though not mutually exclusive components ... : first, self-determination, the belief that the individual is in control of his own destiny; second, self-actualization, the

> conviction that the good life is attained through acting on one's personal needs and desires; third, self-direction, the desire to be free from social constraints. Not only are these important elements of the belief system of most Americans, but I believe that they are at the same time deeply embedded in their character structure. As such, they are powerful determinants of behavior.

Cagan points out that self-determination, self-actualization, and self-direction are important values, but their one-sided emphasis in American culture tends 'to obscure the social nature of human development and to justify a moral posture of selfishness' (ibid.). She further describes that the severance of individual fulfilment and social engagement actually hampers the development of true individuality, and contributes to conformity and subservience as much as it contributes to the feelings and behaviour of superiority. Acknowledgment of interdependence, and a moral posture of concern and care redefine the oppositional relationship between necessity and freedom in terms of a different morality of human relationships. As Bowles and Gintis write (1976: 272), 'the dogma of repressive education is the dogma of necessity which denies freedom. But we must avoid the alternative dogma of freedom which denies necessity'.[6]

The shaping of communal relations and a corresponding consciousness is as much dependent on institutional support as is the creation of its opposite. While educational theory has investigated the processes of critical reflection and self-reflection, and of changing and transforming meaning perspectives – all of which are essential for emancipatory educational practice – it has shed little light on those processes of teaching and learning which contribute towards egalitarian, reciprocal relationships, based on the virtues of love and concern.[7]

Some suggestions have been made by adult educators, although they have hardly entered the mainstream of adult education thinking. In a conference contribution, Annie Brooks (1990) discussed the intuitive, non-cognitive dimension of critical reflection, and its tie to religious beliefs which emphasize social responsibility. In my own work (Hart 1984, 1985, 1990a, and 1990b) I have been pursuing the communal, interactive dimension of emancipatory education.[8]

Educational theory needs to study systematically the abilities, virtues, and sensitivities that are needed for a communal existence, abilities which crystallize around respect and love for life, and which can therefore not be removed from the material and sensuous dimension of life. This means paying attention to the non-cognitive dimensions of learning which are rooted in such life-affirming experiences as joy, pleasure, passion and creativity. It means studying the liberatory potential of intuitive, metaphorical and imaginative-playful modes of thinking and knowing. Adult education can learn much from child education, where the education of the senses, especially in the form of art, has been a traditional theme.[9] I believe that these capacities and modes of knowing are essential prerequisites for engaging in anticipatory, Utopian thought and action. However, they are also vital for an empathetic, imaginative bridging of individual and cultural differences. Maria Lugones (1990) has coined the phrase of 'playful "world"-travelling', an imaginary journey to another person's reality, without forcing one's own reality on to this other person's world. I believe that such an ability is vital for experiencing individual and cultural difference with enjoyment rather than fear, where difference causes appreciation rather than the wish to appropriate it imperialistically or keep this difference at bay as unbridgably 'other'. It is therefore an ability which contributes to community-building in a larger sense of the word.

SUMMARY AND CONCLUSIONS

In this book I proposed to develop a concept of work out of those human endeavours which are based on interactive, non-possessive relations to nature, self, and others, and which are directly oriented towards use and life. I proposed to develop the principles and premises of an education which is similarly productive in the life-giving, life-enhancing sense as production for life. I argued that an education for life must deliberately re-establish the original connection between human work or production and the preservation and improvement of life. Such an education must therefore reappropriate the meaning and reality of human productivity for its own theories and practices. As I described in this book, the consequences of accepting the importance of productivity, understood as a substantive, life-enhancing process, are manifold and far-reaching. Above all, instead of being merely adaptive, with an emphasis on functionality and instrumental rationality, education becomes a critical, transformative project. Furthermore, education becomes an empowering process because it remains attuned to individual experience, and purposefully organizes its own practices in ways which help the learners to reflect upon and understand their individual experience, and because its practices are explicitly oriented towards helping the learners understand their individual experience in the light of an equally understood social reality. Because of its foundation in experience and its future-oriented, transformative outlook, education for life must pay tribute to the organization of time as contained in the structure of experience itself: it must allow a learning rhythm which alternates between short-term learning processes where information is gathered and accumulated and technical skills and abilities are shaped, and long-term learning processes where one's sense of self, one's meaning perspective, and the parameters of experience itself are transformed.

My attempt to outline the contours of an education for life has been an attempt to criticise the distortions and limitations of predominant views on work and education. It was also concerned with a clarification of the proper order within a number of important relationships: the social and the technological, work and its product, the productive process and its material conditions, and the subjective and objective dimensions of work. Finally, I tried to define an alternative concept of work and education out of experiences which have always existed alongside the non-productive or destructive reality of industrial–patriarchal work, although they have been neglected, hidden or denied because they do not follow the rationality of separation and control, do not 'fit' the parameters of current thinking. As I claimed in this book, it is in these experiences that the most important questions and concerns not only for society, but also for education are located. To reveal those experiences, to let the questions contained in them come into view, and to develop corresponding educational programmes and procedures is a task which I see more and more connected with the issue of human survival. In the light of the ongoing destruction of the very foundation of our existence, the erosion of internal and external resources, to ask questions against the grain, and to engage in Utopian thinking becomes a matter of the most serious and conscientious realism. This book is only a beginning, hopefully providing an impetus for many others to build on and continue my work.

NOTES

INTRODUCTION

1 For a detailed critique of various measures of the GNP see Waring 1989.

1 THE NEW INTERNATIONAL DIVISION OF LABOUR

1 The old international division of labour 'meant that raw materials were produced in the colonies or ex-colonies, that they were transported to the industrialized countries in Europe and the USA, and later also Japan, that they were transformed into industrial products which were then marketed either in the industrialized countries themselves, or exported' (Mies 1986: 112). Mies emphasizes that the old international division of labour also relied on cheap labour, and that labour costs 'were kept low partly by force (for example in plantations), by a system of slave labour, or by other forms of labour control (for example, indentureship) which prevented the emergence of the free wage-labourer, the prototype of the industrial worker in the West' (Mies 1986: 112).

2 Industrial relocation now also affects 'capital-intensive crisis-ridden industries (and those that are polluting or incur high antipollution costs), such as automobiles, shipbuilding, steel, and petrochemicals' (Frank 1983: 191). Furthermore, many Third World countries increasingly produce agricultural goods for export, many of which are luxury items like flowers or strawberries (Mies 1986: 114).

3 For a description of the debate behind this term, and the formation of the 'Bielefeld Approach' see Mies 1986: 33, and Mies 1983.

4 Safa (1986: 59) cites a particularly illustrative example of keeping on theoretical blinders even in the face of massive counter-evidence: 'Despite considerable study by the International Labour Organisation and others on the macroeconomic effects of export-processing industries, few have given attention to the type of labor force recruited, other than to characterize it as cheap and unskilled. Many studies do not even mention that the great majority of workers are women. The high rate of female employment represents a radical departure from the pattern of

most multinationals, which generally employ men in highly mechanized, capital-intensive industry.'

5 Motherhood is not the only aspect of women's reality that is 'explained' in biological determinist ways. Popular as well as scientific accounts of female behaviour portray women as being practically all their lives in the grips of their biology, from the debilitating effects of the monthly cycle to the 'hormonal hurricanes' of menopause (Fausto-Sterling 1985). Apart from the fact that female biology has a tendency to appear principally diseased when compared with the norm of male biology, the overall message is that femaleness is explained to a much larger degree by biological 'facts' than maleness which is regarded as rooted primarily in the social domain (see also MacCormack 1980). The view of nineteenth century medical science that 'woman is a pair of ovaries with a human being attached, whereas man is a human being furnished with a pair of testes' (quoted in Fausto-Sterling 1985: 90) is still in currency today although no longer expressed as bluntly. In a peculiar twist of logic, however, modern sociobiologists, on the other hand, today 'explain' and justify male dominance in terms of their (superior) biology (Fausto-Sterling 1985).

6 Although the marriage contract is a form of labour contract, it 'is the only important legal contract in which the terms are not listed' (Cronan 1973: 218). Among other things, this means that the wife has no regulated working hours, there are no 'government standards' of safe working conditions, there are no pension plans, holidays or vacation, etc. As the statistics of wife beating and the occurrence of marital rape (Schechter 1982, Tong 1984) show, the working conditions of the housewife are extremely hazardous and often life-threatening.

7 The many forms of direct violence and coercion – from the barrack-like living or working conditions in global factories, of South African mining camps, of migrant workers in the United States, of 'guest workers' in Western Europe (to name only a few examples) – all testify to the ongoing trend of a diminishing regard for human rights in conjunction with a diminishing importance of free wage labour.

8 Frequently, these assumptions are supported by repressive or openly militaristic political structures that guarantee a 'favourable' employment and investment climate.

2 THE EXPORT OF SEXUAL INEQUALITY

1 In her study of *The Lacemakers of Narsapur* (1982) Mies gives a detailed account of how Indian peasant housewives directly produce for the world market. See also Mies 1986, von Werlhof 1985c.

2 For other examples and studies see Mies 1986: 133; von Werlhof 1985c and 1985a; Bennholdt-Thomsen 1988a and 1988b, and Rogers 1980.

3 See, for instance, Sen and Grown 1987, for a summary for the effect of 'development' on women; see also Beneria 1984, Loufti 1985, Momsen and Townsend 1987, Shiva 1989, Waring 1989, and the publications on

'Women, Work and Development' commissioned by the International Labor Office (1828 L. Street N.W., Washington, DC 20036).

4 For the discussion of a similar situation in East Asia see Grossman 1979, and Fuentes and Ehrenreich 1983. There is a striking resemblance between the creation of a new industrial labour force in certain Third World countries and the creation of the first industrial labour force in the United States which consisted mainly of young farmers' daughters, expected to contribute to the financial well-being of their families rather than to their own independent existence. Like their sisters in multinational-controlled factories they were also not expected to stay in the labour force permanently. Furthermore, in both cases labour discipline was tied to a paternalistic ideology (see Kessler-Harris 1982).

5 There exists an alarming resemblance between employment policies directed at women during the Third Reich of Nazi Germany, and employment practices of multinational corporations. As Tröger (1984) reports, the Nazis were not against women working in the newly Taylorized factories of Germany, but against women working for decent pay, and with access to social insurance benefits. The ideology of motherhood was directly employed to create 'gender suitable' work, i.e. work that paid less, was only temporary, was therefore ineligible for benefits, as well as highly monotonous and repetitive.

6 Sandra is one of the women Fernández-Kelly interviewed.

7 See Waring 1989 for a more recent critique of econometrists' failure to count 'traditional' female labour.

8 UN mid-Decade World Conference for Women, Document # WOM/C, July 11–13, 1980.

3 A NEW SEXIST DIVISION OF LABOUR

1 See Evans and Nelson 1989 on the history of changing myths and ideological justifications for paying women less than men. Their book *Wage Justice* gives a detailed account of the Minnesota campaign to implement pay equity for public employees.

2 Wilson (1987) gives an example of the ideological consequences of the acceptance of the family wage by distorting or entirely neglecting not only Black women's employment history and current situation, but also their many contributions to the survival and well-being of the Black community. Wilson operates entirely within a framework of the (White) middle-class nuclear family where 'the family's', i.e. children's *and* women's economic well-being is entirely dependent on the presence of a male 'breadwinner'. His example also illustrates how 'mainstream' assumptions are always 'malestream' as well.

3 Not only are there many examples of the same activity being alternately considered male or female work depending on the cultural context (Momsen and Townsend 1987), but also examples of typically male work changing into typically female work within the same cultural context (e.g. teachers, clerical workers, healers). Thus, to affix the sexual division of labour to specific tasks is of only limited value.

4 For instance, to name only a few, there are differences with respect to the percentage of Black and White women's employment in personal and institutional service (30 to 18 per cent) and with respect to continued work in paid employment after the birth of children: 'Only White women show a drop in participation rates during the childbearing years' (Lloyd and Niemi 1979: 37). Further, there are major differences with respect to trends in marital status (see Jones 1986: 305). All these factors translate into quite different everyday realities for Black and White women.

5 Recent studies dealing with changes in women's employment conditions due to the introduction of new technologies are particularly promising for a sharpening of our understanding of the sexist division of labour. These changes often either reinforce existing segregation along the lines of work on and with new technology, or they directly sharpen the division among the sexes (see, for instance, Cockburn 1983; Form and McMillen 1983, Machung 1984, Wright 1987, and especially Game and Pringle 1983). Analyses dealing with the over-representation of women in part-time jobs are also very important (see *Working at the Margins* 1986; Beechy and Perkins 1987; Holden and Hansen 1987). The task remains to gather systematically the information made available in these studies and to solidify the understanding of common underlying mechanisms through further research which explicitly looks at differences in work relations.

6 Machung, and others (see Cockburn 1983, Game and Pringle 1983, Strober and Arnold 1987), describe the growing sexual stratification in many work places where the introduction of new technology alters the content and organization of phases of production or work. Apart from management decisions that assign women to the now de-skilled and less desirable aspects of work, male workers often also immediately engage in a power struggle to reserve the less stressful and more prestigious tasks.

7 There are some feminist theorists who are beginning to move away from either exclusively dealing with women's situation on the labour market or with the oppressive conditions of women within the family. See, for instance, Sokoloff (1980: 213) who proposes 'a unity of opposites – housework and market work', and Beechy (1987: 146), who recognizes this unity, revising an earlier position. See also Game and Pringle (1983) for an excellent theoretical analysis of the relationship of women's work to issues of power.

8 Apart from individual exceptions (which are few and far between, see Hochschild 1989), exclusive responsibility is a socially defined state. Thus, proposals for policy changes almost always include the establishment of better childcare facilities as a major 'solution' to the problem of working mothers. These proposals unerringly leave the underlying sexual division of work with children, as well as the whole 'children question', entirely unchallenged. Calls for 'paternity leaves' are a step in the right direction, although by themselves they will not be able to change the overall structure of the sexual division of labour, and the predominant patriarchal-capitalist concept of work.

9 It could be argued that men likewise have to bring their 'manliness' into their work, or sell their masculinity together with their labour power because work as well as workers are both 'gendered'. However, because gender relations are hierarchical and power-bound, 'masculinity' carries a great deal of social and cultural power as well as corresponding material and psychological benefits in addition to its oppressive features. Sexuality means something different for men and for women: where for women it signifies (passive) availability and accessibility, for men it means self-assertion, agency, and control. Furthermore, to the extent to which women are perceived as personifying sexuality *per se*, they have to carry the additional burden of society's overall repressive and aggressive attitudes to the body and to sexuality.

10 The time-honoured tradition of holding mothers responsible for the problems of their children therefore reflects part of the truth. In the absence of any other social group that is equally burdened not only with the expectation but also with the actual task of raising well-adjusted children, the blame for failure can easily fall on women.

11 See especially Bergmann 1986 for a presentation of this view. The recent discussions around the 'mommy track' (see *Business Week*, 20 March 1989) are based on a similar view of female workers with children as being less valuable or productive.

12 To name only a few references where examples of male disloyalty to women workers, and a consistent lack of solidarity on the workplace can be found: Cockburn 1981, 1983, Bergmann 1986, Feldberg 1986, Machung 1984, McKinnon 1979, Strober and Arnold 1987.

4 GOOD WORK AND LIBERAL EDUCATION FOR CAREERS

1 See Nash and Hawthorne (1987) for a recent report on these kinds of efforts.

2 I am explicitly leaving out the other side of the debate on the crisis in higher education where the new Great Books conservatives fetishize 'tradition' into an icon that 'provides a gilt edge leather cover for the blatant economic and military agenda of concurrent reports' (Grumet 1986: 360).

3 Although Schon himself does not talk about liberal learning, his main concept of 'reflection-in-action' underpinning a new approach to professional education necessitates analytic and evaluative cognitive procedures which bear great similarity with 'liberal learning skills' identified explicitly by others as characterizing successful performance in professional occupations (see, for instance, Chickering 1981).

4 This is of course, closely related to the equally inherently patriarchal core of 'liberal education'.

5 For a detailed description of these procedures as developed by Jürgen Habermas see Hart 1985.

6 Carnegie Foundation report on *Higher Education and the American Resurgence*, quoted in AAACE Newsletter vol. 3 no. 6, November 1985, page 5).

7 Quoted in *The New York Times* supplement 'Survey of Continuing Education', 30 August 1981.

8 Klemp (1982), for instance, presents a considerably eroded version of the skills Chickering discusses. Although he himself does not use the concept of liberal education or even liberal learning, the editor of the collection on liberal learning and business careers where Klemp's essay 'Three factors of success' is included, obviously recognized the resemblance of Klemp's factors to the liberal learning skills discussed in the other contributions (Jones 1982). Chickering (1981: 6) himself credits Klemp with 'major contributions' to research 'which identifies the skills, abilities and other characteristics required for effective work'.

9 The publication *Workplace Basics* (Carnevale *et al.* 1988), issued by the American Society for Training and Development and the US Department of Labor (1988) is a case in point.

5 EDUCATING CHEAP LABOUR

1 See also Bluestone and Harrison 1988. For a discussion of the current economic situation and its relation to education see Shor 1986: 127–30, and Spring 1985.

2 However, to base an entire educational curriculum or reform plan on a certain skills shortage can lead to a situation where the 'curriculum for 25 *million* students in high school and college was tilted after 1983 to supply 40,000 engineers plus the 320,000 computer workers cited by the BLS [Bureau of Labor Statistics]' (Shor 1986: 139).

3 As Perelman (1984: 20–1) reports, education has already become a booming business.

4 See also Shor (1986: 64–5) for a discussion of this point.

5 Almost every issue of *Business Week* carries an item on the 'rapidly tightening labor market', expressing fear of full employment. Significantly, the 'flash point' of what counts as full employment has been shifting. In a commentary by Aaron Bernstein, (19 December 1988, p. 106), the 'trigger point' where 'a lower unemployment level will start to fuel inflation' has changed from 4 per cent in the 1960s to about 5 per cent in the 1980s.

6 The following statistics further undermine the simplicity of the 'decline' argument: 'Working women and men with comparable educational backgrounds do not earn comparable salaries, ... Female high school graduates earn 35 per cent less, on the average, than male high school graduates, and women with college degrees earn 34 per cent less than men with college degrees. In fact, women with college degrees earn $1,988 less per year than male high school graduates and female high school graduates earn $2,478 less per year than males with an eighth-grade education' (*Occupational Segregation* 1988: 3).

7 This is not the place to discuss the political uses of skill as regards women's work; I want to refer the reader to the study 'Sex and Skill' by Phillips and Taylor (1980) for a discussion of this problem, as well as to Bergmann (1986) for a number of illustrative examples of the uses of

skill definitions to exclude women from certain jobs, or from training for certain occupations. See also Gaskell (1986) for a critique of the assumptions behind equating women's skills with low skills.

8 This is reflected in their wages as well as working conditions. In Malaysia, for instance, the women work eight hours a day for six days a week, with changing shifts every two weeks, and for $1.65 an hour (see *Voices Rising*, May/June 1987: 21; see also Grossman 1979).

9 See, for instance, the contributions to the special issue of the *Annals of the American Academy of Political and Social Science*, titled 'Unemployment: A global challenge' (June 1987). Furthermore, the policies of the World Bank (International Bank for Reconstruction and Development/IBRD), the major development agency of the world, has for over a decade recognized not only the potential explosiveness of this trend, but also its potential profitability. As Bennholdt-Thomsen reports in her article 'Investment in the poor' (1988a), the IBRD attempts to make the still 'tangible assets, however meagre' (McNamara) available for profit by drawing the poor into commercial agriculture as wageless subsistence producers. While the 'productivity' of the poor increases, their poverty remains unchanged. It would be worth studying similar trends of labour surplus absorption in industrialized countries, particularly those suggestions that praise various forms of 'self-employment' (see, for instance, Handy 1984).

10 By living in a highly segregated city like Chicago, one easily gets the impression that the inner city Black population has been entirely given up by society (including business). Deploring these people's skill levels nevertheless serves an important political purpose: to justify the dismissal or social neglect of these populations.

11 As reported by CBS''60 Minutes' (18 February 1990), employment agencies blatantly and systematically discriminate against minorities, especially those who apply for jobs which bring them in contact with the public.

12 The study team which put together the report on *Enhancing Literacy* (1989) decided on a 'continuum' definition of literacy, creating room for non-readers, those needing basic skills, and those needing upgrading (p. 15). The authors admit, however, that such measures may still be inappropriate for a workplace context (ibid. 15). In Harman's words (1987: 36): 'There simply is no magical point of literacy at which individuals become employable, perform well on their jobs, carry out the responsibilities of citizenship, qualify for citizenship rights, or become good parents'.

13 Johnston and Packer (1987: 79) make other contradictory statements. For instance, in the context of discussing 'the impacts of slow population and labor force growth' they state that 'labor markets will be tighter, due to the slower growth of the workforce and the smaller reservoir of well-qualified workers'; within the context of discussing the factors 'most responsible for the increasing competitiveness of the world economy', on the other hand, they cite 'the glut of natural resources, manufactured goods, *and educated workers*' leading to a 'relentless' competition among producers and workers (op. cit. 49, my emphasis).

14 As Cyert and Mowery (1987: 25–6) report, re-training of currently employed workers whose technical skills have become obsolete in connection with the introduction to new technology is less of a concern to employers than lack of basic skills because this makes such re-training difficult if not impossible.

15 There exists, of course, a large body of critical writings and studies which are written from the perspective of the workers themselves, continuing the tradition Karl Marx started with his famous essay on 'Alienated Labour'. One of the better-known writings is Harry Braverman's *Labor and Monopoly Capital* (1974).

16 'Literacy after NAEP – New beginnings' *Online*, vol. 16, no. 6, January 1988, p. 3.

17 Such a class bias is obviously widely accepted among adult educators. Otherwise, the callous and condescending remarks made by McKenzie could not appear in a collection titled *Selected Writings on Philosophy and Adult Education* (Merriam 1984). McKenzie portrays the average worker as pathologically passive, as 'other directed to the point of intellectual and moral vassalage' (p. 83), with his principle virtue being 'bovine docility' and his 'chief activity' being 'bowing and scraping (p. 84). (Ironically, after such a devastating portrayal of large numbers of Americans, McKenzie calls for a 'unified humanity'.)

18 Apart from the above-mentioned basic skills they include 'basic problem-solving', and the ability to 'think through and take ownership of the problems [workers] unearth' (report from 'Building a Quality Workforce', conference at Washington, DC, see *Chicago Tribune*, 19 July 1988); see also Carnevale *et al.* (1988) who list such skills as 'knowing how to learn', 'creative thinking and problem-solving', 'personal management', 'group effectiveness', and 'leadership'.

19 A historic parallel is the Victorian ideal of true womanhood towards which all women were expected to aspire regardless of the reality of their lives.

20 Today, these informal aspects, frequently constituting a unique worker culture outside or in opposition to officially sanctioned work relations, are directly taken up and incorporated into the training schemes themselves. To the extent to which these schemes represent the perspective of management, hitherto untouched realms of working life are subsumed under a context of utilization and control (see also Chapter 9).

21 See, for instance Klemp 1982, Carnevale *et al.* 1988. Some programmes offered by states trying to lure business into their region promise to instil 'positive attitudes' and to create 'dedicated workers' including 'trainee orientation on the free enterprise system and its value for the worker' as part of an overall favourable investment climate (*Texas Facts*, quoted by Goodman 1979: 30). It seems that in so-called right-to-work states, characterized by a strong anti-union sentiment, an infrastructure is to be created that is to replicate as much as possible the conditions of overseas operations.

6 THE CHANGING FORMS OF SUBSISTENCE LABOUR

1 For examples of this usage of the term see the contributions to *Households and the World-Economy* (Smith *et al.* 1984).

2 The work of mothering has recently been reclaimed by feminist writers who analyse its oppressive reality but also its potential for providing models for creative and constructive work, and for a non-alienating and preserving attitude towards (inner and outer) nature (see, for instance, the collection of articles in Trebilcot 1984; see also Chapter 11).

3 The current debate around the notion of a 'mommy track', instigated by Felice Schwartz' suggestion that companies provide different 'tracks' for women who want to be mothers and for women who want to remain childless, illustrates this point remarkably well (see 'The mommy track', *Business Week*, 20 March 1989).

4 The issue is further complicated by the fact that these 'choices' and corresponding experiences are fundamentally different for White and African-American women. In Jones' account of the history of Black women's work, the desire to be able to stay home and raise children has been a strong, and for the most part unfulfilled one (Jones 1986). Far from being backward, it recognizes Black women's self-interest, and of their experience of wage labour.

5 See Modigliani (1986) for an account of how the pay and conditions of childcare reflect the overall devaluation of female labour; see also a report in the *Chicago Tribune* (8 October 1989). It is interesting to note that Modigliani sees the ultimate cause of this devaluation not merely in the fact that childcare workers do 'women's work', but that children, and what they represent, are devalued in our society. I would enlarge the argument and say that giving birth to and raising children is devalued because it is oriented towards life rather than profit, and because it is inherently tied to the realm of necessity (see next chapter).

7 NECESSITY AND FREEDOM

1 Such a view is possible only if the work of giving birth to and raising children is entirely screened out, literally left in a 'state of nature'.

2 The biologistic view of childbearing as an expression of 'fertility', i.e. a primarily biological rather than social event, is the result of a patriarchal evaluation and treatment of this ability. One of the most dramatic consequences of this 'naturalization' of women's labour and productive capacity can be seen in the systematic dispossession and destruction of female knowledge about birth and birth control, both in Europe during the time of the witch hunts, as well as in the European colonies (Becker *et al.* 1977, Ehrenreich and English 1979, Merchant 1983, Mies 1986). It is probably impossible to measure the extent of damage done not only to female but also to male self-identity in the process of shaping a Western feminine and masculine social character which stems from the ideological expropriation of this creative capacity by rendering it, and

treating it, as a handicap, a burden, a disability, or a compensation for the lack of the actual 'creative tool' (Lacan), i.e. the phallus.

3 See, for instance, Murray Bookchin's body of work, and especially Shiva 1989. In the past decade, feminist critiques of science have emerged as a growing field. See, for instance, Birke 1986, Keller 1985, Harding 1986, Harding and O'Barr 1987, Bleier 1988.

4 It is important to note that well into the nineteenth century the notion of 'nature' retained a number of different meanings, for instance, the association of nature with a realm or state which had not become corrupted by civilization, or with the untamable wildness of primitive peoples or savages. The retention of these meanings accounts for the ambivalent evaluation of femininity and female sexuality, where, on the one hand, women's 'natural' moral purity and civilizing influence was stressed, and, on the other hand, their irrationality in form of uncontrollable passions (Jordanova 1980).

5 As Haraway (1988: 84) correctly points out, 'nature–culture and feminine–masculine lace into networks with each other; the terms do not relate as isomorphisms or unidirectional parallels. That is, the paired distinctions feminine–masculine, body–mind, nature–culture, animal–human, and so on are systematically related to each other, but in many ways'.

6 Shiva (1989) convincingly argues that only such a view of nature, where human beings live in ecological harmony with the natural conditions of their lives, and where they respect and support 'the continued capacity of nature to renew its forests, fields and rivers' (ibid. 115) will guarantee human survival.

8 THE RECONCEPTUALIZATION OF SKILLS

1 Her viewpoint, her examples and her overall approach reveal, however, that the dilemma she talks about is not constituted by 'the body' but rather by the fact that 'laboring bodies' have minds and wills, posing a difficulty or 'dilemma' for those who want to control their labour and the products of their labour.

2 As discussed in Chapter 5, the idea that work in the future will be primarily of the type of knowledge work described by Zuboff has very little foundation in reality. Zuboff (1988) herself describes the predominance of the 'automating', i.e. routinizing and 'de-skilling' use of new technology rather than its 'informating' use which is associated with the need for theoretical understanding and the employment of 'intellective skills'. Although, as she writes, the technology itself contains a potential for using many important reasoning and theoretical abilities as well as a potential for more democratic, participatory work relations, existing social relations point in the direction of greater polarization of (in this sense) skilled and unskilled or routinized labour.

3 Zuboff (1988) provides excellent descriptions of this process, and of the psychological trauma many workers experienced when their workplaces were restructured.

4 Zuboff's account of the restructuring of work 'in the age of the smart machine' (1988) illustrates this mechanism very well. In her descriptions it appears that the early factory owners were, like the early colonialists, confronted with uncivilized savages. They had to tame 'the animality' and 'uncontrollability' of the [worker's] body', (ibid. 29), they were charged with the noble task of freeing 'the production process from the organic limits of the body', as exemplified by the (untamed) worker's 'instinctual' and downright 'dysfunctional, uncontrolled, and irregular behavior' (ibid. 30, 31, 34). It is not a coincidence that Taylor 'scientifically selected' for his first study a worker whom he described as 'a man of the type of the ox, – no rare specimen of humanity, difficult to find and therefore very highly prized' (quoted in Braverman 1974: 108). In both cases, the terminology that emphasizes the body, instincts, or that draws on comparisons with the animal world describes the workers as being in a state of 'nature' rather than 'civilization'.

9 THE TRIUMPH OF INSTRUMENTAL RATIONALITY

1 Of related significance is the technological flipside of ideologically pre-determined consent. Zuboff (1988: 182), for instance, discusses how the incorporation of skills into the design and function of a piece of technology very often 'obviates the necessity of human skills', and thereby also the necessity for conscious human thought and decision-making. She illustrates the logical extreme of this process by the history of weaponry where nuclear weapons have become a form of weaponry 'which has so completely embodied the human skills associated with battle that it has eliminated requirements for both human skill *and* human presence in the conduct of battle (ibid. 183). She quotes Elain Scarry who writes that 'the building-in of skill thus becomes, in its most triumphant form, the building-out of consent'.

2 As I describe elsewhere (Hart 1990b), Mezirow's own use of Habermas' categories is somewhat inconsistent, leading to a liberal, de-politicized version of Habermas' powerful and decidedly radical critical theory (see also Collard and Law, 1989, on this issue). Neither Mezirow nor Marsick mention the problem of dominance relations, although their ideas and the terminology they employ, is soaked with the issue of power.

3 This is the paradigm behind every single management training seminar or course that has been described to me.

4 The suggestions made by Carnevale *et al.* (1988) particularly in the section on 'oral communication', are a case in point. Communication is here reduced entirely to a question of 'voice inflection', 'body language' and 'style'.

10 THE MISEDUCATIVE EXPERIENCE OF WORK

1 In this context it is the sanctity of 'culture' and 'tradition' which canonizes the areas of knowledge the student has to absorb, very much

in the way Freire describes the 'banking method of education'. In the context of work it is the sanctity of the needs of business and industry, and of economic growth, which determine the kinds of skills the workers need to acquire. When seen against the background of the current wave of political and social conservatism, characterized by a strong 'pro-business' and 'pro-family' agenda, it is not surprising that we have recently witnessed a resuscitation of the Great Books approach to education. See, for instance, Bloom 1987, Hirsch 1988.

2 The quasi-automatic association of knowledge work with 'higher skills' therefore mainly feeds on the general allure of new or 'high' technology. In the terms suggested by Zuboff (1988), knowledge work could be of the 'informated' or of 'the automated' kind. As described in an earlier chapter, whereas the former requires substantial technological skills and expertise, the latter requires mainly concentration and endurance.

3 Howard (1986: 103–5) describes similar difficulties in the clerical sector, where the process of translating 'practical action' into the terms of a 'clear-cut and technical problem' has the tendency to cast 'the informal office in a kind of technical cement'.

4 This is the main point behind Noble's account in *Forces of Production* (1984). He describes in detail how the introduction of new technology, and especially an 'unchecked drive to automate' (ibid. 349) are fed by many other considerations besides productivity, which is often the least concern.

5 Hayes (1989) provides excellent examples of such behaviour, culminating in a compulsive attachment to work itself, and spreading to all other areas of life.

6 These assumptions also underly the practice of multi-skilling or 'pay-for-knowledge', another version of 'flexibility', here understood in terms of 'substitutability' (Parker and Slaughter 1988: 110).

11 PRODUCTIVE WORK

1 Probably no other writer has illuminated the minutiae of damages caused by market relations in all, including the most intimate spheres of life, better and more painstakingly than Adorno in his *Minima Moralia* (1974).

12 SUBSISTENCE KNOWING

1 A child raised within the isolation of middle class acceptability is bound to be afraid of otherness, and cannot identify with people who are different if she is to hold on to her sense of self. Such a child will not have the capacity to see herself in others – however different they may be from herself (Lugones 1990).

2 This is true particularly as regards 'expert knowledge' in whose construction the actual producers, i.e. mothers or mothering persons, did not participate.

3 In a similar vein, but within an entirely different context, Dewey (in McDermott 1973: 537) describes the same idea as the 'aesthetic moment' of thought arriving at 'the corporate meanings of objects'.
4 In a conversation Lori Rosenblum pointed out that this is a different, and decidedly positive dimension of the notion that 'a woman's work is never done'.
5 As Mel Paul pointed out during a conversation, Tronto is overly optimistic in her choice of words. Rather than saying '*if* a care-taker has deficient self-knowledge', we should probably all proceed on the basis of an acknowledged deficiency, and consider the gaining of self-knowledge as an ongoing but never-ending achievement. I would add that deficient self-knowledge is not the only source of potential problems. Mothering or care-taking consists in a peculiar and highly volatile mix of authority and dependency. Especially in the absence of strong egalitarian sensibilities and individual identities which are not fixated on power, relations of control can easily assert themselves in many different forms. They may be particularly hard to detect precisely because they occur under the guise of caring and nurturing. Thus, a care-taker might let herself be dominated by the other's needs, or she might make the one she cares for dependent on her and fail to release her from her care-taking power.
6 See, for instance, Culley and Portuges 1985, Belenky *et al.* 1986, Bunch and Pollack 1983, Davis 1985, Minnich *et al.* 1988, Thompson 1983, Weiler 1988.

13 SUMMARY AND CONCLUSIONS: RETHINKING WORK AND EDUCATION

1 The ecology movement, feminist or otherwise, is far from being monolithic, representing diverse viewpoints on problems as well as solutions to ecological crises, some of which replicate the values and structures that led to these crises in the first place. In particular, the branch of the ecology movement which looks at nature as being dependent on us for her survival – rather than the other way round – does not really get at the ultimate causes of environmental destruction. It proposes purely technical solutions, relying on the same means that contributed to the problems. Furthermore, American ecological feminists have been criticized as seeking refuge in a spiritualism which hovers above and beyond the real material structures for whose change it has little to suggest.
2 Both workplaces exist in Chicago, Illinois.
3 The Council for Adult and Experiential Learning (CAEL) has established a number of 'joint ventures' with corporations as well as unions. In contrast with the Boston College experiment, however, employees of participating organizations are matched with programmes at existing educational institutions.
4 The workshops had the following titles: alternative ways of living and working with children; creating family-oriented work cultures; creating

low-stress work environments; creating non-racist work environments; challenging sexist hiring, promotion, and pay systems; female bonding: mentoring and mutual support; eliminating sexual harassment, economic self-sufficiency.

5 For a detailed discussion of this point and descriptions of concrete examples see Shiva 1989.

6 Although I agree with this part of the quote, the rest of it reveals the familiar male as well as Marxist bias against necessity: 'Indeed freedom and individuality arise only through a confrontation with necessity, and personal powers develop only when pitted against a recalcitrant reality'. Thus, an acceptance of necessity is still clad in the terms of battle and resistance in these writers' minds.

7 For a more detailed discussion see Hart 1990b.

8 Other writers have taken up the issue of social responsibility in broader terms by discussing the importance of linking education with larger movements of social change (see, for instance, Heany and Horton 1990). The field of international education, especially in the Third World, is considerably more promising. Here the connections between education and society are much more clearly perceived and articulated (see especially the contributions in *Convergence*, see also the February special issue on 'Education as Transformation', of *Harvard Educational Review*, and critical replies in the February issue of 1982.

9 See, for instance, the work of Maxine Greene. In a book titled *Fostering Critical Reflection in Adulthood* (Mezirow 1990), Greene makes her theme of the liberatory potential of imagination available to adult educators; see also Greene 1984.

BIBLIOGRAPHY

Adorno, T.W. (1974), *Minima Moralia*, London, NLB.

Allen, J. (ed.) (1990), *Lesbian Philosophies and Cultures*, Albany, New York, State University of New York Press.

Apple, M. (1980), 'The Other Side of the Hidden Curriculum. Correspondence Theories and the Labour Process', *Journal of Education*, vol. 162, no. 1.

Appelbaum, E. (1987), 'Technology and the Redesign of Work in the Insurance Industry', in B.D. Wright (ed.), *Women, Work, and Technology*, Ann Arbor, The University of Michigan Press.

Arendt, H. (1958), *The Human Condition*, Chicago, The University of Chicago Press.

Arizpe. L. and Aranda, J. (1986), 'Women in the Strawberry Agribusiness in Mexico', in E. Leacock and H.I. Safa (eds), *Women's Work*, South Hadley, Massachusetts, Bergin and Garvey.

Aronowitz, S. (1980), 'Politics and Higher Education in the 1980's', *Journal of Education*, vol. 162, no. 3.

Aronowitz, S. and Giroux, H.A. (1985), *Education Under Siege*, South Hadley, Massachusetts, Bergin and Garvey.

Barbier, E. (1986), 'Economic Growth: the Political Economy of Resource Misallocation', in P. Ekins (ed.), *The Living Economy*, London, Routledge and Kegan Paul.

Becker, G. *et al.* (1977), *Aus der Zeit der Verzweiflung*, Frankfurt, edition suhrkamp.

Beechy, V. (1987) *Unequal Work*, Norfolk, Thetford Press.

Beechy, V. and Perkins, T. (1987), *A Matter of Hours: Women, Part-time Work, and the Labor Market*, Minneapolis, University of Minnesota Press.

Belenky, M.F. *et al.* (1986), *Women's Ways of Knowing*, New York, Basic Books.

Bennholdt-Thomsen, V. (1984), 'Towards a Theory of the Sexual Division of Labor', in J. Smith *et al.* (eds), *Households and the World Economy*, Beverly Hills, Sage Press.

—— (1988),'The Future of Women's Work and Violence Against Women', in M. Mies (ed.), *Women – The Last Colony*, London, Zed Press.

—— (1988a), '"Investment in the Poor": An Analysis of World Bank Policy', in M. Mies (ed.), *Women – The Last Colony*, London, Zed Press.

—— (1988b), 'Why do Housewives Continue to be Created in the Third World too?', in M. Mies (ed.), *Women – the Last Colony*, London, Zed Press.

Bergmann, B. (1986), *The Economic Emergence of Women*, New York, Basic Books.

Bernstein, A. (1988) 'Where the Jobs are is Where the Skills Aren't', *Business Week*, 19 September 1988.

Bernstein, R. (1967), *John Dewey*, New York, Washington Square Press.

Birke, L. (1986), *Women, Feminism, and Biology*, New York, Methuen.

Bleier, R. (ed.) (1988), *Feminist Approaches to Science*, New York, Pergamon Press.

Bloom, A. (1987), *The Closing of the American Mind*, New York, Simon and Schuster.

Bluestone, B. and Harrison, B. (1982), *The Deindustrialization of America*, New York, Basic Books.

—— (1988), *The Great U-Turn: Corporate Restructuring and the Polarization of America*, New York, Basic Books.

Bookchin, M. (1982), *The Ecology of Freedom*, Palo Alto, California, Cheshire Books.

Bowles, S. and Gintis, H. (1976), *Schooling in Capitalist America*, New York, Basic Books.

Bravermann, H. (1974), *Labor and Monopoly Capital*, New York, Monthly Review Press.

Bridenthal, R. *et al.* (eds) (1984), *When Biology Became Destiny*, New York, Monthly Review Press.

Brooks, A. (1990), 'Making Trouble in Corporate America: Critical Reflection Within a Fortune 500 Company', *Proceedings*, 31st Adult Education Research Conference, Athens, Georgia, The University of Georgia.

Brown, C. and Pechman, J.A. (eds) (1987), *Gender in the Workplace*, Washington, D.C., The Brookings Institute.

Bunch, S. and Pollack, S. (eds) (1983), *Learning Our Way*, Trumansburg, New York, The Crossing Press.

Cagan, E. (1978), 'Individualism, Collectivism, and Radical Educational Reform', *Harvard Educational Review*, vol. 48, no. 2.

Carlson, D. (1982), 'Updating Individualism and the Work Ethic: Corporate Logic in the Classroom', *Curriculum Inquiry*, vol. 12, no. 2.

Carnevale, A. *et al.* (1988), *Workplace Basics*, Washington, D.C., The American Society for Training and Development, US Department of Labor, Employment and Training Administration.

Carter, V. (1987), 'Office Technology and Relations of Control in Clerical Work Organization', in B. D. Wright (ed.), *Women, Work, and Technology*, Ann Arbor, The University of Michigan Press.

Castello, N. and Richardson, M. (eds) (1982), *Continuing Education for the Post-Industrial Society*, Milton Keynes, The Open University Press.

Charner, I. and Rolzinsky, C.A. (eds) (1987), *Responding to the Educational Needs of Today's Workplace*, New Directions for Continuing Education, no. 33, San Francisco, Jossey-Bass.

Chickering, A. W. (1981), 'Education, Work and Human Development', paper presented to the Mid South Regional Conference Supporting Adult Learners, Memphis State University.

Chilcote, R.E. and Johnson, D.L. (eds) (1983), *Theories of Development*, Beverly Hills, Sage Press.

Christian, B. (1983), *Black Feminist Criticism*, New York, Pergamon Press.

Chynoweth, J.K. (1989), *Enhancing Literacy for Jobs and Productivity*, Washington, D.C., The Council of State Policy and Planning Agencies.

Cockburn, C. (1981), 'The Material of Male Power', *Feminist Review*, vol. 9.

—— (1983), *Brothers: Male Dominance and Technological Change*, London, Pluto Press.

Collard, S. and Law, M. (1989), 'The Limits of Perspective Transformation: A Critique of Mezirow's Theory', *Adult Education Quarterly*, vol. 39, no. 2.

Conger, D.S. and Mullen, D. (1982), 'Life Skills', in C. Klevins (ed.), *Materials and Methods in Adult and Continuing Education*, Los Angeles, Klevens Publishers.

Cronan, S. (1973), 'Marriage', in A. Koedt *et al.* (eds), *Radical Feminism*, New York, Quadrangle Books.

Culley, S. and Portuges, C. (eds) (1985), *Gendered Subjects: The Dynamics of Feminist Teaching*, Boston, Routledge and Kegan Paul.

Cunningham, S. (1987), 'Gender and Industrialization in Brazil', in J.H. Momsen and J. Townsend (eds), *Geography of Gender*, Albany, New York, State University of New York Press.

Cyert, R.M. and Mowery, D.C. (eds) (1987), *Technology and Employment*, Washington, D.C., National Academy Press.

Davis, B.H. (ed.) (1985), *Feminist Education*, Norman, Oklahoma, University of Oklahoma Press.

Derber, C. (1987), 'Worker Education for a Changing Economy: New Labor-Academic Partnerships', in I. Charner and C.A. Rolzinski, *Responding to the Educational Needs of Today's Workplace*, New Directions for Continuing Education, no. 33, San Francisco, Jossey-Bass.

Dewey, J. (1958), *Art and Experience*, New York, Capricorn Press.

—— (1966), *Democracy and Education*, New York, The Free Press (Macmillan).

Dole, E. (1989), 'America's Competitive Advantage: A Skilled Workforce', *Adult Learning*, vol. 1, no. 1.

Dole, R.C. (1980), 'Speculations on the Meaning of the Trend Toward Corporate Education', *Phi Delta Kappan*, January.

Ehrenreich, D. and English, D. (1979), *For Her Own Good*, Garden City, New York, Anchor Press (Doubleday).

Ekins, P. (ed.) (1986), *The Living Economy*, London, Routledge and Kegan Paul.

Entwistle, H. (1970), *Education, Work, and Leisure*, London, Routledge and Kegan Paul.

—— (1978), *Class, Culture and Education*, London, Methuen.

Evans, S.M. and Nelson, B.J. (1989), *Wage Justice*, Chicago, University of Chicago Press.

Evers, H. *et al.* (1984), 'Subsistence Reproduction', in J. Smith *et al.* (eds), *Households and the World Economy*, Beverly Hills, Sage Press.

Fahrenbach, H. (ed.) (1973), *Wirklichkeit und Reflexion (Walter Schulz zum 60. Geburtstag)*, Pfullingen, Verlag Guenther Neske.

Fausto-Sterling, A. (1985), *Myths of Gender*, New York, Basic Books.

Feldberg, R.L. (1986), 'Comparable Worth: Toward Theory and Practice in the United States', in B.C. Gelpi *et al.* (eds), *Women and Poverty*, Chicago, The University of Chicago Press.

Fernández-Kelly, M.P. (1983), *For We Are Sold, I and My People*, Albany, New York, State University of New York Press.

—— (1984), '*Maquiladoras*: The View from the Inside', in K.B. Sacks and D. R. Remy (eds), *My Troubles Are Going to Have Trouble With Me*, New Brunswick, New Jersey, Rutgers University Press.

Ferman, L.A. *et al.* (1987), *The Informal Economy*, Annals of the American Academy of Political and Social Science, vol. 493, September.

Fiegl, V. (1990), *Der Krieg gegen die Frauen*, Bielefeld, Tarantel Frauenverlag.

Form, W. and McMillen, D.B. (1983), 'Women, Men, and Machines', *Work and Occupations*, vol. 10, no. 2.

Fox, M.F. and Hesse-Biber, S. (1984), *Women at Work*, Palo Alto, California, Mayfield.

Frank, A.G. (1983), 'Crisis and Transformation of Dependency in the World System', in R.E. Chilcote and D.L. Johnson (eds), *Theories of Development*, Beverly Hills, Sage Press.

Freire, P. (1970), *Pedagogy of the Oppressed*, New York, Seabury Press.

Fromm, E. (1966), *The Sane Society*, Greenwich, Connecticut, Fawcett.

Fuentes, A. and Ehrenreich, B. (1983), *Women in the Global Factory*, Boston, South End Press.

Galeano, E. (1973), *Open Veins of Latin America*, New York, Monthly Review Press.

Game, A. and Pringle, R. (1983), *Gender At Work*, Sydney, George Allen and Unwin.

Gardner, H. (1983), *Frames of Mind: The Theory of Multiple Intelligences*, New York, Basic Books.

Garland, S.B. (1988), 'Why the Underclass Can't Get Out From Under', *Business Week*, 19 September 1988.

Garson, B. (1989), *The Electronic Sweatshop*, New York, Penguin Books.

Gaskell, J. (1986), 'The Social Reproduction of Gender', in R. Hamilton and M. Barrett (eds), *The Politics of Diversity*, London, Verso.

Gelpi, B.C. *et al.* (eds) (1986), *Women and Poverty*, Chicago, The University of Chicago Press.

Gilligan, C. (1982), *In a Different Voice*, Cambridge, Massachusetts, Harvard University Press.

Giroux, H. (1983), *Theory and Resistance in Education*, South Hadley, Massachusetts, Bergin and Garvey Publishers.

Gleeson, D. (1986), 'Further Education, Free Enterprise and the Curriculum', in S. Walker and L. Barton, *Youth, Unemployment and Schooling*, Milton Keynes, The Open University Press.

Glenn, E.N. and Tolbert, C.M. (1987), 'Technology and Emerging Patterns of Stratification for Women of Color: Race and Gender Segregation in Contemporary Occupations', in B.D. Wright (ed.), *Women, Work, and Technology*, Ann Arbor, The University of Michigan Press.

Godelier, M. (1981), 'The Origins of Male Domination', *New Left Review*, no. 127, May–June.

Goodman, R. (1979), *The Last Entrepreneurs*, Boston, South End Press.

Gorz, A. (1985), *Paths to Paradise*, Boston, South End Press.

Green, T.F. (1968), *Work, Leisure and the American Schools*, New York, Random House.

Greene, M. (1984), 'The Art of Being Present: Education for Aesthetic Encounters', *Journal of Education*, vol. 166, no. 2.

—— (1990), 'Realizing Literature's Emancipatory Potential', in J. Mezirow (ed.), *Fostering Critical Reflection in Adulthood*, San Francisco, Jossey-Bass.

Grossman, R. (1979), 'Women's Place in the Integrated Circuit', special joint issue of *South Asian Chronicle*, no. 66 and *Pacific Research*, vol. 9 no. 5–6 (1978).

Grumet, M. (1986), '*The Paideia Proposal*: A Thankless Child Replies', *Curriculum Inquiry*, vol. 16, no. 3.

Haas, G. (1985), *Plant Closures*, Boston, South End Press.

Habermas, J. (1970), *Toward a Rational Society*, Boston, Beacon Press.

—— (1971), *Strukturwandel der Öffentlichkeit*, Neuwied und Berlin, Luchterhand.

—— (1973), 'Wahrheitstheorien', in H. Fahrenbach (ed.), *Wirklichkeit und Reflexion (Walter Schulz zum 60. Geburtstag)*, Pfullingen, Verlag Günther Neske.

—— (1975), *Legitimation Crisis*, Boston, Beacon Press.

—— (1979), *Communication and the Evolution of Society*, Boston, Beacon Press.

—— (1983), untitled paper delivered at the Conference on Hermeneutics and Critical Theory, Bryn Maur College, Bryn Maur, Pennsylvania.

—— (1984), *The Theory of Communication, Volume One*, Boston, Beacon Press.

Hall, R.H. (1986), *Dimensions of Work*, Beverly Hills, Sage Press.

Hamilton, R. and Barrett, M. (eds) (1986), *The Politics of Diversity*, London, Verso.

Handy, C. (1984), *The Future of Work*, Oxford, Basil Blackwell.

Haraway, D. (1988), 'Primatology is Politics by Other Means', in R. Bleier (ed.), *Feminist Approaches to Science*, New York, Pergamon Press.

Harding, S. (1986), *The Science Question in Feminism*, Ithaca, Cornell University Press.

—— and Hintikka, M.B. (eds) (1983), *Discovering Reality*, Dordrecht, Holland, D. Reidel Publishing Company.

—— and O'Barr, J.F. (eds) (1987), *Sex and Scientific Inquiry*, Chicago, The University of Chicago Press.

Harman, D. (1987), *Illiteracy: A National Dilemma*, New York, The Cambridge Book Company.

Hart, M. (1984), 'Toward a Theory of Collective Learning', unpublished doctoral dissertation, Indiana University, Bloomington, Indiana.

—— (1985), 'Thematization of Power, the Search for Common Interests, and Self-Reflection: Towards a Comprehensive Concept of Emancipatory Education', *International Journal of Lifelong Education*, vol. 4, no. 2.

—— (1990a), 'Liberation Through Consciousness Raising', in J. Mezirow (ed.), *Fostering Critical Reflection in Adulthood*, San Francisco, Jossey-Bass.

—— (1990b), 'Critical Theory and Beyond: Further Perspectives on Emancipatory Education', *Adult Education Quarterly*, vol. 40, no. 3.

Hartsock, N.C.M. (1983), 'The Feminist Standpoint: Developing the Ground for a Specifically Feminist Historical Materialism', in S. Harding and M.B. Hintikka (eds), *Discovering Reality*, Dordrecht, Holland, D. Reidel Publishing Company.

Hayes, D. (1989), *Behind the Silicon Curtain*, Boston, South End Press.

Heany, T.W. and Horton, A. (1990), 'Reflective Engagement for Social Change', in J. Mezirow (ed.), *Fostering Critical Reflection in Adulthood*, San Francisco, Jossey-Bass.

Held, V. (1987), 'Feminism and Moral Theory', in E.F. Kittay and D.T. Meyers (eds), *Women and Moral Theory*, Lanham, Maryland, Rowman and Littlefield.

Hirsch, E.D. (1988), *Cultural Literacy*, New York, Vintage Books.

Hochschild, A., with Machung, A. (1989), *The Second Shift*, New York, Viking.

Holden, K.C. and Hansen, L.W. (1987), 'Part-Time Work, Full-Time Work, and Occupational Segregation', in C. Brown and J.A. Pechman (eds), *Gender in the Workplace*, Washington, DC, The Brookings Institute.

Hooks, B. (1984), *Feminist Theory – From Margin to Center, Boston, South End Press*.

Howard, R. (1986), *Brave New Workplace*, New York, Penguin.

Illich, I. (1981), *Shadow Work*, Boston, Marion Boyars.

'An Interview with Bennett Harrison and Barry Bluestone' (1983), *Working Papers*, January–February.

Jaggar, A.M. and Bordo, S.R. (eds) (1989), *Gender/Body/Knowledge*, New Brunswick, Rutgers University Press.

Jay, M. (1973), *The Dialectical Imagination*, Boston, Little and Brown Company.

James, S. (1975), 'Sex, Race and Working Class Power', in S. James and M. Dalla Costa, *Sex, Race and Class*, London, Falling Wall Press and Race Today Publications.

James, S. and Dalla Costa, M. (1975), *Sex, Race and Class*, London, Falling Wall Press and Race Today Publications.

Johnston, W.B. and Packer, A.H. (1987), *Workforce 2000*, Indianapolis, Indiana, Hudson Institute.

Jones, J. (1986), *Labor of Love, Labor of Sorrow*, New York, Vintage Books.

Jones, T.B. (ed.) (1982), *Liberal Learning and Business Careers*, St Paul, Minnesota, Metropolitan State University.

Jordanova, L.J. (1980), 'Natural Facts: A Historical Perspective On Science And Sexuality', in C. MacCormack and M. Strathern (eds), *Nature, Culture and Gender*, Cambridge, Cambridge University Press.

Keller, E.F. (1985), *Reflections on Gender and Science*, New Haven, Yale University Press.

Kessler-Harris, A. (1982), *Out to Work: A History of Wage-Earning Women in the United States*, New York, Oxford University Press.

Kittay, E.F. and Meyers, D.T. (eds) (1987), *Women and Moral Theory*, Lanham, Maryland, Rowman and Littlefield.

Klemp, G.O. (1982), 'Three Factors of Success', in T.B. Jones (ed.), *Liberal Learning and Business Careers*, St Paul, Minnesota, Metropolitan State University.

Knödler-Bunte, E. (1975), 'The Proletarian Sphere and Political Organization: An Analysis of Oskar Negt and Alexander Kluges' *The Public Sphere and Experience*', *New German Critique*, vol. 4.

Koedt, A. *et al.* (eds) (1973), *Radical Feminism*, New York, Quadrangle/The New York Times Book Company.

Kolb, D.A. (1974), *Experiential Learning*, Englewood Cliffs, New Jersey, Prentice-Hall.

Kuttner, B. (1983), 'The Declining Middle', *The Atlantic Monthly*, July.

Kuttner, B. and Freeman, P. (1982), 'Women to the Workhouse', *Working Papers Magazine*, vol. 9, no. 6.

Lauritzen, P. (1989), 'A Feminist Ethic and the New Romanticism - Mothering as a Model of Moral Relations', *Hypatia*, vol. 4, no. 2.

Leacock, E. and Safa, H.I. (eds) (1986), *Women's Work*, South Hadley, Massachusetts, Bergin and Harvey.

Lee, C. (1988), 'Basic Training in the Corporate Schoolhouse', *Training*, vol. 25, no. 4.

Lloyd, C.B. and Niemi, B.T. (1979), *The Economics of Sex Differentials*, New York, Columbia University Press.

Lloyd, G. (1984), *The Man of Reason*, Minneapolis, University of Minnesota Press.

Loufti, M.F. (1985), *Rural Women: Unequal Partners in Development*, Geneva, International Labour Office.

Lugones, M. (1990), 'Playfulness, "World"-Travelling, and Loving Perception', in J. Allen (ed.), *Lesbian Philosophies and Cultures*, Albany, New York, State University of New York Press.

McCarthy, T. (1981), *The Critical Theory of Juergen Habermas*, Cambridge, Massachusetts, The MIT Press.

MacCormack, C., (1980), 'Nature, Culture and Gender: A Critique', in C. MacCormack and M. Strathern (eds), *Nature, Culture and Gender*, Cambridge, Cambridge University Press.

MacCormack, C. and Strathern, M. (eds) (1980), *Nature, Culture and Gender*, Cambridge, Cambridge University Press.

McDermott, J.J. (1973), *The Philosophy of John Dewey*, vol. II, New York, G.P. Putnam' Sons.

McKenzie, L. (1984), 'Adult Education and the Burden of the Future', in S.B. Merriam (ed.), *Selected Writings on Philosophy and Adult Education*, Malabar, Florida, Robert E. Krieger Publishing Company.

Machung, A. (1984), 'Word Processing: Forward for Business, Backward for Women', in K. B. Sacks and D. Remy (eds), *My Troubles Are Going to*

Have Trouble With Me, New Brunswick, New Jersey, Rutgers University Press.

McKinnon, C. (1979), *Sexual Harassment of Working Women: A Case of Sex Discrimination*, New Haven, Connecticut, Yale University Press.

Mansfeld, C. (1983), 'Eine Frau haben, einen Sessel und ein Glas Bier. Warum orientieren sich Menschen in der dritten Welt an westlichen Werten?', *Peripherie*, vol. 4, no. 13.

Marshall, H. (1988), 'Work or Learning', *Educational Researcher*, December.

Marsick, V.J. (1987a), 'New Paradigms for Learning in the Workplace', in V.J. Marsick (ed.), *Learning in the Workplace*, London, Croom Helm.

Marsick, V.J. (ed.) (1987b), *Learning in the Workplace*, London, Croom Helm.

Marx, K. (1963), *Selected Writings*, New York, Penguin.

—— (1967), *Capital. Vol. I*, New York, International Publishers.

—— (1972), *The Grundrisse*, New York, Harper and Row.

May, M. (1985), 'Bread Before Roses: American Workingmen, Labor Unions and the Family Wage', in R. Milkman (ed.), *Women, Work & Protest*, Boston, Routledge and Kegan Paul.

Merchant, C. (1983), *The Death of Nature*, San Francisco, Harper and Row.

Merriam, S. (ed.) (1984), *Selected Writings on Philosophy and Adult Education*, Malabar, Florida, Robert E. Krieger Publishing Company.

Mezirow, J. (ed.) (1990a), *Fostering Critical Reflection in Adulthood*, San Francisco, Jossey-Bass.

Mezirow, J. (1990b), 'Reflection and Meaning in Adult Learning', in J. Mezirow (ed.), *Fostering Critical Reflection in Adulthood*, San Francisco, Jossey-Bass.

Mies, M. (1982), *Housewives in the World Market: The Lacemakers of Narsapur*, London, Zed Press.

—— (1983), 'Subsistenzproduktion, Hausfrauisierung, Kolonisierung', *Beiträge zur Feministischen Theorie und Praxis*, vol. 6, no. 9/10.

—— (1986), *Patriarchy and Accumulation on a World Scale*, London, Zed Press.

Mies, M. (ed.) (1988), *Women – The Last Colony*, London, Zed Press.

Milkman, R. (ed.) (1985), *Women, Work and Protest*, Boston, Routledge and Kegan Paul.

Minnich, E. *et al.* (eds) (1988), *Reconstructing the Academy*, Chicago, The University of Chicago Press.

Mitchell, J. and Oakley, A. (1986), *What is Feminism*, New York, Pantheon Books.

Modigliani, K. (1986), 'But Who Will Take Care of The Children? Childcare, Women, and Devalued Labor', *Journal of Education*, vol. 168, no. 3.

Momsen, J.H. and Townsend, J. (1987) *Geography of Gender*, Albany, New York, State University of New York Press.

Morello, T. (1983), 'Sweatshops in the Sun?', *Far Eastern Economic Review*, 15 September.

Munelly, C. (1987), 'Learning Participation: The Worker's Viewpoint', in V.J. Marsick (ed.), *Learning in the Workplace*, London, Croom Helm.

Nash, N.S. and Hawthorne, E. (1987), *Formal Recognition of Employer-Sponsored Instruction*, ASHE-ERIC Higher Education Reports.

A Nation At Risk, (1983), The National Commission on Excellence in Education, Washington, D.C., The Commission.

Newman, M. (1979), *The Poor Cousin*, London, George Allen and Unwin.

Noble, D. (1984), *Forces of Production*, New York, Alfred A. Knopf.

Noddings, N. (1984), *Caring: A Feminist Approach to Ethics*, Berkeley, University of Colorado Press.

Noll, J.W. (1985), *Taking Sides*, Guildford, Connecticut, The Dushkin Publishing Group.

Occupational Segregation, (1988), Chicago, Women Employed Institute Study.

Parker, M. (1985), *Inside the Circle*, Boston, South End Press.

Parker, M. and Slaughter, J. (1988), *Choosing Sides*, Boston, South End Press.

Payer, E. (1979), 'The World Bank and the Small Farmer', *Journal of Peace Research*, vol. 16, no. 4.

Perelman, L.J. (1984), *The Learning Enterprise: Adult Learning, Human Capital and Economic Development*, Washington, DC, The Council of State Planning Agencies.

Phillips, A. and Taylor, B. (1980), 'Sex and Skill: Notes Towards a Feminist Economics', *Feminist Review*, no. 6.

Pierce, G. (1987), 'Management Workshop: Toward a New Paradigm', in V.J. Marsick (ed.), *Learning in the Workplace*, London, Croom Helm.

Polanyi, M. (1964), *Personal Knowledge*, New York, Harper and Row.

Powers, T.F. (ed.) (1977), *Educating for Careers*, University Park, The Pennsylvania State University Press.

Rifkin, J. (1987), *Time Wars: The Primary Conflict in Human History*, New York, Henry Holt and Company.

Ritchie-Calder, The Lord (1982), 'Education for the Post-Industrial Society', in N. Castello and M. Richardson (eds), *Continuing Education for the Post-Industrial Society*, Milton Keynes, The Open University Press.

Rogers, B. (1980), *The Domestication of Women*, New York, Methuen.

Rollins, J. (1985), *Between Women: Domestics and their Employers*, Philadelphia, Temple University Press.

Rose, H. (1986), 'Women's Work, Women's Knowledge', in J. Mitchell and A. Oakley (eds), *What is Feminism*, New York, Pantheon Books.

Roszak, T. (1986), *The Cult of Information*, New York, Pantheon Books.

Rothwell, S. (1986), 'Working Like Women', in P. Ekins (ed.), *The Living Economy*, London, Routledge and Kegan Paul.

Ruddick, S. (1984), 'Maternal Thinking', in J. Trebilcot (ed.), *Mothering*, Totowa, New Jersey, Rowman and Allanheld.

—— (1989), *Maternal Thinking*, New York, Ballantine Books.

Ryan, A. (ed.) (1979), *The Idea of Freedom*, Oxford, Oxford University Press.

Sacks, K.B. and Remy, D. (eds) (1984), *My Troubles Are Going to Have Troubles With Me*, New Brunswick, New Jersey, Rutgers University Press.

Safa, H.I. (1986), 'Runaway Shops and Female Employment: The Search for Cheap Labor', in E. Leacock, and H.I. Safa (eds), *Women's Work*, South Hadley, Massachusetts, Bergin and Harvey.

Schechter, S. (1982), *Women and Male Violence: The Visions and Struggles of the Battered Women's Movement*, Boston, South End Press.

Schon, D. (1983), *The Reflective Practitioner*, New York, Basic Books.

Schultz, I. (1985), 'Über den Zusammenhang von Zeit, Geld und Geschlecht', *Beiträge zur Feministischen Theorie und Praxis*, vol. 8, no. 15/16.

Schumacher, E.F. (1973), *Small is Beautiful: Economics as if People Mattered*, New York, Harper and Row.

Schutz, A. (1962), *Collected Papers*, The Hague, Martinus Nijhoff.

Scott, B.A, (1986), 'The Decline of Literacy and Liberal Learning', *Journal of Education*, vol. 168, no. 1.

Sen, G. and Grown, C. (1987), *Development, Crises, and Alternative Visions*, New York, Monthly Review Press.

Shiva, V. (1989), *Staying Alive: Women, Ecology and Development*, London, Zed Press.

Shor, I. (1986), *Culture Wars*, New York, Methuen.

Smith, D. (1987), *The Everyday World as Problematic*, Boston, Northeastern University Press.

Smith, J. (1984), 'Nonwage Labor and Subsistence', in J. Smith, J. *et al.* (eds), *Households and the World Economy*, Beverly Hills, Sage Press.

Smith, J. (1986), 'The Paradox of Women's Poverty: Wage-Earning Women and Economic Transformation', in B.C. Gelpi *et al.* (eds), *Women and Poverty*, Chicago, The University of Chicago Press.

Smith, J. *et al.* (1984), *Households and the World Economy*, Beverly Hills, Sage Press.

Sohn-Rethel, A. (1978), *Intellectual and Manual Labour: A Critique of Epistemology*, London, Macmillan.

Sokoloff, N. (1980), *Between Money and Love*, New York, Praeger.

Spikes, F. (1989), 'Educating the Workforce', *Adult Learning*, vol. 1, no. 1.

Spring, J. (1985), 'Education and the Sony War', in J.W. Noll (ed.), *Taking Sides*, Guildford, Connecticut, The Dushkin Publishing Group.

Strober, M.H. and Arnold, C.L. (1987), 'The Dynamics of Occupational Segregation Among Bank Tellers', in C. Brown and J.A. Pechman (eds), *Gender in the Workplace*, Washington, D.C., The Brookings Institute.

Taylor, C. (1979), 'What's Wrong with Negative Liberty', in A. Ryan (ed.), *The Idea of Freedom*, Oxford, Oxford University Press.

Terkel, S. (1974), *Working*, New York, Avon Books.

Thompson, E.P. (1967), 'Time, Work-Discipline and Industrial Capitalism', *Past and Present*, vol. 38, December.

Thompson, J. (1983), *Learning Liberation*, London, Croom Helm.

Tong, R. (1984), *Women, Sex, and the Law*, Totowa, New Jersey, Rowman and Allanheld.

Toward Economic Justice for Women (1985), Women's Economic Agenda Working Group, Washington, DC, Institute for Policy Studies.

Trebilcot, J. (ed.) (1984), *Mothering*, Totowa, New Jersey, Rowman and Allanheld.

Trenchard, E. (1987), 'Rural Women's Work in Sub-Saharan Africa and the Implications for Nutrition', in J.H. Momsen and J. Townsend (eds), *Geography of Gender*, Albany, New York, State University of New York Press.

Tröger, A. (1984), 'The Creation of a Female Assembly-Line Proletariat', in R. Bridenthal *et al.* (eds), *When Biology Became Destiny*, New York, Monthly Review Press.

Tronto, J.C. (1989), 'Women and Caring: What Can Feminists Learn About Morality From Caring?', in A.M. Jaggar and S.R. Bordo (eds), *Gender/Body/Knowledge*, New Brunswick, New Jersey, Rutgers University Press.

Tuana, N. (ed.), *Feminism and Science*, Bloomington, Indiana, Indiana University Press.

Walker, S. and Barton, L. (1986), *Youth, Unemployment and Schooling*, Milton Keynes, The Open University Press.

Wallerstein, I. (1974), 'The Rise and Future Demise of the World Capitalist System: Concepts for Comparative Analysis', *Comparative Studies in Society and History*, vol. 16, no. 4.

—— (1979), *The Capitalist World Economy*, Cambridge, Cambridge University Press.

Waring, M. (1989) *If Women Counted*, New York, Harper and Row.

Watts, A.G. (1983), *Education, Unemployment and the Future of Work*, Milton Keynes, The Open University Press.

Weber, M. (1958), *The Protestant Ethic and the Spirit of Capitalism*, New York, Charles Scribner's Sons.

Weiler, K. (1988), *Women Teaching for Change*, South Hadley, Massachusetts, Bergin and Garvey.

Werlhof, C. von (1983a), 'Neue Formen genossenschaftlicher Agrarproduktion und staatlich verordnete Geschlechtspolarisierung', in C. von Werlhof *et al.*, *Frauen, die letzte Kolonie*, Reinbek bei Hamburg, Rowohlt.

—— (1985a), 'Kredite für Hausfrauen: Traum oder Alptraum?', *Beiträge zur Feministischen Theorie und Praxis*, vol. 8, no. 15/16,

—— (1985b). 'Why Peasants and Housewives do not Disappear in the Capitalist World System', paper delivered at the Annual Meeting of the American Sociological Association, Washington, D.C.

—— (1985c), *Wenn die Bauern wiederkommen*, Bremen, Edition CON.

—— (1988a), 'The Proletarian is Dead: Long Live the Housewife', in M. Mies (ed.), *Women – The Last Colony*, London, Zed Press.

—— (1988b), 'On the Concept of Nature and Society in Capitalism', in M. Mies (ed.), *Women – the Last Colony*, London, Zed Press.

Werlhof, C. von *et al.* (1983), *Frauen, die letzte Kolonie*, Reinbek bei Hamburg, Rowohlt.

Wilson, W.J. (1987), *The Truly Disadvantaged*, Chicago, The University of Chicago Press.

Wirth, A.G. (1983), *Productive Work – In Industry and Schools*, Lanham, Maryland, University Press of America.

Wong, A.E. (1986), 'Planned Development, Social Stratification, and the

Sexual Division of Labor in Singapore', in E. Leacock, and H.I. Safa (eds), *Women's Work*, South Hadley, Massachusetts, Bergin and Harvey.
Working at the Margins (1986), Report by National Association for Working Women, Cleveland, Ohio.
Wright, B.D. (ed.) (1987), *Women, Work, and Technology*, Ann Arbor, The University of Michigan Press.
Zuboff, S. (1988), *In the Age of the Smart Machine*, New York, Basic Books.

INDEX

For Product Safety Concerns and Information please contact our EU representative GPSR@taylorandfrancis.com
Taylor & Francis Verlag GmbH, Kaufingerstraße 24, 80331 München, Germany

www.ingramcontent.com/pod-product-compliance
Lightning Source LLC
LaVergne TN
LVHW010552110826
845149LV00003B/632

* 9 7 8 1 1 3 8 3 1 3 5 4 5 *